"Two perceptive writers recently
wrote a book called
**START-UP NATION.**
We are the start-up nation."
—Benjamin Netanyahu

## Praise for **START-UP NATION**

"A compelling case study, delivered with insightful analysis...an accomplishment, not simply for exposing the roots of Israel's success, but showing what the Israeli case might teach the rest of the world."                                                    —*USA Today*

"Vividly illustrates how Israel has developed a culture where authority not only can be challenged, but must be...a compelling and satisfying work, filled with eye-opening revelations and shot through with rich examples, explanations, and analysis."          —*Barron's*

"Compelling...engrossing...With the scary state of the world economy, it also provides a window of hope for so many suffering locales around the world: Israel has thrived not despite its obstacles but because of them; maybe other places can too."          —*Forbes.com*

"A playbook for every CEO who wants to develop the next generation of corporate leaders."
                —Tom Brokaw, special correspondent for NBC News
                          and author of *The Greatest Generation*

"Both informs and inspires...The best ad for Israel in recent memory." —*Jerusalem Post*

"An eye-opening look at a side of Israel that most people never think about."
—Steven D. Levitt and Stephen J. Dubner,
authors of *Freakonomics*; *The Week*

"Bracing...has huge relevance for those thinking about America's renewal." —*New Republic*

"This is such a good book I don't know where to begin with my raves. It is brilliantly written...Want to know who saved Intel? Read this book!...I'll bet no readers come away from the book without being awed by what Israel has been able to do, and without being impressed by the authors' impressive way of telling this story."
—Growthology.org

"Required reading." —*New York Post*

"It's a book I think every single Arab businessman, Arab bureaucrat, *and* Arab politician should read, because it explains this wide gulf between Israel and the Arab world." —Fareed Zakaria, CNN

"Filled with inspiring insights into what's behind Israel's dynamic economy. This is a timely book and a much-needed celebration of the entrepreneurial spirit."
—Meg Whitman, former president and CEO of eBay

"The authors ground their analysis in case studies and interviews with some of Israel's most brilliant innovators to make this a rich and insightful read not just for business leaders and policy makers but for anyone curious about contemporary Israeli culture."
—*Publishers Weekly*

"Senor and Singer's experience in government, in business, and in journalism—and especially on the ground in the Middle East—comes to life in their illuminating, timely, and often surprising analysis."

—George Stephanopoulos, anchor,
ABC's *Good Morning America*

"Senor and Singer highlight some important lessons and sound instruction for countries struggling to enter the twenty-first century."
—*Kirkus Reviews*

"Dan Senor and Saul Singer have done the impossible...a fascinating and illuminating look at the reasons Israel has become one of the world's prime incubators of technological innovation...an indispensable business book. I wish I had thought to write it."
—Jeffrey Goldberg, *Atlantic*

"Lively, surprising, and fun to read...chockfull of short, punchy narratives...[a] remarkable book." —*New Jersey Jewish Standard*

"Fascinating."

—Clifford May, former *New York Times*
foreign correspondent and president
of the Foundation for Defense of
Democracies; Scripps Howard News Service

"Very often books of this nature digress into pages crammed with all kinds of graphs and statistics that, to put it bluntly, are just plain boring. However, Senor and Singer avoid this with an entertaining prose style, bolstered by meticulous research and many first-hand interviews with people in the know."

—AmericanChronicle.com

"In the end, it is not easy to discover why Israel, a tiny nation of immigrants torn by war, has managed to become the first technology nation. It may be enough, as this fine book does, to shine a spotlight on its success."

—James K. Glassman, *Wall Street Journal*

# START-UP NATION

The Story of Israel's Economic Miracle

## DAN SENOR and SAUL SINGER

A Council on Foreign Relations Book

TWELVE

NEW YORK    BOSTON

Twelve
Hachette Book Group
1290 Avenue of the Americas
New York, NY 10104

www.HachetteBookGroup.com

Twelve is an imprint of Grand Central Publishing.
The Twelve name and logo are trademarks of Hachette Book Group, Inc.

The publisher is not responsible for websites (or their content) that are not owned by the publisher.

Printed in the United States of America

First Trade Edition: September 2011

Printing 14, 2022

Originally published in hardcover by Twelve.

The Library of Congress has cataloged the hardcover edition as follows:

Senor, Dan.
Start-up nation : the story of Israel's economic miracle / Dan Senor and Saul Singer.—1st ed.
    p. cm.
Includes index.
Summary: "What the world can learn from Israel's meteoric economic success."—Provided by the publisher.
ISBN 978-0-446-54146-6
1. Israel—Economic conditions.    I. Singer, Saul.    II. Title.
HC415.25.S455 2009
330.95694—dc22

2009013144

ISBN 978-0-446-54147-3 (pbk.)

*To Campbell Brown and Wendy Singer, who
shared our enthusiasm for this story.*

*To James Senor and Alex Singer, who would have
marveled at what they worked to create.*

# CONTENTS

# FOREWORD

People prefer remembering to imagining. Memory deals with familiar things; imagination deals with the unknown. Imagination can be frightening—it requires risking a departure from the familiar.

The seeds of a new Israel grew from the imagination of an exiled people. The exile was extremely long, some two thousand years. The exile left the Jews with a prayer and without a country. Yet this unbroken prayer nurtured their hope and their bond to the land of their forefathers.

With the establishment of the State of Israel, this great prayer was planted in a small land. The soil was obstinate, and the environment was hostile. On our ancient journey from Egypt to Israel we Jews crossed a huge desert and, in modern times, too, returned home to more desert. We had to create ourselves anew. As a poor people coming home to a poor land, we had to discover the riches of scarcity.

The only capital at our disposal was human capital. The arid land would not yield to financial contributions, only to pioneers who contented themselves with little and who volunteered a lot. They invented new ways of living: kibbutzim, moshavim, development towns, and communities where none existed. They drilled and labored and demanded much from themselves. But they also dreamed and innovated.

They were idealists and intellectuals, yet they chose to till the land with their own hands. When they discovered that the land was infertile and the water insufficient, they turned to invention and technology.

The kibbutz became an incubator, and the farmer a scientist. High-tech in Israel began with agriculture. Even with little land and less water, Israel became an agricultural leader. Though many still consider agriculture the epitome of low-tech, they are mistaken: technology was 95 percent of the secret of Israel's prodigious agricultural productivity.

The hostility of the environment did not subside. Israel was attacked seven times in the first sixty-two years of its existence and subjected to comprehensive diplomatic and economic embargoes. No foreign soldiers came to its aid. The only way we could overcome our attackers' quantitative superiority of weapons was to create an advantage built on courage and technology.

Israel bred creativity proportionate not to the size of our country, but to the dangers we faced. This creativity on the security front, moreover, laid the foundations for civilian industries. Military development is often dual-purpose. Aeronautics, for example, is applicable to civil and military industries alike. The military, in cooperation with civilian industries, became a technological incubator that exposed many young people to sophisticated equipment and managerial experience.

Israel will always be a small country in territory and population. So Israel can never become a large market or develop very large industries. But while size grants the advantages of quantity, smallness creates an opportunity to specialize in quality. Israel's only option has been to pursue quality based on creativity.

"All the experts," Israel's first prime minister, David Ben-Gurion, said, "are experts on what was. There is no expert on what will be." To become an "expert" on the future, vision must replace experience.

I believe that the next decade will be the most surprising decade yet in the scientific and industrial domains because of three simultaneous developments:

The first is the rise of artificial intelligence. The capabilities of the computer have grown a million-fold in the past twenty-five years.

The second is the outpouring of scientific discovery that will result from the growing number of scientists in the world (mainly in China and India), coupled with advances in technology.

The third is the advent of nanotechnology, which will enable the deciphering of the brain of man, the most marvelous creation of the cosmos. This will reveal human potential, open communication systems, and create societal challenges in ways we cannot yet imagine.

With just these three changes, we shall be able to see phenomena that are far beyond today's horizons. We shall be able to prevent or overcome illnesses, circumvent obstacles, and travel higher into space and deeper into the oceans. Maybe we will penetrate the greatest mystery of all: the code of the existence of man and the secret story of human creativity.

Israel is now preparing itself for this great journey, helping other travelers and being helped by them.

The book before you, *Start-Up Nation*, is an eye-opener. It should be taken as an interim report on the history of Israel, a country that is itself a perpetual start-up. In it, Dan Senor and Saul Singer tell the story of people who defied what existed and challenged the conventional—who created the "Israeli secret" and positioned their country as a critical research and development center for the world's leading technology companies.

At the gateway to this dynamic and exciting decade, Israel is building on its head start in contributing to the new age of discovery. The next years will continue Israel's commitment to a better tomorrow, with a readiness to take risks and seek renewal. We hope that by rising to embrace this new frontier we will not only play our part in bringing peace to the region, but will also continue to make an even greater contribution to fulfilling humanity's dreams of health, prosperity, and freedom for everyone, everywhere.

Shimon Peres

# AUTHORS' NOTE

This is a book about innovation and entrepreneurship, and how one small country, Israel, came to embody both.

This is not a book about technology, even though we feature many high-tech companies. While we are fascinated by technology and its impact on the modern age, our focus is the ecosystem that generates radically new business ideas.

This book is part exploration, part argument, and part storytelling. The reader might expect the book to be organized chronologically, around companies, or according to the various key elements that we have identified in Israel's model for innovation. These organizational blueprints tempted us, but we ultimately rejected them all in favor of a more mosaiclike approach.

We examine history and culture, and use selected stories of companies to try to understand where all of this creative energy came from and the forms in which it is expressed. We have interviewed economists and studied their perspectives, but we come at our subject as students of history, business, and geopolitics. One of us (Dan) has a background in business and government, the other (Saul) in government and journalism. Dan lives in New York and has studied in Israel and lived, worked, and traveled in the Arab world; Saul grew up in the United States and now lives in Jerusalem.

Dan has invested in Israeli companies. None of these companies are profiled in this book, but some people Dan has invested with are. We will note this where appropriate.

While our admiration for the untold story of what Israel has accomplished economically was a big part of what motivated us to write this book, we do cover areas where Israel has fallen behind. We also examine threats to Israel's continued success—most of which will likely surprise the reader, since they do not relate to those that generally preoccupy the international press.

We delve briefly into two other areas: why American innovation industries have not taken better advantage of the entrepreneurial talent offered by those with U.S. military training and experience, in contrast to the practice in the Israeli economy; and why the Arab world is having difficulty in fostering entrepreneurship. These subjects deserve in-depth treatment beyond the scope of this book; entire books could be written about each.

Finally, if there is one story that has been largely missed despite the extensive media coverage of Israel, it is that key economic metrics demonstrate that Israel represents the greatest concentration of innovation and entrepreneurship in the world today.

This book is our attempt to explain that phenomenon.

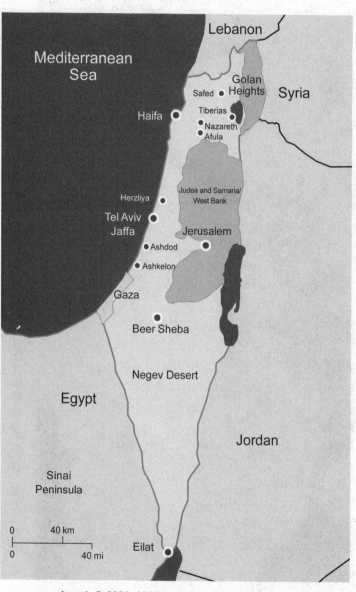

Mediterranean
Sea

Lebanon

Golan
Heights

Syria

Safed

Tiberias

Haifa

Nazareth

Afula

Herzliya

Judea and Samaria/
West Bank

Tel Aviv
Jaffa

Jerusalem

Ashdod

Ashkelon

Gaza

Beer Sheba

Negev Desert

Egypt

Jordan

Sinai
Peninsula

0        40 km

0              40 mi

Eilat

Israel. © 2003–2009 Koret Communications Ltd.
www.koret.com. Reprinted by permission.

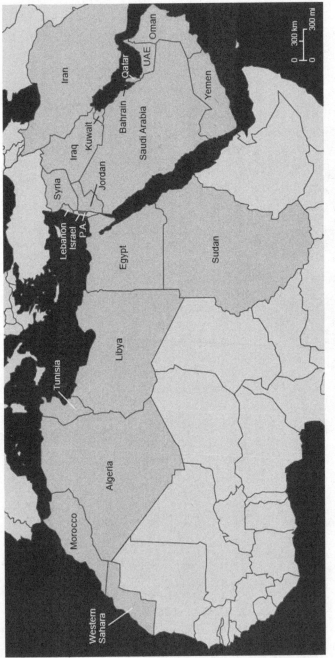

Israel and the region. © 2003–2009 Koret Communications Ltd. www.koret.com.
Reprinted by permission.

# START-UP NATION

# Introduction

*Nice speech, but what are you going to do?*

—SHIMON PERES TO SHAI AGASSI

THE TWO MEN MADE AN ODD COUPLE as they sat, waiting, in an elegant suite in the Sheraton Seehof, high up in the Swiss Alps. There was no time to cut the tension with small talk; they just exchanged nervous glances. The older man, more than twice the age of the younger and not one to become easily discouraged, was the calmer of the two. The younger man normally exuded the self-confidence that comes with being the smartest person in the room, but repeated rejections had begun to foster doubt in his mind: Would he really be able to pull off reinventing three megaindustries? He was anxious for the next meeting to begin.

It was not clear why the older man was subjecting himself to this kind of hassle and to the risk of humiliation. He was the world's most famous living Israeli, an erudite two-time prime minister and Nobel Prize winner. At eighty-three years old, Shimon Peres certainly did not need another adventure.

Just securing these meetings had been a challenge. Shimon Peres was a perennial fixture at the annual Davos World Economic Forum. For the press, waiting to see whether this or that Arab potentate would shake Peres's hand was an easy source of drama at what was otherwise a dressed-up business conference. He was one of the famous leaders CEOs typically wanted to meet.

So when Peres invited the CEOs of the world's five largest carmakers to meet with him, he expected that they would show up. But it was early 2007, the global financial crisis was not yet on the horizon, the auto industry was not feeling the pressure it would a year later, and the American Big Three—GM, Ford, and Chrysler—didn't bother to respond. Another top automaker had arrived, but he'd spent the entire twenty-five minutes explaining that Peres's idea would never work. He wasn't interested in hearing about the Israeli leader's utopian scheme to switch the world over to fully electric vehicles, and even if he had been, he wouldn't dream of launching it in a tiny country like Israel. "Look, I've read Shai's paper," the auto executive told Peres, referring to the white paper Peres had sent with the invitation. "He's fantasizing. There is no car like that. We've tried it, and it can't be built." He went on to explain that hybrid cars were the only realistic solution.

Shai Agassi was the younger man making the pitch alongside Peres. At the time, Agassi was an executive at SAP, the largest enterprise software company in the world. Agassi had joined the German tech giant in 2000, after it bought his Israeli start-up, TopTier Software, for $400 million. The sale had proved that though the tech bubble had just burst, some Israeli companies could still garner precrash values.

Agassi founded TopTier when he was twenty-four. Fifteen years later, he headed two SAP subsidiaries, was the youngest and only non-German member of SAP's board, and had been short-listed for CEO. Even if he missed the ring at thirty-nine, he could be pretty confident that someday it would be his.

Yet here Agassi was, with the next president of Israel, trying to instruct an auto executive on the future of the auto industry. Even he was beginning to wonder if this entire idea was preposterous, especially since it had begun as nothing more than a thought experiment.

At what Agassi calls "Baby Davos"—the Forum for Young Leaders—two years before, he had taken seriously a challenge to the group to come up with a way to make the world a "better place" by 2030. Most participants proposed tweaks to their businesses. Agassi came up with an idea so ambitious that most people thought him naive. "I decided that the most important thing to do was to figure out how to take a single country off of oil," he told us.

Agassi believed that if just one country was able to become completely oil-independent, the world would follow. The first step was to find a way to run cars without oil.

This alone was not a revolutionary insight.

He explored some exotic technologies for powering cars, such as hydrogen fuel cells, but they all seemed like they would forever be ten years away. So Agassi decided to focus on the simplest system of all: battery-powered electric vehicles. The concept was one that had been rejected in the past as too limiting and expensive, but Agassi thought he had a solution to make the electric car not just viable for consumers but preferable. If electric cars could be as cheap, convenient, and powerful as gas cars, who wouldn't want one?

Something about coming from an embattled sliver of a country—home to just one one-thousandth of the world's population—makes Israelis skeptical of conventional explanations about what is possible. If the essence of the Israeli condition, as Peres later told us, was to be "dissatisfied," then Agassi typified Israel's national ethos.

But if not for Peres, even Agassi might not have dared to pursue his own idea. After hearing Agassi make his pitch for oil independence, Peres called him and said, "Nice speech, but what are you going to *do*?"[1]

Until that point, Agassi says, he "was merely solving a puzzle"— the problem was still just a thought experiment. But Peres put the challenge before him in clear terms: "Can you really do it? Is there anything more important than getting the world off oil? Who will do it if you don't?" And finally, Peres added, "What can I do to help?"[2]

Peres was serious about helping. Just after Christmas 2006 and into the first few days of 2007, he orchestrated for Agassi a whirl-wind of more than fifty meetings with Israel's top industry and government leaders, including the prime minister. "Each morning, we would meet at his office and I would debrief him on the previous day's meetings, and he'd get on the phone and begin scheduling the next day's meetings," Agassi told us. "These are appointments I could never have gotten without Peres."

Peres also sent letters to the five biggest automakers, along with Agassi's concept paper, which was how they found themselves in a Swiss hotel room, waiting on what was likely to be their last chance. "Up until that first meeting," Agassi said, "Peres had only heard about the concept from me, a software guy. What did I know? But he took a risk on me." The Davos meetings were the first time Peres had personally tested the idea on people who actually worked in the auto industry. And the first industry executive they'd met had not only shot down the idea but spent most of the meeting trying to talk Peres out of pursuing it. Agassi was mortified. "I had completely embarrassed this international statesman," he said. "I made him look like he did not know what he was talking about."

But now their second appointment was about to begin. Carlos Ghosn, the CEO of Renault and Nissan, had a reputation in the business world as a premier turnaround artist. Born in Brazil to Lebanese parents, he is famous in Japan for taking charge of Nissan, which was suffering massive losses, and in two years turning a profit. The grateful Japanese reciprocated by basing a comic-book series on his life.

Peres began to speak so softly that Ghosn could barely hear him, but Agassi was astounded. After the pounding they had just received in the previous meeting, Agassi expected that Peres might say something like, "Shai has this crazy idea about building an electric grid. I'll let him explain it, and you can tell him what you think." But rather than pulling back, Peres grew even more energetic than before in making the pitch, and more forceful.

Oil is finished, he said; it may still be coming out of the ground, but the world doesn't want it anymore. More importantly, Peres told Ghosn, it is financing international terrorism and instability. "We don't need to defend against incoming Katyusha rockets," he pointed out, "if we can figure out how to cut off the funding that launches them in the first place."

Then Peres tried to preempt the argument that the technology alternative just didn't exist yet. He knew that all the big car companies were flirting with a bizarre crop of electric mutations—hybrids, plug-in hybrids, tiny electric vehicles—but none of them heralded a new era in motor vehicle technology.

Just then, again about five minutes into Peres's pitch, the visitor stopped him. "Look, Mr. Peres," Ghosn said, "I read Shai's paper"—Agassi and Peres tried not to wince, but they felt they knew where this meeting was heading—"and he is absolutely right. We are exactly on the same page. We think the future is electric. We have the car, and we think we have the battery."

Peres was almost caught speechless. Just minutes ago they'd received an impassioned lecture on why the fully electric car would never work and why hybrids were the way to go. But Peres and Agassi knew that hybrids were a road to nowhere. What's the point of a car with two separate power plants? Existing hybrids cost a fortune and increase fuel efficiency by only 20 percent. They wouldn't get countries off oil. In Peres and Agassi's view, hybrids were like treating a gunshot wound with a Band-aid.

But they had never heard all this from an actual carmaker. Peres couldn't help blurting out, "So what do you think of hybrids?"

"I think they make no sense," Ghosn said confidently. "A hybrid is like a mermaid: if you want a fish, you get a woman; if you want a woman, you get a fish."

The laughter from Peres and Agassi was genuine, mixed with a large dose of relief. Had they found a true partner for their vision? Now it was Ghosn's turn to be worried. Though he was optimistic, all the classic obstacles to electric vehicles still remained: the batteries were too expensive, they had a range less than half that of a tank of gas, and they took hours to recharge. So long as consumers were being asked to pay a premium in price and convenience, clean cars would remain a niche market.

Peres said that he'd had all the same misgivings, until he had met Agassi. This was Agassi's cue to explain how all these liabilities could be addressed using existing technology, not some miracle battery that wouldn't be available for decades.

Ghosn's attention shifted from Peres to Agassi, who dove right in.

Agassi explained his idea, as simple as it was radical: electric cars *seemed* expensive only because batteries were expensive. But selling the car with the battery is like trying to sell gas cars with enough gasoline to run them for several years. When you factor in operating costs, electric cars are actually much cheaper—seven cents a mile for electric (including both the battery and the electricity to charge it) compared to ten cents a mile for gas, assuming gas costs $2.50 a gallon. If the price of gas is as high as $4.00 per gallon, this cost gap becomes a chasm. But what if you didn't have to pay for the battery when you bought the car and—as with any other fuel—spread the cost of the battery over the life of the car? Electric cars could become at least as cheap as gasoline cars, and the cost of the battery *with* the electricity to charge it would be significantly cheaper than what people were used to paying at the pump. Suddenly, the economics of the electric car would turn upside down. Furthermore, over the long run, this already sizable electric cost advantage would be certain to increase as batteries became cheaper.

Overcoming the price barrier was the biggest breakthrough, but it wasn't sufficient for electric vehicles to become, as Agassi called it, the "Car 2.0" that would replace the transportation model introduced by Henry Ford almost a century ago. A five-minute fill-up will last a gas car three hundred miles. How, Ghosn wondered, can an electric car compete with that?

Agassi's solution was infrastructure: wire thousands of parking spots, build battery swap stations, and coordinate it all over a new "smart grid." In most cases, charging the car at home and the office would easily be enough to get you through the day. On longer drives, you could pull into a swap station and be off with a fully charged battery in the time it takes to fill a tank of gas. He'd recruited a former Israeli army general—a man skilled at managing complex military logistics—to become the company's local Israeli CEO and lead the planning for the grid and the national network of charging/parking spots.

The key to the model would be that consumers would own their cars, but Agassi's start-up, called Better Place, would own the batteries. "Here's how it works," he later explained. "Think cell phones. You go to a cell provider. If you want, you can pay full price for a phone and make no commitment. But most people commit for two or three years and get a subsidized or free phone. They end up paying for the phone as they pay for their minutes of air time."[3]

Electric vehicles, Agassi explained, could work the same way: Better Place would be like a cellular provider. You would walk in to a car dealer, sign up for a plan based on miles instead of minutes, and get an electric car. But the buyer wouldn't own the car battery; Better Place would. So the company could spread the cost of the battery—and the car, too—over four or more years. For the price consumers are used to paying each month for gas, they could pay for the battery and the electricity needed to run it. "You get to go completely green for less than it costs to buy and run a gas car," Agassi said.

Agassi picked up where Peres had left off on another question: Why start with Israel, of all places? The first reason was size, he told Ghosn. Israel was the perfect "beta" country for electric cars. Not only was it small but, due to the hostility of its neighbors, it was a sealed "transportation island." Because Israelis could not drive beyond their national borders, their driving distances were always within one of the world's smallest national spaces. This limited the number of battery swap stations Better Place would have to build in the early phase. By isolating Israel, Agassi told us with an impish smile, Israel's adversaries had actually created the perfect laboratory to test ideas.

Second, Israelis understand not only the financial and environmental costs of being dependent on oil but also the security costs of pumping money into the coffers of less-than-savory regimes. Third, Israelis are natural early adopters—they were recently number one in the world in time spent on the Internet and have a cell phone penetration of 125 percent, meaning lots of people have more than one.

No less importantly, Agassi knew that in Israel he would find the resources he needed to tackle the tricky software challenge of creating a "smart grid" that could direct cars to open charging spots and manage the charging of millions of cars without overloading the system. Israel, the country with the highest concentration of engineers and research and development spending in the world, was a natural place to attempt this. Agassi actually wanted to go even further. After all, if Intel could mass-produce its most sophisticated chips in Israel, why couldn't Renault-Nissan build cars there? Ghosn's response was that it would work only if they could produce at least fifty thousand cars a year. Peres didn't blink, and committed to an annual production of one hundred thousand cars. Ghosn was on board, provided Peres could make good on his promise.

Agassi was caught between three possible commitments. He needed a country, a car company, and the money, but to get any one of them he first needed the other two. For example, when Peres and Agassi had gone to then prime minister Ehud Olmert to secure his commitment to make Israel the first country to free itself from oil, the premier had set two conditions: Agassi had to sign on a top-five carmaker and raise the $200 million needed to develop the smart grid, turning half a million parking spaces into charging spots, and building swap stations. Now Agassi had the carmaker, and it was time to fulfill Olmert's second condition: money.

Still, Agassi had heard enough to believe that his idea could take off. Stunning the tech world, he quit his job at SAP to found Better Place. (It took four conversations to convince the SAP management that he was serious about quitting.)

But investors around the globe were not jumping at a plan that involved reimagining some of the largest, most powerful industries in the world: cars, oil, and electricity. Plus, since the cars were useless without the infrastructure, the charging grid would have to be developed and deployed *before* the cars were released in significant numbers. That meant spending most of the $200 million to wire the entire country up front—an enormous capital expenditure that would make investors' heads spin. Ever since the tech bubble had burst in 2000, venture capitalists were much less venturesome; no one wanted to spend tons of money up front, well before the first dollar of revenue showed up.

Except for one investor, that is—Israeli billionaire Idan Ofer, who had just made the largest ever Israeli investment in China by buying a major stake in the Chinese car manufacturer Chery Automobile. Six months before, Ofer had also bought an oil refinery. So he knew a thing or two about the auto and oil industries. When Mike Granoff, an early American investor in Better Place, suggested tapping Ofer, Agassi said, "Why would he help me put him out of his two newest businesses?" But Agassi had nothing to lose.

Forty-five minutes into their meeting, Ofer told Agassi he was in for $100 million. He later increased his stake by another $30 million and told his Chinese auto team he wanted it to build electric cars.

Agassi raised the $200 million, making Better Place the fifth-largest start-up in history.[4] With Israel in place as the first test case, others were quick to follow. As of this writing, Denmark, Australia, the San Francisco Bay Area, Hawaii, and Ontario—Canada's most populous province—have all announced that they will join the Better Place plan. Better Place was the only foreign company asked to compete in developing an electric vehicle system for Japan, a highly unusual step for the historically protectionist Japanese government.

Among the many skeptics is Thomas Weber, the Mercedes research and development chief. He said that in 1972 his company had actually built an electric bus with a swappable battery, called the LE 306, and discovered that changing a battery could cause electrocution or fire.

Better Place's answer has been a working battery swap station. Using one is like pulling into a car wash. Only, once the driver pulls in, a large rectangular metal plate—much like the lifts at the back end of moving trucks—rises up from underneath the car. The car then retracts the thick two-inch metal hooks securing the enormous blue battery, releasing it so it rests on the plate. The plate moves back down, drops the spent battery in a charging station, picks up a full battery, and lifts it into place under the car. Total time for the completed automated swap: sixty-five seconds.

Agassi is proud of how his team solved the engineering problem of precisely, instantly, and reliably releasing a battery that weighs hundreds of pounds. They employed the same hooks used to hold five-hundred-pound bombs in place on air force bombers. There was no room for error in a bomb-release mechanism; the battery would be just as secure, yet removable, in electric cars.

If it succeeds, the global impact of Better Place on economics, politics, and the environment might well transcend that of the most important technology companies in the world. And the idea will have spread from Israel throughout the world.

Companies like Better Place and entrepreneurs like Shai Agassi don't appear every day. Yet a glance at Israel shows why it is not so surprising that, as Boston's Battery Ventures investor Scott Tobin predicted, "the next big idea will come from Israel."[5]

Technology companies and global investors are beating a path to Israel and finding unique combinations of audacity, creativity, and drive everywhere they look. Which may explain why, in addition to boasting the highest density of start-ups in the world (a total of 3,850 start-ups, one for every 1,844 Israelis),[6] more Israeli companies are listed on the NASDAQ exchange than all companies from the entire European continent.

And it's not just the New York stock exchanges that have been drawn to Israel, but also the most critical and fungible measure of technological promise: venture capital.

In 2008, per capita venture capital investments in Israel were 2.5 times greater than in the United States, more than 30 times greater than in Europe, 80 times greater than in China, and 350 times

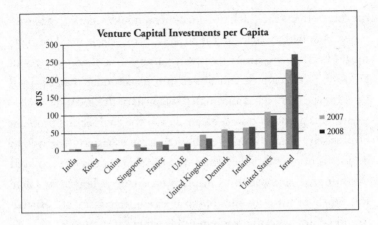

FIGURE I.1. *Sources:* Dow Jones, VentureSource; Thomson Reuters;
U.S. Central Intelligence Agency, *World Fact Book*, 2007, 2008.

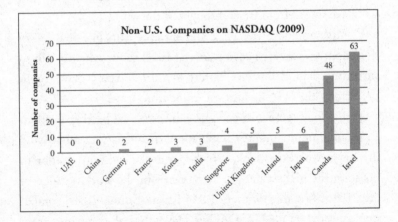

FIGURE I.2. *Source:* NASDAQ, http://www.nasdaq.com/asp/
NonUsOutput.asp, May 2009.

greater than in India. Comparing absolute numbers, Israel—a
country of just 7.1 million people—attracted close to $2 billion in
venture capital, as much as flowed to the United Kingdom's 61
million citizens or to the 145 million people living in Germany

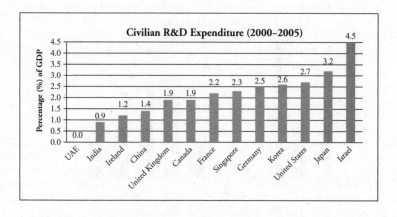

**FIGURE I.3.** *Source:* **UNDP (United Nations Development Programme) Report, 2007/2008.**

and France combined.[7] And Israel is the only country to experience a meaningful increase in venture capital from 2007 to 2008, as figure I.1 shows.[8]

After the United States, Israel has more companies listed on the NASDAQ than any other country in the world, including India, Korea, Singapore, and Ireland, as figure I.2 shows. And, as figure I.3 makes clear, Israel is the world leader in the percentage of the economy that is spent on research and development.

Israel's economy has also grown faster than the average for the developed economies of the world in most years since 1995, as a chart on page 14 illustrates (figure I.4).

Even the wars Israel has repeatedly fought have not slowed the country down. During the six years following 2000, Israel was hit not just by the bursting of the global tech bubble but by the most intense period of terrorist attacks in its history and by the second Lebanon war. Yet Israel's share of the global venture capital market did not drop—it *doubled*, from 15 percent to 31 percent. And the Tel Aviv stock exchange was higher on the last day of the Lebanon

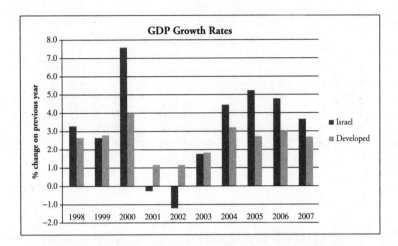

**FIGURE I.4.** *Sources:* "Miracles and Mirages," *Economist*, April 13, 2008; "GDP Growth Rates by Country and Region, 1970–2007," Swivel, http://www.swivel.com/data_columns/spreadsheet/2085677.

war than on the first, as it was after the three-week military operation in the Gaza Strip in 2009.

The Israeli economic story becomes even more curious when one considers the nation's dire state just a little over a half century ago. Shai Agassi's family immigrated to Israel from Iraq in 1950, two years after Israel's founding. The Agassis were part of a flood of a million refugees fleeing as a wave of violent pogroms swept the Arab world after the State of Israel's founding. At the time, the fledgling Jewish state simultaneously faced two seemingly insurmountable challenges: fighting an existential war for independence and absorbing masses of refugees from postwar Europe and the surrounding Arab countries.

Israel's population doubled in the first two years of its existence. Over the next seven years, the country grew by another third. Two out of three Israelis were new arrivals. Right off the boat, many refugees were given a gun they had no idea how to use and sent to fight. Some of those who had survived Nazi concentration camps fell in battle even before their names could be recorded. Proportionately, more Israelis died in the war for Israel's establishment than Americans in both world wars combined.

Those who survived had to struggle to thrive in a stagnant economy. "Everything was rationed," complained one new arrival. "We had coupon books, one egg a week, long lines."[9] The average standard of living for Israelis was comparable to that of Americans in the 1800s.[10] How, then, did this "start-up" state not only survive but morph from a besieged backwater to a high-tech powerhouse that has achieved fiftyfold economic growth in sixty years? How did a community of penniless refugees transform a land that Mark Twain described as a "desolate country... a silent, mournful expanse,"[11] into one of the most dynamic entrepreneurial economies in the world?

The fact that this question has been treated only in piecemeal fashion is unbelievable to Israeli political economist Gidi Grinstein: "Look, we doubled our economic situation relative to America while multiplying our population fivefold and fighting three wars. This is totally unmatched in the economic history of the world." And, he told us, the Israeli entrepreneur continues to perform in unimaginable ways.[12]

While the Holy Land has for centuries attracted pilgrims, lately it has been flooded by seekers of a different sort. Google's CEO and chairman, Eric Schmidt, told us that the United States is the number one place in the world for entrepreneurs, but "after the U.S., Israel is the best." Microsoft's Steve Ballmer has called Microsoft "an Israeli company as much as an American company" because of the size and centrality of its Israeli teams.[13] Warren Buffett, the apostle of risk aversion, broke his decades-long record of not buying any foreign company with the purchase of an Israeli company—for $4.5 billion—just as Israel began to fight the 2006 Lebanon war.

It is impossible for major technology companies to ignore Israel, and most haven't; almost half of the world's top technology companies have bought start-ups or opened research and development centers in Israel. Cisco alone has acquired nine Israeli companies and is looking to buy more.[14]

"In two days in Israel, I saw more opportunities than in a year in the rest of the world," said Paul Smith, senior vice president of Philips Medical.[15] Gary Shainberg, British Telecom's VP for technology and innovation, told us, "There are more new innovative ideas, as opposed to recycled ideas—or old ideas repackaged in a new box—coming out of Israel than there are out in [Silicon] Valley now. And it doesn't slow during global economic downturns."[16]

Though Israel's technology story is becoming more widely known, those exposed to it for the first time are invariably baffled. As an NBC Universal vice president sent to scout for Israeli digital media companies wondered, "Why is all this happening in Israel? I've never seen so much chaos and so much innovation all in one tiny place."[17]

That is the mystery this book aims to solve. Why Israel and not elsewhere?

One explanation is that adversity, like necessity, breeds inventiveness. Other small and threatened countries, such as South Korea, Singapore, and Taiwan, can also boast growth records that are as impressive as Israel's. But none of them have produced an entrepreneurial culture—not to mention an array of start-ups—that compares with Israel's.

Some people conjecture that there is something specifically Jewish at work. The notion that Jews are "smart" has become deeply embedded in the Western psyche. We saw this ourselves; when we told people we were writing a book about why Israel is so innovative, many reacted by saying, "It's simple—Jews are smart, so it's no surprise that Israel is innovative." But pinning Israel's success on a stereotype obscures more than it reveals.

For starters, the idea of a unitary Jewishness—whether genetic or cultural—would seem to have little applicability to a nation that, though small, is among the most heterogeneous in the world. Israel's tiny population is made up of some seventy different nationalities. A Jewish refugee from Iraq and one from Poland or Ethiopia did not share a language, education, culture, or history—at least not for the two previous millennia. As Irish economist David McWilliams explains, "Israel is quite the opposite of a uni-dimensional, Jewish country....It is a monotheistic melting pot of a diaspora that brought back with it the culture, language and customs of the four corners of the earth."[18]

While a common prayer book and a shared legacy of persecution count for something, it was far from clear that this disparate group could form a functioning country at all, let alone one that would excel at—of all things—teamwork and innovation.

Indeed, Israel's secret seems to lie in something more than just the talent of individuals. There are lots of places with talented people, certainly with many times the number of engineers that Israel has to offer. Singaporean students, for example, lead the world in science and mathematics test scores. Multinationals have set up shop in places like India and Ireland, too. "But we don't set up our mission critical work in those countries," an American executive from eBay told us. "Google, Cisco, Microsoft, Intel, eBay...the list goes on. The best-kept secret is that we all live and die by the work of our Israeli teams. It's much more than just outsourcing call centers to India or setting up IT services in Ireland. What we do in Israel is unlike what we do anywhere else in the world."[19]

Another commonly cited factor in Israel's success is the country's military and defense industry, which has produced successful spin-off companies. This is part of the answer, but it does not explain why other countries that have conscription and large militaries do not see a similar impact on their private sectors. Pointing to the military just shifts the question: What is it about the Israeli military that seems to foster entrepreneurship? And even with the influence of the military, why is it that defense, counterterrorism, and homeland security companies today represent less than 5 percent of Israel's gross domestic product?

The answer, we contend, must be broader and deeper. It must lie in the stories of individual entrepreneurs like Shai Agassi, which are emblematic of the state itself. As we will show, it is a story not just of talent but of tenacity, of insatiable questioning of authority, of determined informality, combined with a unique attitude toward failure, teamwork, mission, risk, and cross-disciplinary creativity. Israel is replete with such stories. But Israelis themselves have been too busy building their start-ups to step back and try to stitch together how it happened and what others—governments, large companies, and start-up entrepreneurs—can learn from their experience.

It would be hard to imagine a time when understanding the story of Israel's economic miracle could be more relevant. While the United States continues to be rated the world's most competitive economy, there is a widespread sense that something fundamental has gone wrong.

Even before the global financial crisis that began in 2008, observers of the innovation race were sounding alarms. "India and China are a tsunami about to overwhelm us," predicted Stanford Research Institute's Curtis Carlson. He forecasts that America's information technology, service, and medical-devices industries are about to be lost, costing "millions of jobs... like in the 1980s when the Japanese surged ahead." The only way out, says Carlson, is "to learn the tools of innovation" and forge entirely new, knowledge-based industries in energy, biotechnology, and other science-based sectors.[20]

"We are rapidly becoming the fat, complacent Detroit of nations," says former Harvard Business School professor John Kao. "We are... milking aging cows on the verge of going dry... [and] losing our collective sense of purpose along with our fire, ambition, and determination to achieve."[21]

The economic downturn has only sharpened the focus on innovation. The financial crisis, after all, was triggered by the collapse of real estate prices, which had been inflated by reckless bank lending and cheap credit. In other words, global prosperity had rested on a speculative bubble, not on the productivity increases that economists agree are the foundation of sustainable economic growth.

According to the pioneering work of Nobel Prize winner Robert Solow, technological innovation is the ultimate source of productivity and growth.[22] It's the only proven way for economies to consistently get ahead—especially innovation born by start-up companies. Recent Census Bureau data show that most of the net employment gains in the United States between 1980 and 2005 came from firms younger than five years old. Without start-ups, the average annual net employment growth rate would actually have been negative. Economist Carl Schramm, president of the Kauffman Foundation, which analyzes entrepreneurial economics, told us that "for the United States to survive and continue its economic leadership in the world, we must see entrepreneurship as our central comparative advantage. Nothing else can give us the necessary leverage."[23]

It is true that there are many models of entrepreneurship, including microentrepreneurship (the launching of household businesses) and the establishment of small companies that fill a niche and never grow beyond it. But Israel specializes in high-growth entrepreneurship—start-ups that wind up transforming entire global industries. High-growth entrepreneurship is distinct in that it uses specialized talent—from engineers and scientists to business managers and marketers—to commercialize a radically innovative idea.

This is not to suggest that Israelis are immune from the universally high failure rate of start-ups. But Israeli culture and regulations reflect a unique attitude to failure, one that has managed to repeatedly bring failed entrepreneurs back into the system to constructively use their experience to try again, rather than leave them permanently stigmatized and marginalized.

As a recent report by the Monitor Group, a global management consulting firm, described it, "When [entrepreneurs] succeed, they revolutionize markets. When they fail, they still [keep] incumbents under constant competitive pressure and thus stimulate progress." And the Monitor study shows that entrepreneurship is the main engine for economies to "evolve and regenerate."[24]

The question has become, as a *BusinessWeek* cover put it, "Can America Invent Its Way Back?"[25] The magazine observed that "beneath the gloom, economists and business leaders across the political spectrum are slowly coming to an agreement: Innovation is the best—and maybe the only—way the U.S. can get out of its economic hole."

In a world seeking the key to innovation, Israel is a natural place to look. The West needs innovation; Israel's got it. Understanding where this entrepreneurial energy comes from, where it's going, how to sustain it, and how other countries can learn from the quintessential start-up nation is a critical task for our times.

# PART I

## The Little Nation That Could

# CHAPTER 1

# Persistence

*Four guys are standing on a street corner...*
*an American, a Russian, a Chinese man, and an Israeli....*
*A reporter comes up to the group and says to them:*
*"Excuse me.... What's your opinion on the meat shortage?"*
*The American says: What's a shortage?*
*The Russian says: What's meat?*
*The Chinese man says: What's an opinion?*
*The Israeli says: What's "Excuse me"?*

—MIKE LEIGH, *Two Thousand Years*

SCOTT THOMPSON LOOKED AT HIS WATCH.[1] He was running behind. He had a long list of to-dos to complete by the end of the week, and it was already Thursday. Thompson is a busy guy. As president and former chief technology officer of PayPal, the largest Internet payment system in the world, he runs the Web's alternative to checks and credit cards. But he'd promised to give twenty minutes to a kid who claimed to have a solution to the problem of online payment scams, credit card fraud, and electronic identity theft.

Shvat Shaked did not have the brashness of an entrepreneur, which was just as well, since most start-ups, Thompson knew, didn't go anywhere. He did not look like he had the moxie of even a typical PayPal junior engineer. But Thompson wasn't going to say no to this meeting, not when Benchmark Capital had requested it.

Benchmark had made a seed investment in eBay, back when it was being run out of the founders' apartment as a quirky exchange site for collectible Pez dispensers. Today, eBay is an $18 billion public company with sixteen thousand employees around the world. It's also PayPal's parent company. Benchmark was considering an investment in Shaked's company, Israel-based Fraud Sciences. To help with due diligence, the Benchmark partners asked Thompson, who knew a thing or two about e-fraud, to check Shaked out.

"So what's your model, Shvat?" Thompson asked, eager to get the meeting over with. Shifting around a bit like someone who hadn't quite perfected his one-minute "elevator pitch," Shaked began quietly: "Our idea is simple. We believe that the world is divided between good people and bad people, and the trick to beating fraud is to distinguish between them on the Web."

Thompson suppressed his frustration. This was too much, even as a favor to Benchmark. Before PayPal, Thompson had been a top executive at credit card giant Visa, an even bigger company that was no less obsessed with combating fraud. A large part of the team at most credit card companies and online vendors is devoted to vetting new customers and fighting fraud and identity theft, because that's where profit margins can be largely determined and where customer trust is built or lost.

Visa and the banks it partnered with together had tens of thousands of people working to beat fraud. PayPal had two thousand, including some fifty of their best PhD engineers, trying to stay ahead of the crooks. And this kid was talking about "good guys and bad guys," as if he were the first to discover the problem.

"Sounds good," Thompson said, not without restraint. "How do you do that?"

"Good people leave traces of themselves on the Internet—digital footprints—because they have nothing to hide," Shvat continued in his accented English. "Bad people don't, because they try to hide themselves. All we do is look for footprints. If you can find them, you can minimize risk to an acceptable level and underwrite it. It really is that simple."

Thompson was beginning to think that this guy with the strange name had flown in not from a different country but rather a different planet. Didn't he know that fighting fraud is a painstaking process of checking backgrounds, wading through credit histories, building sophisticated algorithms to determine trustworthiness? You wouldn't walk into NASA and say, "Why build all those fancy spaceships when all you need is a slingshot?"

Still, out of respect for Benchmark, Thompson thought he'd indulge Shaked for a few more minutes. "So where did you learn how to do this?" he asked.

"Hunting down terrorists," Shaked said matter-of-factly. His unit in the army had been tasked with helping to catch terrorists by tracking their online activities. Terrorists move money through the Web with fictitious identities. Shvat's job was to find them online.

Thompson had heard enough from this "terrorist hunter," too much even, but he had a simple way out. "Have you tried this at all?" he asked.

"Yes," Shaked said with quiet self-assurance. "We've tried it on thousands of transactions, and we were right about all of them but four."

*Yeah, right,* Thompson thought to himself. But he couldn't help becoming a bit more curious. How long did that take? he asked.

Shaked said his company had analyzed forty thousand transactions over five years, since its founding.

"Okay, so here's what we're going to do," Thompson said, and he proposed that he give Fraud Sciences one hundred thousand Pay-Pal transactions to analyze. These were consumer transactions Pay-Pal had already processed. PayPal would have to scrub some of the personal data for legal privacy reasons, which would make Shvat's job more difficult. "But see what you can do," Thompson offered, "and get back to us. We'll compare your results with ours."

Since it had taken Shvat's start-up five years to go through their first forty thousand transactions, Thompson figured he wouldn't be seeing the kid again anytime soon. But he wasn't asking anything unfair. This was the sort of scaling necessary to determine whether his bizarre-sounding system was worth anything in the real world.

The forty thousand transactions Fraud Sciences had previously processed had been done manually. Shaked knew that to meet Pay-Pal's challenge he would have to automate his system in order to handle the volume, do so without compromising reliability, and crunch the transactions in record time. This would mean taking the system he'd tested over five years and turning it upside down, quickly.

Thompson gave the transaction data to Shvat on a Thursday. "I figured I was off the hook with Benchmark," he recalled. "We'd never hear from Shvat again. Or at least not for months." So he was surprised when he received an e-mail from Israel on Sunday. It said, "We're done."

Thompson didn't believe it. First thing Monday morning, he handed Fraud Sciences' work over to his team of PhDs for analysis; it took them a week to match the results up against PayPal's. But by Wednesday, Thompson's engineers were amazed at what they had seen so far. Shaked and his small team produced more accurate results than PayPal had, in a shorter amount of time, and with incomplete data. The difference was particularly pronounced on the transactions that had given PayPal the most trouble—on these,

Fraud Sciences had performed 17 percent better. This was the category of customer applicants, Thompson told us, that PayPal initially rejected. But in light of what PayPal now knows from monitoring the rejected customers' more recent credit reports, Thompson said, those rejections were a mistake: "They are good customers. We should never have rejected them. They slipped through our system. But how did they *not* slip through Shaked's system?"

Thompson realized that he was looking at a truly original tool against fraud. With even less data than PayPal had, Fraud Sciences was able to more accurately predict who would turn out to be a good customer and who would not. "I was sitting here, dumbfounded," Thompson recalled. "I didn't get it. We're the best in the business at risk management. How is it that this fifty-five-person company from Israel, with a crackpot theory about 'good guys' and 'bad guys,' managed to beat us?" Thompson estimated that Fraud Sciences was five years ahead of PayPal in the effectiveness of its system. His previous company, Visa, would never have been able to come up with such thinking, even if given ten or fifteen years to work on it.

Thompson knew what he had to tell Benchmark: PayPal could not afford to risk letting its competitors get hold of Fraud Sciences' breakthrough technology. This was not a company Benchmark should invest in; PayPal needed to acquire the company. Immediately.

Thompson went to eBay's CEO, Meg Whitman, to bring her into the loop. "I told Scott that it was impossible," Whitman related. "We're the market leader. Where on earth did this tiny little company come from?" Thompson and his team of PhDs walked her through the results. She was astounded.

Now Thompson and Whitman had a truly unexpected problem on their hands. What could they tell Shvat? If Thompson told this start-up's CEO that he had handily beaten the industry leader, the start-up's team would realize they were sitting on something invaluable. Thompson knew that PayPal had to buy Fraud Sciences, but how could he tell Shvat the test results without jacking up the company's price and negotiating position?

So he stalled. He responded to Shaked's anxious e-mails by saying PayPal needed more time for analysis. Finally, he said he would share the results in person the next time the Fraud Sciences team was in San Jose, hoping to buy more time. Within a day or two, Shaked was on Thompson's doorstep.

What Thompson did not know, however, was that the Fraud Sciences founders—Shaked and Saar Wilf, who served together in Israel's elite army intelligence unit, called 8200—were not interested in selling their company to PayPal. They just wanted Thompson's blessing as they proceeded down a checklist of due diligence requirements for Benchmark Capital.

Thompson went back to Meg: "We need to make a decision. They're here." She gave him the go-ahead: "Let's buy it." After some valuation work, they offered $79 million. Shaked declined. The Fraud Sciences board, which included the Israeli venture firm BRM Capital, believed the company was worth at least $200 million.

Eli Barkat, one of the founding partners of BRM, explained to us his theory behind the company's future value: "The first generation of technology security was protecting against a virus invading your PC. The second generation was building a firewall against hackers." Barkat knew something about both these threats, having funded and built companies to protect against them. One of them, Checkpoint—an Israeli company also started by young alumni from Unit 8200—is worth $5 billion today, is publicly traded on the NASDAQ, and includes among its customers the majority of Fortune 100 companies and most national governments around the world. The third generation of security would be protecting against hacking into e-commerce activity. "And this would be the biggest market yet," Barkat told us, "because up until then, hackers were just having fun—it was a hobby. But with e-commerce taking off, hackers could make real money."

Barkat also believed that Fraud Sciences had the best team and the best technology to defend against Internet and credit card fraud. "You've got to understand the Israeli mentality," he said. "When you've been developing technology to find terrorists—when lots of innocent lives hang in the balance—then finding thieves is pretty simple."

After negotiations that lasted only a few days, Thompson and Shaked agreed on $169 million. Thompson told us that the PayPal team thought it could get away with a lower price. When the negotiating process began and Shaked stuck to the higher number, Thompson assumed it was just a bluff. "I figured I'd never seen such a convincing poker face. But what was really going on was that the Fraud Sciences guys had a view of what their company was worth. They were not sales guys. They weren't hyping it. Shaked just played it straight. He basically said to us, 'This is our solution. We know it is the best. This is what we think it's worth.' And that really was the end of it. There was a matter-of-factness that you just don't see that often."

Soon after, Thompson was on a plane to visit the company he had just purchased. During the last leg of the twenty-hour flight from San Francisco, about forty-five minutes before landing, as he sipped his coffee to wake up, he happened to glance at the screen in the aisle that showed the plane's trajectory on a map. He could see the little airplane icon at the end of its flight path, about to land in Tel Aviv. That was fine, until he noticed what else was on the map, which at this point showed only places that were pretty close by. He could see the names and capitals of the countries in the region, arrayed in a ring around Israel: Beirut, Lebanon; Damascus, Syria; Amman, Jordan; and Cairo, Egypt. For a moment, he panicked: "I bought a company there? I'm flying into a war zone!" Of course, he'd known all along who Israel's neighbors were, but it had not quite sunk in how small Israel was and how closely those neighbors ringed it. "It was as if I were flying into New York and suddenly saw Iran where New Jersey was supposed to be," he recalled.

It didn't take long after he stepped off the plane, however, before he was at ease in a place that was not shockingly unfamiliar, and that treated him to some pleasant surprises. His first big impression was in the Fraud Sciences parking lot. Every car had a PayPal bumper sticker on it. "You'd never see that kind of pride or enthusiasm at an American company," he told us.

The next thing that struck Thompson was the demeanor of the Fraud Sciences employees during the all-hands meeting at which he spoke. Each face was turned raptly to him. No one was texting, surfing, or dozing off. The intensity only increased when he opened the discussion period: "Every question was penetrating. I actually started to get nervous up there. I'd never before heard so many unconventional observations—one after the other. And these weren't peers or supervisors, these were junior employees. And they had no inhibition about challenging the logic behind the way we at PayPal had been doing things for years. I'd never seen this kind of completely unvarnished, unintimidated, and undistracted attitude. I found myself thinking, Who works for whom?"

What Scott Thompson was experiencing was his first dose of Israeli *chutzpah*. According to Jewish scholar Leo Rosten's description of Yiddish—the all-but-vanished German-Slavic language from which modern Hebrew borrowed the word—*chutzpah* is "gall, brazen nerve, effrontery, incredible 'guts,' presumption plus arrogance such as no other word and no other language can do justice to."[2] An outsider would see *chutzpah* everywhere in Israel: in the way university students speak with their professors, employees challenge their bosses, sergeants question their generals, and clerks second-guess government ministers. To Israelis, however, this isn't *chutzpah*, it's the normal mode of being. Somewhere along the way—either at home, in school, or in the army—Israelis learn that assertiveness is the norm, reticence something that risks your being left behind.

This is evident even in popular forms of address in Israel. Jon Medved, an entrepreneur and venture capital investor in Israel, likes to cite what he calls the "nickname barometer": "You can tell a lot about a society based on how [its members] refer to their elites. Israel is the only place in the world where everybody in a position of power—including prime ministers and army generals— has a nickname used by all, including the masses."

Israel's current and former prime ministers Benjamin Netanyahu and Ariel Sharon are "Bibi" and "Arik." A former Labor Party leader is Binyamin "Füad" Ben-Eliezer. A recent Israel Defense Forces (IDF) chief of staff is Moshe "Bogey" Yaalon. In the 1980s, the legendary IDF chief was Moshe "Moshe VeHetzi" (Moshe-and-a-Half) Levi—he was six foot six. Other former IDF generals in Israeli history were Rehavam "Gandhi" Zeevi, David "Dado" Elazar, and Rafael "Raful" Eitan. A famous Shinui Party leader was Yosef "Tommy" Lapid. A top minister in successive Israeli governments is Isaac "Bugie" Herzog. These nicknames are used not behind the officials' backs but, rather, openly, and by everyone. This, Medved argues, is representative of Israel's level of informality.

Israeli attitude and informality flow also from a cultural tolerance for what some Israelis call "constructive failures" or "intelligent failures." Most local investors believe that without tolerating a large number of these failures, it is impossible to achieve true innovation. In the Israeli military, there is a tendency to treat all performance—both successful and unsuccessful—in training and simulations, and sometimes even in battle, as value-neutral. So long as the risk was taken intelligently, and not recklessly, there is something to be learned.

As Harvard Business School professor Loren Gary says, it is critical to distinguish between "a well-planned experiment and a roulette wheel."[3] In Israel, this distinction is established early on in military training. "We don't cheerlead you excessively for a good performance, and we don't finish you off permanently for a bad performance," one air force trainer told us.[4]

Indeed, a 2006 Harvard University study shows that entrepreneurs who have failed in their previous enterprise have an almost one-in-five chance of success in their next start-up, which is a higher success rate than that for first-time entrepreneurs and not far below that of entrepreneurs who have had a prior success.[5]

In *The Geography of Bliss*, author Eric Weiner describes another country with a high tolerance for failure as "a nation of born-agains, though not in a religious sense."[6] This is certainly true for Israeli laws regarding bankruptcy and new company formation, which make it the easiest place in the Middle East—and one of the easiest in the world—to birth a new company, even if your last one went bankrupt. But this also contributes to a sense that Israelis are always hustling, pushing, and looking for the next opportunity.

Newcomers to Israel often find its people rude. Israelis will unabashedly ask people they barely know how old they are or how much their apartment or car cost; they'll even tell new parents—often complete strangers on the sidewalk or in a grocery store—that they are not dressing their children appropriately for the weather. What is said about Jews—two Jews, three opinions—is certainly true of Israelis. People who don't like this sort of frankness can be turned off by Israel, but others find it refreshing, and honest.

"We did it the Israeli way; we argued our case to death."[7] That's how Shmuel "Mooly" Eden (he has a nickname, too) glibly sums up a historic showdown between Intel's top executives in Santa Clara and its Israeli team. It, too, was a case study in *chutzpah*.

The survival of Intel would turn on the outcome. But this fierce, months-long dispute was about more than just Intel; it would determine whether the ubiquitous laptop computer—so much taken for granted today—would ever exist.

Eden is a leader of Intel's Israeli operation—the largest private-sector employer in the country—which today exports $1.53 billion annually.[8] He told us the story of Intel in Israel, and Intel's battles with Israel.

Throughout most of the history of modern computing, the speed of data processing—how much time it takes your computer to do anything—was determined by the speed of a chip's transistors. The transistors flipped on and off, and the order in which they did so produced a code, much like letters are used to make words. Together, millions of flips could record and manipulate data in endless ways. The faster the transistors could be made to flip on and off (the transistor's "clock speed"), the more powerful the software they could run, transforming computers from glorified calculators to multimedia entertainment and enterprise machines.

But until the 1970s, computers were used predominantly by rocket scientists and big universities. Some computers took up whole rooms or even buildings. The idea of a computer on your office desk or in your home was the stuff of science fiction. All that began to change in 1980, when Intel's Haifa team designed the 8088 chip, whose transistors could flip almost five million times per second (4.77 megahertz), and were small enough to allow for the creation of computers that would fit in homes and offices.

IBM chose Israel's 8088 chip as the brains for its first "personal computer," or PC, launching a new era of computing. It was also a major breakthrough for Intel. According to journalist Michael Malone, "With the IBM contract, Intel won the microprocessor wars."[9]

From then on, computing technology continued to get smaller and faster. By 1986, Intel's only foreign chip factory was producing the 386 chip. Built in Jerusalem, its processing speed was 33 megahertz. Though a small fraction of today's chip speeds, Intel called it "blazing"—it was almost seven times faster than the 8088. The company was solidly on the path imagined by one of its founders, Gordon

Moore, who predicted that the industry would shrink transistors to half their size every eighteen to twenty-four months, roughly doubling a chip's processing speed. This constant halving was dubbed "Moore's law," and the chip industry was built around this challenge to deliver faster and faster chips. IBM, Wall Street, and the business press all caught on, too—clock speed and size was how they measured the value of new chips.

This was proceeding well until about 2000, when another factor came into the mix: power. Chips were getting smaller and faster, just as Moore had predicted. But as they did, they also used more power and generated more heat. Chips overheating would soon become a critical problem. The obvious solution was a fan, but, in the case of laptops, the fan needed to cool the chips would be much too big to fit inside. Industry experts dubbed this dead end the "power wall."

Intel's Israeli team was the first group within the company to see this coming. Many late nights at Intel's Haifa facility were dedicated to hot coffee, cold takeout, and ad hoc brainstorming sessions about how to get around the power wall. The Israeli team was more focused than anyone on what the industry called "mobility"—designing chips for laptop computers and, eventually, for all sorts of mobile devices. Noticing this tendency, Intel put their Israeli branch in charge of building mobility chips for the whole company.

Even given this responsibility, Israelis still resisted fitting into the Intel mainstream. "The development group in Israel, even before it was tasked as the mobility group, pushed ideas for mobility that went against the common wisdom at Intel," explained Intel Israel's chief, David "Dadi" Perlmutter, a graduate of the Technion (Israel's MIT) who'd started designing chips at Intel Israel in 1980.[10] One of these unconventional ideas was a way to get around the power wall. Rony Friedman was one of Intel Israel's top engineers at the time. Just for fun, he had been tinkering with a way to produce low-power chips, which went blatantly against the prevailing orthodoxy that the only way to make chips faster was to deliver more power to their transistors. This, he thought, was a bit like making cars go faster by revving their engines harder. There was definitely a connection between the speed of the engine and the speed of the car, but at some point the engine would go too fast, get too hot, and the car would have to slow down.[11]

Friedman and the Israeli team realized that the solution to the problem was something like a gear system in a car: if you could change gears, you could run the engine more slowly while still making the car go faster. In a chip, this was accomplished differently, by splitting the instructions fed into the chip. But the effect was similar: the transistors in Intel Israel's low-power chips did not need to flip on and off as fast, yet, in a process analogous to shifting a car into high gear, they were able to run software faster.

When Intel's Israel team euphorically introduced its innovation to headquarters in Santa Clara, the engineers thought their bosses would be thrilled. What could be better than a car that goes faster without overheating? Yet what the Israeli team saw as an asset— that the engine turned more slowly—headquarters saw as a big problem. After all, the entire industry measured the power of chips by how fast the *engine* turned: clock speed.

It did not matter that Israeli chips ran software faster. The computer's engine—composed of its chip's transistors—wasn't turning on and off fast enough. Wall Street analysts would opine on the attractiveness (or unattractiveness) of Intel's stock based on performance along a parameter that said, *Faster clock speed: Buy; Slower clock speed: Sell.* Trying to persuade the industry and the press that this metric was obsolete was a nonstarter. This was especially the case because Intel had itself created—through Moore's law—the industry's Pavlovian attachment to clock speed. It was tantamount to trying to convince Ford to abandon its quest for more horsepower or telling Tiffany's that carat size does not matter.

"We weren't in the mainstream—clock speed was king and we were on the outside," Israel's Rony Friedman recalls.[12]

The head of Intel's chip division, Paul Otellini, tried to mothball the whole project. The clock-speed doctrine was enshrined among Intel's brass, and they weren't about to hold a seminar to decide whether or not to change it.

The "seminar" is part of a culture that Israelis know well, going back to the founding of the state. From the end of March to the end of May 1947, David Ben-Gurion—Israel's George Washington—conducted an inquiry into the military readiness of Jewish Palestine, in anticipation of the war he knew would come when Israel declared independence. He spent days and nights meeting with, probing, and listening to military men up and down the ranks. More than six months before the United Nations passed its partition plan for dividing Palestine into a Jewish and an Arab state, Ben-Gurion was keenly aware that the next phase in the Arab-Israeli conflict would be very different from the war the pre-state Jewish militias had been fighting; they needed to step back, in the midst of ongoing fighting, and plan for the existential threats that were nearing.

At the end of the seminar, Ben-Gurion wrote of the men's confidence in their readiness: "We have to undertake difficult work—to uproot from the hearts of men who are close to the matter the belief that they have something. In fact, they have nothing. They have good will, they have hidden capacities, but they have to know: to make a shoe one has to study cobbling."[13]

Intel's Otellini didn't know it, but his Israeli team was giving him a similar message. They saw that Intel was headed for the "power wall." Instead of waiting to ram into it, the Israelis wanted Otellini to avert it by taking a step back, discarding conventional thinking, and considering a fundamental change in the company's technological approach.

The executives in Santa Clara were ready to strangle the Israeli team, according to some of those on the receiving end of Intel Israel's "pestering." The Israelis were making the twenty-hour trip between Tel Aviv and California so frequently that they seemed omnipresent, always ready to corner an executive in the hallway or even a restroom—anything to argue their case. David Perlmutter spent one week each month in the Santa Clara headquarters, and he used much of his time there to press the Israeli team's case.

One point the Israelis tried to make was that while there was risk in abandoning the clock-speed doctrine, there was even greater risk in sticking with it. Dov Frohman, the founder of Intel Israel, later said that to create a true culture of innovation, "fear of loss often proves more powerful than the hope of gain."[14]

Frohman had long tried to cultivate a culture of disagreement and debate at Intel Israel, and he had hoped this ethos would infect Santa Clara. "The goal of a leader," he said, "should be to maximize resistance—in the sense of encouraging disagreement and dissent. When an organization is in crisis, lack of resistance can itself be a big problem. It can mean that the change you are trying to create isn't radical enough...or that the opposition has gone underground. If you aren't even aware that the people in the organization disagree with you, then you are in trouble."

In time, the Israelis outlasted—and outargued—their U.S. supervisors. Each time the Israelis showed up, they had better research and better data, one Intel executive recalled. Soon they had a seemingly bulletproof case as to where the industry was heading. Intel could either lead in that direction, the Israelis told management, or become obsolete.

Finally, this time as CEO, Otellini changed his mind. It had become impossible to counter the Israelis' overwhelming research—not to mention their persistence. In March 2003, the new chip—code-named Banias after a natural spring in Israel's north—was released as the Centrino chip for laptops. Its clock speed was only a bit more than half of the reigning 2.8 gigahertz Pentium chips for desktops, and it sold for more than twice the price. But it gave laptop users the portability and speed they needed.

The switch to the Israeli-designed approach came to be known in Intel and the industry as the "right turn," since it was a sharp change in approach from simply going for higher and higher clock speeds without regard to heat output or power needs. Intel began to apply the "right turn" paradigm not just to chips for laptops but to chips for desktops, as well. Looking back, the striking thing about Intel Israel's campaign for the new architecture was that the engineers were really just doing their jobs. They cared about the future of the whole company; the fight wasn't about winning a battle within Intel, it was about winning the war with the competition.

As a result, the new Israeli-designed architecture, once derided within the company, was a runaway hit. It became the anchor of Intel's 13 percent sales growth from 2003 to 2005. But Intel was not clear of industry threats yet. Despite the initial success, by 2006, new competition caused Intel's market share to plummet to its lowest point in eleven years. Profits soon plunged 42 percent as the company cut prices to retain its dominant position.[15]

The bright spot in 2006, however, came in late July when Otellini unveiled the Core 2 Duo chips, Intel's successors to the Pentium. The Core Duo chips applied Israel's "right turn" concept plus another Israeli development, called dual-core processing, that sped chips up even further. "These are the best microprocessors we've ever designed, the best we've ever built," he told an audience of five hundred in a festive tent at Intel's Santa Clara headquarters. "This is not just incremental change; it's a revolutionary leap." Screens lit up with images of the proud engineers behind the new chip; they were joining the celebration via satellite, from Haifa, Israel. Though Intel's stock was down 19 percent over the whole year, it jumped 16 percent after the July announcement. Intel went on to release forty new processors over a one-hundred-day period, most of them based on the Israeli team's design.

"It's unbelievable that, just a few years ago, we were designing something that no one wanted," says Friedman, who is still based in Haifa but now leads development teams for Intel around the world. "Now we're doing processors that should carry most of Intel's revenue—we can't screw up."

What began as an isolated outpost an ocean away had become Intel's lifeline. As Doug Freedman, an analyst for American Technology Research, put it, the Israeli team "saved the company." Had midlevel developers in the Haifa plant not challenged their corporate superiors, Intel's global position today would be much diminished.

Intel Israel's search for a way around the power wall also produced another dividend. We don't think of computers as using a lot of electricity—we leave them on all the time—but, collectively, they do. Intel's ecotechnology executive, John Skinner, calculated the amount of power that Intel's chips would have used if the company had kept developing them in the same way, rather than making the "right turn" toward the Israeli team's low-power design: a saving of 20 terawatt hours of electricity over a two-and-a-half-year period. That's the amount of power it would take to run over 22 million 100-watt bulbs for an entire year, twenty-four hours a day, seven days a week. Skinner noted, "We calculated about a $2 billion savings in electricity costs.... It's equivalent to a small number of coal-fired power plants or taking a few million cars off the road.... We're very proud that we are dramatically reducing the carbon dioxide footprint of our own company."[16]

The significance of the Intel Israel story is not, however, just that the team in Haifa came up with a revolutionary solution that turned the company around. A good idea alone could not have carried the day against a seemingly intransigent management team.

There had to be willingness to take on higher authorities, rather than simply following directives from the top. Where does this impudence come from?

Dadi Perlmutter recalls the shock of an American colleague when he witnessed Israeli corporate culture for the first time. "When we all emerged [from our meeting], red faced after shouting, he asked me what was wrong. I told him, 'Nothing. We reached some good conclusions.'"

That kind of heated debate is anathema in other business cultures, but for Israelis it's often seen as the best way to sort through a problem. "If you can get past the initial bruise to the ego," one American investor in Israeli start-ups told us, "it's immensely liberating. You rarely see people talk behind anybody's back in Israeli companies. You always know where you stand with everyone. It does cut back on the time wasted on bullshit."

Perlmutter later moved to Santa Clara and became Intel's executive vice president in charge of mobile computing. His division produces nearly half of the company's revenues. He says, "When I go back to Israel, it's like going back to the old culture of Intel. It's easier in a country where politeness gets less of a premium."

The cultural differences between Israel and the United States are actually so great that Intel started running "cross-cultural seminars" to bridge them. "After living in the U.S. for five years, I can say that the interesting thing about Israelis is the culture. Israelis do not have a very disciplined culture. From the age of zero we are educated to challenge the obvious, ask questions, debate everything, innovate," says Mooly Eden, who ran these seminars.

As a result, he adds, "it's more complicated to manage five Israelis than fifty Americans because [the Israelis] will challenge you all the time—starting with 'Why are you my manager; why am I not your manager?'"[17]

# CHAPTER 2

# Battlefield Entrepreneurs

*The Israeli tank commander who has fought in one of the*
*Syrian wars is the best engineering executive in the world.*
*The tank commanders are operationally the best, and they are*
*extremely detail oriented. This is based on twenty years of*
*experience—working with them and observing them.*

—ERIC SCHMIDT

On October 6, 1973, as the entire nation was shut down for the holiest day of the Jewish year, the armies of Egypt and Syria launched the Yom Kippur War with a massive surprise attack. Within hours, Egyptian forces breached Israel's defensive line along the Suez Canal. Egyptian infantry had already overrun the tank emplacements to which Israeli armored forces were supposed to race in case of attack, and hundreds of enemy tanks were moving forward behind this initial thrust.

It was just six years after Israel's greatest military victory, the Six-Day War, an improbable campaign that captured the imagination of the entire world. Just before that war, in 1967, it looked like the nineteen-year-old Jewish state would be crushed by Arab armies poised to invade on every front. Then, in six days of battle, Israel simultaneously defeated the Egyptian, Jordanian, and Syrian forces and expanded its borders by taking the Golan Heights from Syria, the West Bank and East Jerusalem from Jordan, and the Gaza Strip and Sinai Peninsula from Egypt.

All this gave Israelis a sense of invincibility. Afterward, no one could imagine the Arab states risking another all-out attack. Even in the military, the sense was that if the Arabs dared attack, Israel would vanquish their armies as quickly as it had in 1967.

So on that October day in 1973, Israel was not prepared for war. The thin string of Israeli forts facing the Egyptians across the Suez Canal was no match for the overwhelming Egyptian invasion. Behind the destroyed front line, three Israeli tank brigades stood between the advancing Egyptian army and the Israeli heartland. Only one was stationed close to the front.

That brigade, which was supposed to defend a 120-mile front with just fifty-six tanks, was commanded by Colonel Amnon Reshef. As he raced with his men to engage the invading Egyptians, Reshef saw his tanks getting hit one after another. But there were no Egyptian enemy tanks or antitank guns in sight. What sort of device was obliterating his men?

At first he thought the tanks were being hit by rocket-propelled grenades (RPGs), the classic handheld antitank weapon used by infantry forces. Reshef and his men pulled back a bit, as they had been trained, so as to be out of the short range of the RPGs. But the tanks kept exploding. The Israelis realized they were being hit by something else—something seemingly invisible.

As the battle raged, a clue emerged. The tank operators who survived a missile hit reported to the others that they'd seen nothing, but those *next* to them mentioned having seen a red light moving toward the targeted tanks. Wires were found on the ground leading to stricken Israeli tanks. The commanders had discovered Egypt's secret weapon: the Sagger.

Designed by Sergei Pavlovich Nepobedimyi, whose last name literally means "undefeatable" in Russian, the Sagger was created in 1960. The new weapon had initially been provided to Warsaw Pact countries, but it was first put to sustained use in combat by the Egyptian and Syrian armies during the Yom Kippur War. The IDF's account of its own losses on both the southern and northern fronts was 400 tanks destroyed and 600 disabled but returned to battle after repairs. Of the Sinai division's 290 tanks, 180 were knocked out the first day. The blow to the IDF's aura of invincibility was substantial. About half of the losses came from RPGs, the other half from the Sagger.

The Sagger was a wire-guided missile that could be fired by a single soldier lying on the ground. Its range—the distance from which it could hit and destroy a tank—was 3,000 meters (or 1.86 miles), ten times that of an RPG. The Sagger was also far more powerful.[1]

Each shooter could work alone and did not even need a bush to hide behind—a shallow depression in the desert sand would do. A shooter had only to fire in the direction of a tank and use a joystick to guide the red light at the back of the missile. So long as the soldier could see the red light, the wire that remained connected to the missile would allow him to guide it accurately and at great distance into the target.[2]

Israeli intelligence knew about the Saggers before the war, and had even encountered them in Egyptian cross-border attacks during the War of Attrition, which began just after the 1967 war. But the top brass thought the Saggers were merely another antitank weapon, not qualitatively different from what they had successfully contended with in the 1967 war. Thus, in their view, doctrines to oppose them already existed, and nothing was developed to specifically address the Sagger threat.

Reshef and his men had to discover for themselves what type of weapon was hitting them and how to cope with it, all in the heat of battle.

Drawing on the men's reports, Reshef's remaining officers real-ized that the Saggers had some weaknesses: they flew relatively slowly, and they depended on the shooter's retaining eye contact with the Israeli tank. So the Israelis devised a new doctrine: when any tank saw a red light, all would begin moving randomly while firing in the direction of the unseen shooter.

The dust kicked up by the moving tanks would obscure the shooter's line of sight to the missile's deadly red light, and the return fire might also prevent the shooter from keeping his eye on the light.

This brand-new doctrine proved successful, and after the war it was eventually adopted by NATO forces. It had not been honed over years of gaming exercises in war colleges or prescribed out of an operations manual; it had been *improvised* by soldiers at the front.

As usual in the Israeli military, the tactical innovation came from the bottom up—from individual tank commanders and their offi-cers. It probably never occurred to these soldiers that they should ask their higher-ups to solve the problem, or that they might not have the authority to act on their own. Nor did they see anything strange in their taking responsibility for inventing, adopting, and disseminating new tactics in real time, on the fly.

Yet what these soldiers were doing *was* strange. If they had been working in a multinational company or in any number of other armies, they might not have done such things, at least not on their own. As historian Michael Oren, who served in the IDF as a liaison to other militaries, put it, "The Israeli lieutenant probably has greater command decision latitude than his counterpart in any army in the world."[3]

This latitude, evidenced in the corporate culture we examined in the previous chapter, is just as prevalent, if not more so, in the Israeli military. Normally, when one thinks of military culture, one thinks of strict hierarchies, unwavering obedience to superiors, and an acceptance of the fact that each soldier is but a small, uninformed cog in a big wheel. But the IDF doesn't fit that description. And in Israel pretty much everyone serves in the military, where its culture is worked into Israel's citizens over a compulsory two- to three-year service.

The IDF's downward delegation of responsibility is both by necessity and by design. "All militaries claim to value improvisation: read what the Chinese, French, or British militaries say—they all talk about improvisation. But the words don't tell you anything," said Edward Luttwak, a military historian and strategist who wrote *The Pentagon and the Art of War* and co-wrote *The Israeli Army*. "You have to look at structure."[4]

To make his point, Luttwak began rattling off the ratios of officers to enlisted personnel in militaries around the world, ending with Israel, whose military pyramid is exceptionally narrow at the top. "The IDF is deliberately understaffed at senior levels. It means that there are fewer senior officers to issue commands," says Luttwak. "Fewer senior officials means more individual initiative at the lower ranks."

Luttwak points out that the Israeli army has very few colonels and an abundance of lieutenants. The ratio of senior officers to combat troops in the U.S. Army is 1 to 5; in the IDF, it's 1 to 9. The same is true in the Israeli Air Force (IAF), which, though larger than French and British air forces, has fewer senior officers. The IAF is headed by a two-star general, a lower rank than is typical in other Western militaries.

For the United States, the more top-heavy approach may well be necessary; after all, the U.S. military is much larger, fights its wars as far as eight thousand miles from home, and faces the unique logistical and command challenges of deploying over multiple continents.

Yet regardless of whether each force is the right size and structure for the tasks it faces, the fact that the IDF is lighter at the top has important consequences. The benefit was illuminated for us by Gilad Farhi, a thirty-year-old major in the IDF. His career path was fairly typical: from a soldier in a commando unit at age eighteen, to commanding an infantry platoon, then a company, he was next appointed a spokesman of the Southern Command. After that he became the deputy commander of Haruv, an infantry battalion. Now he is the commander of an incoming class of one of the IDF's most recent infantry regiments.

We met him at a base on a barren edge of the Jordan Valley. As he strode toward us, neither his youth nor his attire (a rumpled standard-issue infantry uniform) would have pegged him as commander of the base. We interviewed him the day before his new class of recruits was to arrive. For the next seven months, Farhi would be in charge of basic training for 650 soldiers, most of them fresh out of high school, plus about 120 officers, squad commanders, sergeants, and administrative staff.[5]

"The most interesting people here are the company commanders," Farhi told us. "They are absolutely amazing people. These are kids—the company commanders are twenty-three. Each of them is in charge of one hundred soldiers and twenty officers and sergeants, three vehicles. Add it up and that means a hundred and twenty rifles, machine guns, bombs, grenades, mines, whatever. Everything. Tremendous responsibility."

Company commander is also the lowest rank that must take responsibility for a territory. As Farhi put it, "If a terrorist infiltrates that area, there's a company commander whose name is on it. Tell me how many twenty-three-year-olds elsewhere in the world live with that kind of pressure."

Farhi illustrated a fairly typical challenge facing these twenty-three-year-olds. During an operation in the West Bank city of Nablus, one of Farhi's companies had an injured soldier trapped in a house held by a terrorist. The company commander had three tools at his disposal: an attack dog, his soldiers, and a bulldozer.

If he sent the soldiers in, there was a high risk of additional casualties. And if he sent the bulldozer to destroy the house, this would risk harming the injured soldier.

To further complicate matters, the house shared a wall with a Palestinian school, and children and teachers were still inside. From the roof of the school, journalists were documenting the whole scene. The terrorist, meanwhile, was shooting at both the Israeli forces and the journalists.

Throughout much of the standoff, the company commander was on his own. Farhi could have tried to take charge from afar, but he knew he had to give his subordinate latitude: "There were an infinite number of dilemmas there for the commander. And there wasn't a textbook solution." The soldiers managed to rescue the injured soldier, but the terrorist remained inside. The commander knew that the school staff was afraid to evacuate the school, despite the danger, because they did not want to be branded "collaborators" by the terrorists. And he knew that the journalists would not leave the roof of the school, because they didn't want to miss breaking news. The commander's solution: empty the school using smoke grenades.

Once the students, teachers, and journalists had been safely evacuated, the commander decided it was safe to send in the bulldozer to drive the terrorist out of the adjacent building. Once the bulldozer began biting into the house, the commander unleashed the dog to neutralize the terrorist. But while the bulldozer was knocking down the house, another terrorist the Israelis didn't know about came out of the school next door. The soldiers outside shot and killed this second terrorist. The entire operation took four hours. "This twenty-three-year-old commander was alone for most of the four hours until I got there," Farhi told us.

"After an event like that, the company commander goes back to the base and his soldiers look at him differently," Farhi continued. "And he himself is different. He is on the line—responsible for the lives of a lot of people: his soldiers, Palestinian schoolchildren, journalists. Look, he didn't conquer Eastern Europe, but he had to come up with a creative solution to a very complex situation. And he is only twenty-three years old."

We then heard from a brigadier general about Yossi Klein, a twenty-year-old helicopter pilot in the 2006 Lebanon war. He was ordered to evacuate a wounded soldier from deep in southern Lebanon. When he piloted his chopper to the battlefield, the wounded soldier lay on a stretcher surrounded by a dense overgrowth of bushes that prevented the helicopter from landing or hovering close enough to the ground to pull the stretcher on board.[6]

There were no manuals on how to deal with such a situation, but if there had been, they would not have recommended what Klein did. He used the tail rotor of his helicopter like a flying lawn mower to chop down the foliage. At any point, the rotor could have broken off, sending the helicopter crashing into the ground. But Klein succeeded in trimming the bushes enough so that, by hovering close to the ground, he could pick up the wounded soldier. The soldier was rushed to the hospital in Israel and his life was saved.

Speaking of the company commanders who served under him, Farhi asked, "How many of their peers in their junior year in colleges have been tested in such a way?...How do you train and mature a twenty-year-old to shoulder such responsibility?"

The degree to which authority devolves to some of the most junior members of the military has at times surprised even Israeli leaders. In 1974, during the first premiership of Yitzhak Rabin, a young female soldier from the IDF's Unit 8200—the same unit in which the founders of Fraud Sciences later served—was kidnapped by terrorists. Major General Aharon Zeevi-Farkash (known as

Farkash), who headed the unit—Israel's parallel to the U.S. National Security Agency—recalled Rabin's disbelief: "The kidnapped girl was a sergeant. Rabin asked us to provide him an itemization of what she knew. He was worried about the depth of classified information that could be forced out of her. When he saw the briefing paper, Rabin told us we needed an immediate investigation; it's impossible that a sergeant would know so many secrets that are critical to Israel's security. How did this happen?"

Rabin's reaction was especially surprising since he had been the IDF chief of staff during Israel's Six-Day War. Farkash continued the story: "So I told him, 'Mr. Prime Minister, this individual sergeant is not alone. It was not a mistake. All the soldiers in Unit 8200 must know these things because if we limited such information to officers, we simply would not have enough people to get the work done—we don't have enough officers.' And in fact, the system was not changed, because it's impossible for us, given the manpower constraints, to build a different system."[7]

Farkash, who today runs a company that provides innovative security systems for corporate and residential facilities, quipped that compared to the major powers, Israel is missing four "generals": "general territory, general manpower, general time, and general budget." But nothing can be done about the shortage of general manpower, Farkash says. "We cannot allocate as many officers as other countries do, so we have sergeants that are doing the work of lieutenant colonels, really."

This scarcity of manpower is also responsible for what is perhaps the IDF's most unusual characteristic: the role of its reserve forces. Unlike in other countries, reserve forces are the backbone of Israel's military.

In most militaries, reserve forces are constructed as appendages to the standing army, which is the nation's main line of defense. Israel, however, is so small and outnumbered by its adversaries that, as was clear from the beginning, no standing army could be large enough to defend against an all-out assault. Shortly after the War of Independence, Israel's leaders decided on a unique reserves-dominated military structure, whereby reservists would not only man whole units but would be commanded by reserve officers as well. Reserve units of other militaries may or may not be commanded by officers from the standing army, but they are given weeks or even months of refresher training before being sent into battle. "No army had relied for the majority of its troops on men who were sent into combat one or two days after their recall," says Luttwak.

No one really knew whether Israel's unique reserve system would work, because it had never been tried. Even today, Israel is the only army in the world to have such a system. As U.S. military historian Fred Kagan explained, "It's actually a terrible way to manage an army. But the Israelis are excellent at it because they had no other choice."[8]

Israel's reserve system is not just an example of the country's innovation; it is also a catalyst for it. Because hierarchy is naturally diminished when taxi drivers can command millionaires and twenty-three-year-olds can train their uncles, the reserve system helps to reinforce that chaotic, antihierarchical ethos that can be found in every aspect of Israeli society, from war room to classroom to boardroom.

Nati Ron is a lawyer in his civilian life and a lieutenant colonel who commands an army unit in the reserves. "Rank is almost meaningless in the reserves," he told us, as if this were the most natural thing in the world. "A private will tell a general in an exercise, 'You are doing this wrong, you should do it this way.'"[9]

Amos Goren, a venture capital investor with Apax Partners in Tel Aviv, agrees. He served full-time in the Israeli commandos for five years and was in the reserves for the next twenty-five years. "During that entire time, I never saluted anybody, ever. And I wasn't even an officer. I was just a rank-and-file soldier."[10]

Luttwak says that "in the reserve formations, the atmosphere remains resolutely civilian in the midst of all the trappings of military life."

This is not to say that soldiers aren't expected to obey orders. But, as Goren explained to us, "Israeli soldiers are not defined by rank; they are defined by what they are good at." Or, as Luttwak said, "Orders are given and obeyed in the spirit of men who have a job to do and mean to do it, but the hierarchy of rank is of small importance, especially since it often cuts across sharp differences in age and social status."

When we asked Major General Farkash why Israel's military is so antihierarchical and open to questioning, he told us it was not just the military but Israel's entire society and history. "Our religion is an open book," he said, in a subtle European accent that traces back to his early years in Transylvania. The "open book" he was referring to was the Talmud—a dense recording of centuries of rabbinic debates over how to interpret the Bible and obey its laws—and the corresponding attitude of questioning is built into Jewish religion, as well as into the national ethos of Israel.

As Israeli author Amos Oz has said, Judaism and Israel have always cultivated "a culture of doubt and argument, an open-ended game of interpretations, counter-interpretations, reinterpretations, opposing interpretations. From the very beginning of the existence of the Jewish civilization, it was recognized by its argumentativeness."[11]

Indeed, the IDF's lack of hierarchy pervades civilian life. It can even break down civilian hierarchies. "The professor acquires respect for his student, the boss for his high-ranking clerk.... Every Israeli has his friends 'from the reserves' with whom he might not otherwise have any kind of social contact," says Luttwak. "Sleeping in bare huts or tents, eating dull army food, often going without a shower for days, reservists of widely different social backgrounds meet on an equal footing; Israel is still a society with fewer class differences than most, and the reserve system has contributed to keeping it that way."

The dilution of hierarchy and rank, moreover, is not typical of other militaries. Historian and IDF reserve officer Michael Oren—now serving as Israel's ambassador to the United States—described a typical scene at an Israeli army base from when he was in a military liaison unit: "You would sit around with a bunch of Israeli generals, and we all wanted coffee. Whoever was closest to the coffee pot would go make it. It didn't matter who—it was common for generals to be serving coffee to their soldiers or vice versa. There is no protocol about these things. But if you were with American captains and a major walked in, everyone would stiffen. And then a colonel would walk in and the major would stiffen. It's extremely rigid and hierarchical in the U.S. Rank is very, very important. As they say in the American military, 'You salute the rank, not the person.'"[12]

In the IDF, there are even extremely unconventional ways to challenge senior officers. "I was in Israeli army units where we threw out the officers," Oren told us, "where people just got together and voted them out. I witnessed this twice personally. I actually liked the guy, but I was outvoted. They voted out a colonel." When we asked Oren in disbelief how this worked, he explained, "You go and you say, 'We don't want you. You're not good.' I mean, everyone's on a first-name basis.... You go to the person above him and say, 'That guy's got to go.'... It's much more performance-oriented than it is about rank."

Retired IDF General Moshe "Bogey" Yaalon, who served as chief of staff of the army during the second intifada, told us a similar story from the second Lebanon war. "There was an operation conducted by a reserve unit in the Lebanese village of Dabu. Nine of our soldiers and officers were killed, and others were injured, including my nephew. And the surviving soldiers blamed the battalion commander for his incompetent management of the operation. The soldiers at the company level went to the brigade commander to complain about the battalion commander. Now, the brigade commander, of course, did his own investigation. But the battalion commander was ultimately forced to step down because of a process that was initiated by his subordinates."[13]

Yaalon believes that this unique feature of Israel's military is critical to its effectiveness: "The key for leadership is the soldiers' confidence in their commander. If you don't trust him, if you're not confident in him, you can't follow him. And in this case, the battalion commander failed. It might be a professional failure, like in this case. It might be a moral failure in another case. Either way, the soldier has to know that it is acceptable—and encouraged—for him to come forward and to talk about it."

Former West Point professor Fred Kagan concedes that Americans can learn something from the Israelis. "I don't think it's healthy for a commander to be constantly worrying if his subordinates will go over his head, like they do in the IDF," he told us. "On the other hand, the U.S. military could benefit from some kind of 360-degree evaluation during the promotion board process for officers. Right now in our system the incentives are all one-sided. To get promoted, an officer just has to please more senior officers. The junior guys get no input."

The conclusion Oren draws from displays of what most militaries—and Fred Kagan—would call insubordination is that the IDF is in fact "much more consensual than the American army." This might seem strange, since the U.S. Army is called a "volunteer" army (not unpaid, but in the sense of free choice), while the IDF is built on conscription.

Yet, Oren explains, "in this country there's an unwritten social contract: we are going to serve in this army provided the government and the army are responsible toward us.... The Israeli army is more similar, I would imagine, to the Continental Army of 1776 than it is to the American army of 2008.... And by the way, George

Washington knew that his 'general' rank didn't mean very much—that he had to be a great general, and that basically people were there out of volition."

The Continental Army was an extreme example of what Oren was describing, since its soldiers would decide on an almost daily basis whether to continue to volunteer. But it was a "people's army," and so is the IDF. As Oren describes it, like the Continental Army, the IDF has a scrappy, less formal, more consensual quality because its soldiers are fighting for the existence of their country, and its ranks are composed of a broad cross section of the people they are fighting for.

It's easy to imagine how soldiers unconcerned with rank have fewer qualms about telling their boss, "You're wrong." This *chutzpah*, molded through years of IDF service, gives insight into how Shvat Shaked could have lectured PayPal's president about the difference between "good guys and bad guys" on the Web, or how Intel Israel's engineers decided to foment a revolution to overturn not only the fundamental architecture of their company's main product but the way the industry measured value. Assertiveness versus insolence; critical, independent thinking versus insubordination; ambition and vision versus arrogance—the words you choose depend on your perspective, but collectively they describe the typical Israeli entrepreneur.

# PART II

## Seeding a Culture of Innovation

# CHAPTER 3

# The People of the Book

*Go far, stay long, see deep.*

—OUTSIDE MAGAZINE

THE ELEVATION OF LA PAZ, BOLIVIA, is 11,220 feet and El Lobo is one floor higher. El Lobo is a restaurant, hostel, social club, and the only source of Israeli food in town. It is run by its founders, Dorit Moralli and her husband, Eli, both from Israel.[1]

Almost every Israeli trekker in Bolivia is likely to come through El Lobo, but not just to get food that tastes like it's from home, to speak Hebrew, and to meet other Israelis. They know they will find something else there, something even more valuable: the Book. Though spoken of in the singular, the Book is not one book but an amorphous and evolving collection of journals, dispersed throughout some of the most remote locations in the world. Each journal is a handwritten "Bible" of advice from one traveler to another. And while the Book is no longer exclusively Israeli, its authors and readers tend to be from Israel.

El Lobo's incarnation of the Book was created in 1986, Dorit recalls, just one month after her restaurant opened. Four Israeli backpackers came in and asked, "Where's the Book?" When she looked mystified, they explained that they meant a book where people could leave recommendations and warnings for other travelers. They went out and bought a blank journal and donated it to the restaurant, complete with the first entry, in Hebrew, about a remote jungle town they thought other Israelis might like.

The Book predated the Internet—it actually started in Israel in the 1970s—but even in today's world of blogs, chat rooms, and instant messaging, this primitive, paper-and-pen-based institution is still going strong. El Lobo has become a regional Book hub, with six volumes: a successor to the original Book started in 1989, along with separate Books for Brazil, Chile, Argentina, Peru, and the northern part of South America. There are other Books stationed throughout Asia. While the original was written only in Hebrew, today's Books are written in a wide array of languages.

"The polyglot entries were random, frustrating, and beautiful, a carnival of ideas, pleas, boasts, and obsolete phone numbers," *Outside* magazine reported on the venerable 1989 volume. "One page recommended the 'beautikul girls' [*sic*] in a certain disco; the next tipped a particular ice cave as 'a must' (at least until someone else scrawled a huge 'NO!' over that entry). This was followed by a half-page in Japanese and a dense passage in German, with bar charts of altitude and diagrams of various plants....After that there was a full-page scrawl devoted to buying a canoe in the rainforests of Peru's Manu National Park, with seven parentheticals and a postscript that wrapped around the margins sideways; a warning against so-and-so's couscous; and an ornate four-color drawing of a toucan named Felipe."

Though it has become internationalized, the Book remains a primarily Israeli phenomenon. Local versions of the Book are maintained and pop up wherever the "wave"—what Hebrew University sociologist Darya Maoz calls the shifting fashions in Israeli travel destinations—goes. Many young Israeli trekkers simply go from Book to Book, following the flow of advice from an international group of adventure seekers, among whom Hebrew seems to be one of the most common tongues.

A well-known joke about Israeli travelers applies equally well in Nepal, Thailand, India, Vietnam, Peru, Bolivia, or Ecuador. A hotelkeeper sees a guest present an Israeli passport and asks, "By the way, how many are you?" When the young Israeli answers, "Seven million," the hotelkeeper presses, "And how many are still back in Israel?"

It is hardly surprising that people in many countries think that Israel must be about as big and populous as China, judging from the number of Israelis that come through. "More than any other nationality," says *Outside*, "[Israelis] have absorbed the ethic of global tramping with ferocity: Go far, stay long, see deep."

Israeli wanderlust is not only about seeing the world; its sources are deeper. One is simply the need for release after years of confining army service. Yaniv, an Israeli encountered by the *Outside* reporter, was typical of many Israeli travelers: "He had overcompensated for years of military haircuts by sprouting everything he could: His chin was a wispy scruff and his sun-bleached hair had twirled into a mix of short dreads and Orthodox earlocks, all swept up into a kind of werewolf 'do. 'The hair is because of the army,' Yaniv admitted. 'First the hair, then the travel.'"

But it's more than just the army. After all, these young Israelis probably don't run into many veterans from other armies, as military service alone does not induce their foreign peers to travel. There is another psychological factor at work—a reaction to physical and diplomatic isolation. "There is a sense of a mental prison living here, surrounded by enemies," says Yair Qedar, editor of the Israeli travel magazine *Masa Acher*. "When the sky opens, you get out."

Until recently, Israelis could not travel to a single neighboring country, though Beirut, Damascus, Amman, and Cairo are all less than a day's drive from Israel. Peace treaties with Egypt and Jordan have not changed this much, though many curious Israelis have now visited these countries. In any event, this slight opening has not dampened the urge to break out of the straitjacket that has been a part of Israel's modern history from the beginning—from before the beginning.

Long before there was a State of Israel, there was already isolation. An early economic boycott can be traced back to 1891, when local Arabs asked Palestine's Ottoman rulers to block Jewish immigration and land sales. In 1922, the Fifth Palestine Arab Congress called for the boycott of all Jewish businesses.[2]

A longer official boycott by the twenty-two-nation Arab League, which banned the purchase of "products of Jewish industry in Palestine," was launched in 1943, five years before Israel's founding. This ban extended to foreign companies from any country that bought from or sold to Israel (the "secondary" boycott), and even to companies that traded with these blacklisted companies (the "tertiary" boycott). Almost all the major Japanese and Korean car manufacturers—including Honda, Toyota, Mazda, and Mitsubishi—complied with the secondary boycott, and their products could not be found on Israeli roads. A notable exception was Subaru, which for a long time had the Israeli market nearly to itself but was barred from selling in the Arab world.[3]

Every government of the Arab League established an official Office of the Boycott, which enforced the primary boycott, monitored the behavior of secondary and tertiary targets, and identified new prospects. According to Christopher Joyner of George Washington University, "Of all the contemporary boycotts, the League of Arab States' boycott against Israel is, ideologically, the most virulent; organizationally, the most sophisticated; politically, the most protracted; and legally, the most polemical."[4]

The boycott has at times taken on unusual targets. In 1974, the Arab League blacklisted the entire Baha'i faith because the Baha'i temple in Haifa is a successful tourist attraction that has created revenue for Israel. Lebanon forbade the showing of the Walt Disney production *Sleeping Beauty* because the horse in the film bears the Hebrew name Samson.[5]

In such a climate, it is natural that young Israelis seek both to get away from an Arab world that has ostracized them and to defy such rejectionism—as if to say, "The more you try to lock me in, the more I will show you I can get out." For the same reason, it was natural for Israelis to embrace the Internet, software, computer, and telecommunications arenas. In these industries, borders, distances, and shipping costs are practically irrelevant. As Israeli venture capitalist Orna Berry told us, "High-tech telecommunications became a national sport to help us fend against the claustrophobia that is life in a small country surrounded by enemies."[6]

This was a matter of necessity, rather than mere preference or convenience.

Because Israel was forced to export to faraway markets, Israeli entrepreneurs developed an aversion to large, readily identifiable manufactured goods with high shipping costs, and an attraction to small, anonymous components and software. This, in turn, positioned Israel perfectly for the global turn toward knowledge- and innovation-based economies, a trend that continues today.

It is hard to estimate how much the Arab boycott and other international embargoes—like France's military ban—have cost Israel over the past sixty years, in terms of lost markets and the difficulties imposed on the nation's economic development. Estimates range as high as $100 billion. Yet the opposite is just as difficult to guess: What is the value of the attributes that Israelis have developed as a result of the constant efforts to crush their nation's development?

Today, Israeli companies are firmly integrated into the economies of China, India, and Latin America. Because, as Orna Berry says, telecommunications became an early priority for Israel, every major telephone company in China relies on Israeli telecom equipment and software. And China's third-largest social-networking Web site, which services twenty-five million of the country's young Web surfers, is actually an Israeli start-up called Koolanoo, which means "all of us" in Hebrew. It was founded by an Israeli whose family emigrated from Iraq.

In the ultimate demonstration of nimbleness, the Israeli venture capitalists who invested in Koolanoo when it was a Jewish social-networking site have utterly transformed its identity, moving all of its management to China, where young Israeli and Chinese executives work side by side.

Gil Kerbs, an Israeli alumnus of Unit 8200, also spends a lot of time in China. When he left the IDF, he picked up and moved to Beijing to study Chinese intensively, working one-on-one with a local instructor—for five hours each day for a full year—while also holding a job at a Chinese company, so he could build a business network there. Today he is a venture capitalist in Israel, specializing in the Chinese market. One of his Israeli companies is providing voice-biometric technology to China's largest retail bank. He told us that Israelis actually have an easier time doing business in China than in Europe. "For one, we were in China before the 'tourists' arrived," he says, referring to those who have only in recent years identified China as an emerging market. "Second, in China there is no legacy of hostility to Jews. So it's actually a more welcoming environment for us."[7]

Israelis are far ahead of their global competitors in penetrating such markets, in part because they had to leapfrog the Middle East and search for new opportunities. The connection between the young Israeli backpackers dispersed around the globe and Israeli technology entrepreneurs' penetration of foreign markets is clear. By the time they are out of their twenties, not only are most Israelis tested in discovering exotic opportunities abroad, but they aren't afraid to enter unfamiliar environments and engage with cultures very different from their own. Indeed, military historian Edward Luttwak estimates that many postarmy Israelis have visited over a dozen countries by age thirty-five.[8] Israelis thrive in new economies and uncharted territory in part because they have been out in the world, often in pursuit of the Book.

One example of this avid internationalism is Netafim, an Israeli company that has become the largest provider of drip irrigation systems in the world. Founded in 1965, Netafim is a rare example of a company that bridges Israel's low-tech, agricultural past to the current boom in cleantech.

Netafim was created by Simcha Blass, the architect of one of the largest infrastructure projects undertaken in the early years of the state. Born in Poland, he was active in the Jewish self-defense units organized in Warsaw during World War I. Soon after arriving in Israel in the 1930s, he became chief engineer for Mekorot, the national water company, and planned the pipeline and canal that would bring water from the Jordan River and Sea of Galilee to the arid Negev.

Blass got the idea for drip irrigation from a tree growing in a neighbor's backyard, seemingly "without water." The giant tree, it turns out, was being nourished by a slow leak in an underground water pipe. When modern plastics became available in the 1950s, Blass realized that drip irrigation was technically feasible. He patented his invention and made a deal with a cooperative settlement located in the Negev Desert, Kibbutz Hatzerim, to produce the new technology.

Netafim was pioneering not just because it developed an innovative way to increase crop yields by up to 50 percent while using 40 percent less water, but because it was one of the first kibbutz-based industries. Until then the kibbutzim—collective communities— were agriculture-based. The idea of a kibbutz factory that exported to the world was a novelty.

But Netafim's real advantage was having no inhibition about traveling to far-flung places in pursuit of markets that desperately needed its products—places where, in the 1960s and '70s, entrepreneurs from the West simply did not visit. As a result, Netafim now operates in 110 countries over five continents. In Asia it has offices in Vietnam, Taiwan, New Zealand, China (two offices), India, Thailand, Japan, Philippines, Korea, and Indonesia. In South America it has a presence in Argentina, Brazil, Chile, Colombia, Ecuador, and Peru. Netafim also has eleven offices in Europe and the former Soviet Union, one in Australia, and one in North America.

And because Netafim's technology became so indispensable, a number of foreign governments that historically had been hostile to Israel began to open diplomatic channels. Netafim is active in former Soviet bloc Muslim states like Azerbaijan, Kazakhstan, and Uzbekistan, which led to warmer relations with Israel's government after the dissolution of the Soviet Union. In 2004, then trade minister Ehud Olmert tagged along on a Netafim trip to South Africa in the hope of forming new strategic alliances there. The trip resulted in $30 million in contracts for Netafim, plus a memorandum of understanding between the two governments on agriculture and arid lands development.

Israeli entrepreneurs and executives, though, have themselves been known to engage in self-appointed diplomatic missions on behalf of the state. Many of Israel's globe-trotting businesspeople are not just technology evangelists but endeavor to "sell" the entire Israeli economy. Jon Medved—the inventor of the "nickname barometer" to measure informality—is one such example.

Raised in California, Medved was trained in political activism, not engineering. His first career was as a Zionist organizer. He moved to Israel in 1981 and made a small living by going on speaking tours to preach about the future of Israel to Israelis. But a conversation he had in 1982 with an executive at Rafael, one of Israel's largest defense contractors, burst Medved's bubble. He was told, unceremoniously, that what he was doing was a waste of time and energy. Israel didn't need more professional Zionists or politicians, the executive stated flatly; Israel needed businesspeople. Medved's father had started a small company in California that built optical transmitters and receivers. So Medved began pitching his father's product in Israel. Instead of going from kibbutz to kibbutz to sell the future of Zionism, he went from company to company to sell optical technology.

Later, he got into the investment business and founded Israel Seed Partners, a venture capital firm, in his Jerusalem garage. His fund grew to over $260 million and he invested in sixty Israeli companies, including Shopping.com, which was bought by eBay, and Compugen and Answers.com, both of which went public on the NASDAQ. In 2006, Medved left Israel Seed to launch and manage a start-up himself—Vringo, a company that pioneered video ringtones for cell phones, which has quickly penetrated the European and Turkish markets.

But his own company is less important. Regardless of what Medved is doing for his enterprises, he spends a lot of time—*too much* time, his investors complain—preaching about the Israeli economy. On every trip abroad, Medved lugs a portable projector and laptop loaded with a memorable slide presentation chronicling the accomplishments of the Israeli tech scene. In speeches—and in conversations with anyone who will listen—Medved celebrates all the Israeli landmark "exits" in which companies were bought or went public, and catalogs dozens of "made in Israel" technologies.

In his presentations he says only half-jokingly that if Israel followed the lead of "Intel Inside"—Intel's marketing campaign to highlight the ubiquity of its chips—with similar "Israel Inside" stickers, they would show up on almost everything people around the world touch, and he ticks off a litany of examples: from computers, to cell phones, to medical devices and miracle drugs, to Internet-based social networks, to cutting-edge sources of clean energy, to the food we eat, to the registers in the supermarkets in which we shop.

Medved then hints to the multinationals in the room that they are likely to be missing something if they have not already set up shop in Israel. He finds out in advance of each presentation which companies' executives will be in the audience and is then certain to mention which of their competitors are already in Israel. "The reason that Israel is inside almost everything we touch is because almost every company we touch is inside Israel. Are you?" he asks, peering into the audience.

Medved has taken on a role that, in any other country, would typically belong to the local chamber of commerce, minister of trade, or foreign secretary.

But the start-ups Medved champions in his presentations are rarely companies in which he has invested. He's always torn when he prepares for these speeches: "Do I talk up Vringo among the promising new companies coming out of Israel? It's a no-brainer, right? It's good exposure for the company." But he resists the urge. "My pitch is about Israel. My American investors beat me up over this—'You wind up plugging your competitors but not your own company.' They're right. But they're missing the larger point."

Medved is in perpetual motion. He's given the presentation fifty times a year for the last fifteen years. All told, almost eight hundred times, at technology conferences and universities around the world, in over forty countries, and to scores of international dignitaries visiting Israel.

Alex Vieux, CEO of *Red Herring* magazine, told us that he has been to "a million high-tech conferences, on multiple continents. I see Israelis like Medved give presentations all the time, alongside their peers from other countries. The others are always making a pitch for their specific company. The Israelis are always making a pitch for Israel."[9]

# CHAPTER 4

# Harvard, Princeton, and Yale

*The social graph is very simple here.*
*Everybody knows everybody.*

—Yossi Vardi

DAVID AMIR MET US AT HIS JERUSALEM HOME in his pilot's uniform, but there was nothing *Top Gun* about him. Soft-spoken, thoughtful, and self-deprecating, he looked, even in uniform, more like an American liberal arts student than the typical pilot with crisp military bearing. Yet as he explained with pride how the Israeli Air Force trained some of the best pilots in the world—according to numerous international competitions as well as their record in battle—it became easy to see how he fit in.[1]

While students in other countries are preoccupied with deciding which college to attend, Israelis are weighing the merits of different military units. And just as students elsewhere are thinking about what they need to do to get into the best schools, many Israelis are positioning themselves to be recruited by the IDF's elite units.

Amir decided when he was just twelve years old that he wanted to learn Arabic, partly because he knew even then that it might help him get accepted into the best intelligence units.

But the pressure to get into those units really intensifies when Israelis are seventeen years old. Every year, the buzz builds among high school junior and senior classes all across Israel. Who has been asked to try out for the pilot's course? Who for the different *sayarot*, the commando units of the navy, the paratroopers, the infantry brigades, and, most selective of all, the Sayeret Matkal, the chief of staff's commando unit?

And which students will be asked to try out for the elite intelligence units, such as 8200, where Shvat Shaked and his cofounder of Fraud Sciences served? Who will go to Mamram, the IDF's computer systems division? And who will be considered for Talpiot, a unit that combines technological training with exposure to all the top commando units' operations?

In Israel, about one year before reaching draft age, all seventeen-year-old males and females are called to report to IDF recruiting centers for an initial one-day screening that includes aptitude and psychological exams, interviews, and a medical evaluation. At the end of the day, a health and psychometric classification is determined and service possibilities are presented to the young candidate in a personal interview. Candidates who meet the health, aptitude, and personality requirements are offered an opportunity to take additional qualifying tests for service in one of the IDF's elite units or divisions.

Tests for the paratrooper brigade, for example, occur three times each year, often months before candidates' scheduled draft dates. Young civilians submit themselves to a rigorous two days of physical and mental testing, where an initial group of about four thousand candidates is winnowed down to four hundred future draftees for different units. These four hundred paratroopers can volunteer to participate in the field test and screening process for the special forces, which is an intensive five-day series of eleven repeating drills, each lasting several hours and always conducted under severe time constraints and increasing physical and mental pressure. During the entire time, rest periods are short and sleep almost nonexistent, as is food and the time in which to eat it. Participants describe the five days as one long blur where day and night are indistinguishable. No watches or cell phones are allowed—the screeners want to make the experience as disorienting as possible. At the end of the five days, each soldier is ranked.

The twenty top-ranking soldiers for each unit immediately begin the twenty-month training period. Those who complete the training together remain as a team throughout their regular and reserve service. Their unit becomes a second family. They remain in the reserves until they are in their mid-forties.

While it's difficult to get into the top Israeli universities, the nation's equivalent of Harvard, Princeton, and Yale are the IDF's elite units. The unit in which an applicant served tells prospective employers what kind of selection process he or she navigated, and what skills and relevant experience he or she may already possess.

"In Israel, one's academic past is somehow less important than the military past. One of the questions asked in every job interview is, Where did you serve in the army?" says Gil Kerbs, an intelligence unit alumnus who—after pursuing the Book—today works in Israel's venture capital industry, specializing in China's technology market. "There are job offers on the Internet and want ads that specifically say 'meant for 8200 alumni.' The 8200 alumni association now has a national reunion. But instead of using the time together to reflect on past battles and military nostalgia, it is forward-looking. The alumni are focused on business networking. Successful 8200 entrepreneurs give presentations at the reunion about their companies and industries."[2]

As we've seen, the air force and Israel's elite commando units are well known for their selectivity, the sophistication and difficulty of their training, and the quality of their alumni. But the IDF has a unit that takes the process of extreme selectivity and extensive training to an even higher level, especially in the realm of technological innovation. That unit is Talpiot.

The name Talpiot comes from a verse in the Bible's Song of Songs that refers to a castle's turrets; the term connotes the pinnacle of achievement. Talpiot has the distinction of being both the most selective unit and the one that subjects its soldiers to the longest training course in the IDF—forty-one months, which is longer than the entire service of most soldiers. Those who enter the program sign on for an extra six years in the military, so their minimum service is a total of nine years.

The program was the brainchild of Felix Dothan and Shaul Yatziv, both Hebrew University scientists. They came up with the idea following the debacle of the 1973 Yom Kippur War. At that time, the country was still reeling from being caught flat-footed by a surprise attack, and from the casualties it had suffered. The war was a costly reminder that Israel must compensate for its small size and population by maintaining a qualitative and technological edge. The professors approached then IDF chief of staff Rafael "Raful" Eitan with a simple idea: take a handful of Israel's most talented young people and give them the most intensive technology training that the universities *and* the military had to offer.

Started as a one-year experiment, the program has been running continuously for thirty years. Each year, the top 2 percent of Israeli high school students are asked to try out—two thousand students. Of these, only one in ten pass a battery of tests, mainly in physics and mathematics. These two hundred students are then run through two days of intensive personality and aptitude testing.

Once admitted into the program, Talpiot cadets blaze through an accelerated university degree in math or physics while they are introduced to the technological needs of all IDF branches. The academic training they receive goes beyond what the typical university student would receive in Israel or anywhere else—they study more, in less time. They also go through basic training with the paratroopers. The idea is to give them an overview of all the major IDF branches so that they understand both the technology and military needs—and especially the connection between them.

Providing the students with such a broad range of knowledge is not, however, the ultimate goal of the course. Rather, it is to transform them into mission-oriented leaders and problem solvers.

This is achieved by handing them mission after mission, with minimal guidance. Some assignments are as mundane as organizing a conference for their fellow cadets, which requires coordinating the speakers, facilities, transportation, and food. Others are as complicated as penetrating a telecommunications network of a live terrorist cell.

But more typical is forcing the soldiers to find cross-disciplinary solutions to specific military problems. For example, a team of cadets had to solve the problem of the severe back pain suffered by IDF helicopter pilots from the choppers' vibrations. The Talpiot cadets first determined how to measure the impact of the choppers' vibrations on the human vertebrae. They designed a customized seat, installed it in a helicopter simulator, and cut a hole in its backrest. Next they put a pen on a pilot's back, had him "fly" in the simulator, and used a high-speed camera inserted in the backrest hole to photograph the marks caused by the different vibrations. Finally, after studying the movements by analyzing computerized data generated from the movement information in the photos, they redesigned the chopper seats.

Assuming they survive the first two or three years of the course, these cadets become "Talpions," a title that carries prestige in both military and civilian life.

The Talpiot program as a whole is under Mafat, the IDF's internal research and development arm, which is parallel to America's DARPA (the Defense Advanced Research Projects Agency). Mafat has the coveted and sensitive job of assigning each Talpion to a specific unit in the IDF for their next six years of regular service.

From the beginning, the hyperelitism of the Talpiot program has attracted critics. The program almost didn't get off the ground because military leaders did not think it would be worthwhile to invest so much in such a small group. Recently, some detractors have claimed that the program is a failure because most of the graduates do not stay in the military beyond the required nine years and do not end up in the IDF's senior ranks.

However, though Talpiot training is optimized to maintain the IDF's technological edge, the same combination of leadership experience and technical knowledge is ideal for creating new companies. Although the program has produced only about 650 graduates in thirty years, they have become some of Israel's top academics and founders of the country's most successful companies. NICE Systems, the global corporation behind call-monitoring systems used by eighty-five of the Forbes 100 companies, was founded by a team of Talpions. So was Compugen, a leader in human-genome decoding and drug development. Many of the Israeli technology companies traded on the NASDAQ were either founded by a Talpion or have alumni situated in key roles.

So the architects of Talpiot, Dothan and Yatziv, vigorously reject the criticisms. First, they argue that the interservice competition for Talpions within the IDF—which at times has had to be settled by the prime minister—speaks for itself. Second, they claim that the Talpions easily pay back the investment during their required six years of service. Third, and perhaps most importantly, the two-thirds of Talpiot graduates who end up either in academia or in technology companies continue to make a tremendous contribution to the economy and society, thereby strengthening the country in different ways.

Talpions may represent the elite of the elite in the Israeli military, but the underlying strategy behind the program's development—to provide broad and deep training in order to produce innovative, adaptive problem solving—is evident throughout much of the military and seems to be part of the Israeli ethos: to teach people how to be very good at a lot of things, rather than excellent at one thing.

The advantage that Israel's economy—and its society—gains from this equally dispersed national service experience was driven home to us by neither an Israeli nor an American. Gary Shainberg looks more like a sailor (of the compact, stocky variety) than a tech geek, perhaps because he is an eighteen-year veteran of the British navy. Now vice president for technology and innovation at British Telecom, he met us late one evening in a Tel Aviv bar. He was on one of his many business trips to Israel, en route to the gulf—to Dubai, actually.

"There is something about the DNA of Israeli innovation that is unexplainable," Shainberg said. But he did have the beginnings of a theory. "I think it comes down to maturity. That's because nowhere else in the world where people work in a center of technology innovation do they also have to do national service."[3]

At eighteen, Israelis go into the army for a minimum of two to three years. If they don't reenlist, they typically enroll at a university. "There's a massive percentage of Israelis who go to university out of the army compared to anywhere else in the world," said Shainberg.

In fact, according to the Organisation for Economic Co-operation and Development (OECD), 45 percent of Israelis are university-educated, which is among the highest percentages in the world. And according to a recent *IMD World Competitiveness Yearbook*, Israel was ranked second among sixty developed nations on the criterion of whether "university education meets the needs of a competitive economy."[4]

By the time students finish college, they're in their mid-twenties; some already have graduate degrees, and a large number are married. "All this changes the mental ability of the individual," Shainberg reasoned. "They're much more mature; they've got more life experience. Innovation is all about finding ideas."

Innovation often depends on having a different perspective. Perspective comes from experience. Real experience also typically comes with age or maturity. But in Israel, you get experience, perspective, and maturity at a younger age, because the society jams so many transformative experiences into Israelis when they're barely out of high school. By the time they get to college, their heads are in a different place than those of their American counterparts.

"You've got a whole different perspective on life. I think it's that later education, the younger marriage, the military experience—and I spent eighteen years in the [British] navy, so I can sort of empathize with that sort of thing," Shainberg went on. "In the military, you're in an environment where you have to think on your feet. You have to make life-and-death decisions. You learn about discipline. You learn about training your mind to do things, especially if you're frontline or you're doing something operational. And that can only be good and useful in the business world."

This maturity is especially powerful when mixed with an almost childish impatience.

Since their country's founding, Israelis have been keenly aware that the future—both near and distant—is always in question. Every moment has strategic importance. As Mark Gerson, an American entrepreneur who has invested in several Israeli start-ups, described it, "When an Israeli man wants to date a woman, he asks her out that night. When an Israeli entrepreneur has a business idea, he will start it that week. The notion that one should accumulate credentials before launching a venture simply does not exist. This is actually good in business. Too much time can only teach you what can go wrong, not what could be transformative."[5]

For Amir, as for many other conscripts, the IDF provided him with an exciting opportunity to test and prove himself. But the IDF offers recruits another valuable experience: a unique space within Israeli society where young men and women work closely and intensely with peers from different cultural, socioeconomic, and religious backgrounds. A young Jew from Russia, another from Ethiopia, a secular sabra (native-born Israeli) from a swanky Tel Aviv suburb, a yeshiva student from Jerusalem, and a kibbutznik from a farming family might all meet in the same unit. They'll spend two to three years serving together full-time, and then spend another twenty-plus years of annual service in the reserves.

As we've seen, the IDF was structured to rely heavily on reserve forces, since there is no way for such a small country to maintain a sufficiently large standing army. So for combat soldiers, connections made in the army are constantly renewed through decades of reserve duty. For a few weeks a year, or sometimes just a week at a time, Israelis depart from their professional and personal lives to train with their military unit. Not surprisingly, many business connections are made during the long hours of operations, guard duty, and training.

"Every five years Harvard Business School hosts a class reunion," says Tal Keinan, an Israeli HBS grad. "It's fun. It helps keep your network intact. We spend two days visiting with classmates, sitting in lectures. But imagine a reunion every year, and that it lasts for two to four weeks. And it's with the unit you had spent three years with in the army. And instead of sitting in lectures, you're doing security patrols along the border. It nourishes an entirely different kind of lifelong bond."[6]

Indeed, relationships developed during military service form another network in what is already a very small and interconnected country. "The whole country is one degree of separation," says Yossi Vardi, the godfather of dozens of Internet start-ups and one of the champion networkers in the wired world. Like Jon Medved, Vardi is one of Israel's legendary business ambassadors.

Vardi says he knows of Israeli companies that have stopped using help-wanted ads: "It's now all word of mouth. . . . The social graph is very simple here. Everybody knows everybody; everybody was serving in the army with the brother of everybody; the mother of everybody was the teacher in their school; the uncle was the commander of somebody else's unit. Nobody can hide. If you don't behave, you cannot disappear to Wyoming or California. There is a very high degree of transparency."[7] The benefits of this kind of interconnectedness are not limited to Israel, although in Israel they are unusually intense and widespread.

Unsurprisingly, the IDF has many things in common with other militaries around the world, including equally grueling tryouts for their elite units. However, most of the other militaries' selection processes differ in that they must choose from among volunteer recruits. They are not able to scour the records of every high school student and invite the highest achievers to compete against their most talented peers for a few coveted spots.

In the United States, for example, the military is limited to choosing only from among those potential recruits who express interest. Or as one U.S. recruiter put it, "In Israel, the military gets to select the best. In the U.S., it's the other way around. We can only hope that the best choose us."[8]

The American military goes to great lengths to seek out the best and hope that they may be interested in serving in the U.S. military. Take the United States Military Academy at West Point's freshman class each year. The median grade point average hovers around 3.5, and the admissions department can rattle off all sorts of statistics to quantify the leadership aptitude of its student cadets, including the number who were varsity team captains in high school (60 percent), who were high school class presidents (14 percent), and so on. And the admissions department keeps an extremely comprehensive database of all inquiring prospective applicants, often going back to elementary school. As author David Lipsky writes in his book about West Point, *Absolutely American*, "Drop a line to West Point in the sixth grade and you'll receive correspondence from admissions every six months until you hit high school, when the rate doubles." Approximately fifty thousand high school juniors open West Point prospective files each year, which culminates in a freshman class of twelve hundred cadets. At the end of the five-year program, each graduate has received an education valued at a quarter of a million dollars.[9]

But even with extraordinary outreach efforts, like West Point admissions, a number of the senior leaders of the U.S. armed forces are frustrated that they cannot gain access to the academic records of a broad cross section of Americans. And without that access, they cannot target a tailored recruitment pitch.

A conversation with an American military man underscores the economic value of the Israeli system. Colonel John Lowry, a marine infantry officer, joined the Marine Corps after high school and has been in active duty or reserves for the past twenty-five years. He earned an MBA from Harvard Business School and went on to climb the corporate ranks at Harley-Davidson, the multibillion-dollar premium motorcycle manufacturer. He did so while fulfilling his commitment to the reserves, serving stints in the Horn of Africa, the Persian Gulf, and, prior to his business career, Operation Desert Storm. Lowry commands one thousand marines and travels to various reserve bases across the country for two weekends each month, in addition to annual month-long call-ups. Lowry also helps oversee a number of Harley factory plants and manages about one thousand employees.[10]

By day he is a senior business executive, but by night he trains marines preparing for tours in Iraq. He transitions seamlessly between these two worlds. He only wishes that the kind of military experience he had was as common in the American business world as it is among Israeli entrepreneurs.

"The military gets you at a young age and teaches you that when you are in charge of something, you are responsible for everything that happens...and everything that does not happen," Lowry told us. "The phrase 'It was not my fault' does not exist in the military culture." This comment sounds a lot like Farhi's point from chapter 2 about company commanders taking ownership of whatever happens in their territory. "No college experience disciplines you to think like that...with high stakes and intense pressure," says Lowry, a graduate of Princeton. "When you are under that kind of pressure, at that age, it forces you to think three or four chess moves ahead... with everything you do...on the battlefield...and in business."

The Marine Corps network is important to Lowry. His military peers are a built-in board of advisers for him. "It's another world of friendships, outside of work, but many of them are connected to my line of work," he notes. "Just the other day I spoke with one fellow officer who is in management at Raytheon, based in Abu Dhabi. Many of these guys I've known anywhere from five years to twenty-five years."

The military is also much better than college for inculcating young leaders with a sense of what he calls social range: "The people you are serving with come from all walks of life; the military is this great purely merit-based institution in our society. Learning how to deal with anybody—wherever they come from—is something that I leverage today in business when dealing with my suppliers and customers."

If all this sounds similar to our description of the IDF's role in fostering Israel's entrepreneurial culture, it should. While a majority of Israeli entrepreneurs were profoundly influenced by their stint in the IDF, a military background is hardly common in Silicon Valley or widespread in the senior echelons of corporate America.

As Israeli entrepreneur Jon Medved—who has sold several startups to large American companies—told us, "When it comes to U.S. military résumés, Silicon Valley is illiterate. It's a shame. What a waste of the kick-ass leadership talent coming out of Iraq and Afghanistan. The American business world doesn't quite know what to do with them."[11]

This gulf between business and the military is symptomatic of a wider divide between America's military and civilian communities, which was identified by the leadership of West Point over a decade ago. In the summer of 1998, Lieutenant General Daniel Christman, the superintendent of West Point, and General John Abizaid, commandant at West Point, were driving on the New Jersey Turnpike and pulled off at a roadside food and gas station mall for a quick meal at Denny's. Despite the clearly visible stars on their Class B green army uniforms, the hostess smiled and enthusiastically expressed her gratitude to Generals Christman and Abizaid for the cleanliness of the public parks. She thought they were staff of the parks department.[12]

Despite the military leadership's outreach, too few young Americans today feel any connection to their contemporaries in the military, let alone have actually ever known one who has served. Even after two new war fronts, today only 1 in 221 Americans are in active-duty service. Compare that to the end of the Second World War, when 1 in 10 Americans were serving. Tom Brokaw, author of *The Greatest Generation*, told us that after World War II a young man who had not served would have a hard time getting a good job in business. "There must be something wrong with him" was how Brokaw characterized a typical reaction of employers back then to nonvets looking for private-sector jobs.[13]

But the way David Lipsky describes it, when the draft ended in 1975, after the Vietnam War, an opposite climate began to settle in: "Civilian culture and military culture shook hands, exchanged phone numbers, and started to lose track of each other."

The economic implications of this drift were driven home to us by Al Chase, who runs an executive recruitment firm focused on the placement of U.S. military officers in private enterprises ranging from small start-ups to large Fortune 100 companies such as PepsiCo and GE. Having placed hundreds of vets, he knows what kind of entrepreneurial acumen is formed by battlefield experience. According to Chase, the Cold War military was different. Young officers could go an entire career without acquiring real battlefield experience. But the Iraq and Afghanistan wars have changed that. Almost every young officer has served multiple tours.[14]

As we've seen firsthand in Iraq, the post-9/11 wars have largely been counterinsurgencies, where critical decisions have been made by junior commanders. General David Petraeus's counterinsurgency strategy in Iraq, for example, was predicated on U.S. troops' not just being present and patrolling local Iraqi residential neighborhoods in order to provide security for Iraqi civilians but actually living in the neighborhoods. This is different from the way most U.S. military troops have fought in earlier wars, including in the early years of the Iraq war. Back then, U.S. soldiers and marines lived in forward operating bases (FOBs), enormous self-contained complexes that roughly replicate bases back in the States. A typical FOB could house tens of thousands of troops—if not more. But the soldiers and marines in neighborhood bases in Iraq since 2007 have numbered in only the tens or low hundreds. This alone gives smaller units much more independence from the division in their daily operations, and the junior commander is given more authority to make decisions and improvise.

Nathaniel Fick was a marine captain who fought in the Afghanistan and Iraq wars, before pursuing a dual-degree program at Harvard Business School and the Kennedy School of Government and penning a book about his experiences called *One Bullet Away*. He told us that he was trained to think about fighting the "three-block war." In Iraq and Afghanistan, he said, "Marines could be passing out rice on one city block, doing patrols to keep the peace on another block, and engaged in a full-on firefight on the third block. All in the same neighborhood."[15]

Junior commanders in America's new wars find themselves playing the role of small-town mayor, economic-reconstruction czar, diplomat, tribal negotiator, manager of millions of dollars' worth of assets, and security chief, depending on the day.

And, as in the IDF, today's junior commanders are also more inclined to challenge senior officers in ways they typically would not have in the past. This is partly from serving multiple tours and having watched their peers get killed as a result of what junior officers often believe are bad decisions, lack of strategy, or lackluster resources provided by higher-ups. As American military analyst Fred Kagan explained it, U.S. soldiers and marines "have caught up with the Israelis in the sense that a junior guy who has been deployed multiple times will dispense with the niceties towards superiors." There is a correlation between battlefield experience and the proclivity of subordinates to challenge their commanders.

Given all this battlefield entrepreneurial experience, the vets coming out of the Iraq and Afghanistan wars are better prepared than ever for the business world, whether building start-ups or helping lead larger companies through the current turbulent period.

Al Chase advises vets not to be intimidated by others in the job market who have already been in the business world and know the "nomenclature." Vets, he said, bring things to the table that their business peers could only dream about, including a sense of proportionality—what is truly a life-or-death situation and what is something less than that; what it takes to motivate a workforce; how to achieve consensus under duress; and a solid ethical base that has been tested in the crucible of combat.

Brian Tice, an infantry officer, was a captain in the U.S. Marine Corps when he decided that he wanted to make the transition to business. By that time he was thirty years old and had completed five deployments—including assignments in Haiti and Afghanistan—and was in the middle of his sixth, in Iraq. He wrote his essays for his applications to Stanford's MBA program on a laptop in a burnt-out Iraqi building near the Al Asad Air Base, in the violent Al Anbar Province of western Iraq. He had to complete his application at odd hours because his missions always took place in the middle of the night. As an operations officer for a unit of 120 marines, Tice had to build the "package" for each operation against insurgents and al Qaeda—determine how much force, how many marines, and how much air support were needed. So the only time he could rest and plan future operations was during the day.[16]

Based over eight thousand miles from Stanford's campus, he couldn't meet the school's requirement for an in-person interview. So the admissions department scheduled one over the phone, which he did between sniper operations and raids, while standing in an open expanse of desert. Tice asked the admissions officer to excuse the blaring noise of helicopters flying overhead, and had to cut the interview short when mortars landed nearby.

More and more American military officers are applying for MBA programs and, like Captain Tice, are going to extraordinary lengths to do so. In 2008, of aspiring MBA applicants that took the Graduate Management Admission Test (GMAT), 15,259, or 6 percent, had military experience. At the University of Virginia's Darden School of Business, the number of military applicants rose 62 percent from 2007 to 2008. The first-year class in 2008 had 333 students, 40 of whom were from the military, including 38 who had served in Afghanistan or Iraq.

The Graduate Management Admission Council, which administers the GMAT, has made it a priority to better organize the path from war front to business school. It has launched its Operation MBA program, which helps members of the armed forces find B-schools that waive application fees or offer generous financial aid packages and even tuition deferrals for cash-strapped vets. And the council is even setting up GMAT test centers on military bases, one of which was opened in 2008 at Fort Hood in Texas; another is planned to open at Yokota Air Base in Japan.

Yet the capacity of U.S. corporate recruiters and executives to make sense of combat experience and its value in the business world is limited. As Jon Medved explained, most American businesspeople simply do not know how to read a military résumé. Al Chase told us that a number of the vets he's worked with have walked a business interviewer through all their leadership experiences from the battlefield, including case studies in high-stakes decision making and management of large numbers of people and equipment in a war zone, and at the end of it the interviewer has said something along the lines of "That's very interesting, but have you ever had a real job?"

In Israel it is the opposite. While Israeli businesses still look for private-sector experience, military service provides the critical standardized metric for employers—all of whom know what it means to be an officer or to have served in an elite unit.

# CHAPTER 5

# Where Order Meets Chaos

*Doubt and argument—this is a syndrome of the Jewish
civilization and this is a syndrome of today's Israel.*

—AMOS OZ

ABOUT THIRTY NATIONS have compulsory military service that
lasts longer than eighteen months. Most of these countries
are developing or nondemocratic or both. But among first-world
countries, only three require such a lengthy period of military
service: Israel, South Korea, and Singapore. Not surprisingly, all
three face long-standing existential threats or have fought wars for
survival in recent memory.[1]

For Israel, the threat to its existence began before it had become
a sovereign nation. Beginning in the 1920s, the Arab world resisted
the establishment of a national Jewish state in Palestine, then sought
to defeat or weaken Israel in numerous wars. South Korea has lived
under a constant threat from North Korea, which has a large standing army poised just a few miles from Seoul, South Korea's capital.
And Singapore lives with memories of the occupation by Japan

during World War II, its recent struggle for independence, which culminated in 1965, and the volatile period that followed.

Singaporean National Service was introduced in 1967. "We had to defend ourselves. It was a matter of survival. As a small country with a small population, the only way we could build a force of sufficient size...was through conscription," explained Defense Minister Teo Chee Hean. "It was a decision not taken lightly given the significant impact that conscription would have on every Singaporean. But there was no alternative."[2]

At independence, Singapore had only two infantry regiments, and they had been created and were commanded by the British. Two-thirds of the soldiers were not even residents of Singapore. Looking for ideas, the city-state's first defense minister, Goh Keng Swee, called Mordechai Kidron, the former Israeli ambassador to Thailand, whom he had gotten to know while the two men were working in Asia. "Goh told us that they thought that only Israel, a small country surrounded by Muslim countries,...could help them build a small, dynamic army," Kidron has said.[3]

Singapore gained independence twice over the course of just two years. The first was independence from the British in 1963, as part of Malaysia. The second was independence from Malaysia, in 1965, to stave off civil war. Singapore's current prime minister, Goh Chok Tong, described his country's relations with Malaysia as having remained tense after an "unhappy marriage and acrimonious divorce." Singaporeans also feared threats from Indonesia, all while an armed Communist insurgency was looming just to Singapore's north, in Indochina.

In response to Goh's pleas for help, the IDF tasked Lieutenant Colonel Yehuda Golan with writing two manuals for the nascent Singaporean army: one on combat doctrine and the structure of a defense ministry and another on intelligence institutions. Later, six

IDF officers and their families moved to Singapore to train soldiers and create a conscription-based army.

Along with compulsory service and a career army, Singapore also adopted elements of the IDF's model of reserve service. Every soldier who completes his regular service is obligated to serve for short stints every year, until the age of thirty-three.

For Singapore's founding generation, national service was about more than just defense. "Singaporeans of all strata of society would train shoulder to shoulder in the rain and hot sun, run up hills together, and learn to fight as a team in jungles and built-up areas. Their common experience in National Service would bond them, and shape the Singapore identity and character," Prime Minister Goh said on the Singaporean military's thirty-fifth anniversary.

"We are still evolving as a nation," Goh continued. "Our forefathers were immigrants.... They say that in National Service, everyone— whether Chinese, Malay, Indian, or Eurasian—is of the same color: a deep, sunburnt brown! When they learn to fight as one unit, they begin to trust, respect, and believe in one another. Should we ever have to go to war to defend Singapore, they will fight for their buddies in their platoon as much as for the country."[4]

Substitute "Israel" for "Singapore," and this speech could have been delivered by David Ben-Gurion.

Although Singapore's military is modeled after the IDF—the testing ground for many of Israel's entrepreneurs—the "Asian Tiger" has failed to incubate start-ups. Why?

It's not that Singapore's growth hasn't been impressive. Real per capita GDP, at over U.S. $35,000, is one of the highest in the world, and real GDP growth has averaged 8 percent annually since the nation's founding. But its growth story notwithstanding, Singapore's leaders have failed to keep up in a world that puts a high premium on a trio of attributes historically alien to Singapore's culture: initiative, risk-taking, and agility.

A growing awareness of the risk-taking gap prompted Singapore's finance minister, Tharman Shanmugaratnam, to drop in on Nava Swersky Sofer, an Israeli venture capitalist who went on to run Hebrew University's technology transfer company. The university company, called Yissum, is among the top ten academic programs in the world, measured by the commercialization of academic research. Shanmugaratnam had one question for her: "How does Israel do it?" He was nearby for a G-20 meeting, but he skipped the last day of the summit to come to Israel.

Today the alarm bells are being sounded even by Singapore's founding father, Lee Kuan Yew, who served as prime minister for three decades. "It's time for a new burst of creativity in business," he says. "We need many new tries, many start-ups."[5]

There is a similar feeling in Korea, another country that has a military draft and a sense of external threat, and yet, as in Singapore and not as in Israel, these attributes have not produced a start-up culture. Korea, clearly, has no shortage of large technology companies. Erel Margalit, an Israeli entrepreneur with a stable of media start-ups, actually sees Korea as fertile ground for his cutting-edge companies. "America is the queen of content," Margalit said, "but it is still in the broadcast era, while China and Korea are in the interactive age."[6]

So why doesn't Korea produce nearly as many start-ups per capita as Israel? We turned to Laurent Haug for insight. Haug is the creator and force behind the Lift conferences, which focus on the nexus between technology and culture. Since 2006, his gatherings have alternated between Geneva, Switzerland, and Jeju, Korea. We asked Haug why there were not more start-ups in Korea, despite the great affinity Koreans have for technology.

"The fear of losing face, and the bursting of the Internet bubble in 2000," he told us. "In Korea, one should not be exposed while failing. Yet in early 2000, many entrepreneurs jumped on the bandwagon of the new economy. When the bubble burst, their public failure left a scar on entrepreneurship." Haug was surprised to hear from the director of a technology incubator in Korea that a call for projects received only fifty submissions, "a low figure when you know how innovative and forward-thinking Korea really is." To Haug, who has also explored the Israeli tech scene, "Israelis seem to be on the other side of the spectrum. They don't care about the social price of failure and they develop their projects regardless of the economic or political situation."[7]

So when Swersky Sofer hosts visitors from Singapore, Korea, and many other countries, the challenge is how to convey the cultural aspects that make Israel's start-up scene tick. Conscription, serving in the reserves, living under threat, and even being technologically savvy are not enough. What, then, are the other ingredients?

"I'll give you an analogy from an entirely different perspective," Tal Riesenfeld told us matter-of-factly. "If you want to know how we teach improvisation, just look at Apollo. What Gene Kranz did at NASA—which American historians hold up as model leadership—is an example of what's expected from many Israeli commanders in the battlefield." His response to our question about Israeli innovation seemed completely out of context, but he was speaking from experience. During his second year at Harvard Business School, Riesenfeld launched a start-up with one of his fellow Israeli commandos. They presented their proposal at the Harvard business plan competition and beat out the seventy other teams for first place.[8]

After graduating from HBS at the top of his class, Riesenfeld turned down an attractive offer from Google in order to start Tel Aviv–based EyeView. Earlier, Riesenfeld had made it through one of the most selective recruitment and training programs in the Israeli army.

While he was at HBS, Riesenfeld studied a case that compared the lessons of the *Apollo 13* and *Columbia* space shuttle crises.[9] The 2003 *Columbia* mission has a special resonance for Israelis. One of its crew members—air force colonel Ilan Ramon, the first Israeli astronaut—was killed when *Columbia* disintegrated. But Ramon had been an Israeli hero long before. He was a pilot in the daring 1981 air force mission that destroyed Iraq's nuclear facility, Osirak.

HBS professors Amy Edmondson, Michael Roberto, and Richard Bohmer spent two years researching and comparing the *Apollo* and *Columbia* crises. They produced a study that became the basis for one of Riesenfeld's classes, analyzing the lessons learned from a business-management perspective. When Riesenfeld first read the HBS case, in 2008, the issues it presented were immediately familiar to the ex-commando. But why had Riesenfeld mentioned the case to us? What was the connection to Israel, or to its innovation economy?

The *Apollo 13* crisis occurred on April 15, 1970, when the spaceship had traveled three-fourths of the way to the moon. It was less than a year after Neil Armstrong and Buzz Aldrin had stepped off *Apollo 11*. NASA was riding high. But when *Apollo 13* was two days into its mission, traveling two thousand miles per hour, one of its primary oxygen tanks exploded. This led astronaut John Swigert to utter what has by now become a famous line: "Houston, we've had a problem."

The flight director, Gene Kranz, was in charge of managing the mission—and the crisis—from the Johnson Space Center in Houston. He was immediately presented with rapidly worsening readouts. First he was informed that the crew had enough oxygen for eighteen minutes; a moment later that was revised to seven minutes; then it became four minutes. Things were spiraling out of control.

After consulting several NASA teams, Kranz told the astronauts to move into the smaller lunar excursion module, which was designed to detach from *Apollo* for short subtrips in space. The excursion module had its own small supply of oxygen and electricity. Kranz later recalled that he had to figure out a way to "stretch previous resources, barely enough for two men for two days, to support three men for four days."

Kranz then directed a group of teams in Houston to lock themselves in a room until they could diagnose the oxygen problem and come up with ways to get the astronauts back into *Apollo* and then home. This was not the first time these teams had met. Kranz had assembled them months in advance, in myriad configurations, and practice drills each day had gotten them used to responding to random emergencies of all shapes and sizes. He was obsessed with maximizing interaction not only within teams but between teams and NASA's outside contractors. He made sure that they were all in proximity during training, even if it meant circumventing civil service rules barring contractors from working full-time on the NASA premises. Kranz did not want there to be any lack of familiarity between team members who one day might have to deal with a crisis together.

Three days into the crisis, Kranz and his teams had managed to figure out creative ways to get *Apollo* back to earth while consuming a fraction of the power that would typically be needed. As the *New York Times* editorialized, the crisis would have been fatal had it not been for the "NASA network whose teams of experts performed miracles of emergency improvisation."[10]

It was an incredible feat and a riveting story. *But*, we asked Riesenfeld, *what's the connection to Israel?* Fast-forward to February 1, 2003, he told us, sixteen days into the *Columbia* mission, when the space shuttle exploded into pieces as it reentered the earth's atmosphere. We now know that a piece of insulating foam—weighing 1.67 pounds—had broken off the external fuel tank during takeoff. The foam struck the leading edge of the shuttle's left wing, making a hole that would later allow superheated gases to rip through the wing's interior.

There were over two weeks of flight time between takeoff—when the foam had first struck the wing—and the explosion. Could something have been done during this window to repair *Columbia*?

After reading the HBS study, Riesenfeld certainly thought so. He pointed to the handful of midlevel NASA engineers whose voices had gone unheard. As they watched on video monitors during a post-launch review session, these engineers saw the foam dislodge. They immediately notified NASA's managers. But they were told that the foam "issue" was nothing new—foam dislodgments had damaged shuttles in previous launches and there had never been an accident. It was just a maintenance problem. *Onward.*

The engineers tried to push back. This broken piece of foam was "the largest ever," they said. They requested that U.S. satellites—already in orbit—be dispatched to take additional photos of the punctured wing. Unfortunately, the engineers were overruled again. Management would not even acquiesce to their secondary request to have the astronauts conduct a spacewalk to assess the damage and try to repair it in advance of their return to earth.

NASA had seen foam dislodgments before; since they hadn't caused problems in the past, they should be treated as routine, management ruled; no further discussion was necessary. The engineers were all but told to go away.

This was the part of the HBS study that Riesenfeld focused on. The study's authors explained that organizations were structured under one of two models: a standardized model, where routine and systems govern everything, including strict compliance with timelines and budgets, or an experimental model, where every day, every exercise, and every piece of new information is evaluated and debated in a culture that resembles an R&D laboratory.

During the *Columbia* era, NASA's culture was one of adherence to routines and standards. Management tried to shoehorn every new piece of data into an inflexible system—what Roberta Wohlstetter, a military intelligence analyst, describes as our "stubborn attachment to existing beliefs."[11] It's a problem she has encountered in the world of intelligence analysis, too, where there is often a failure of imagination when assessing the behavior of enemies.

NASA's transformation from the *Apollo* culture of exploration to the *Columbia* culture of rigid standardization began in the 1970s, when the space agency requested congressional funding for the new shuttle program. The shuttle had been promoted as a reusable spacecraft that would dramatically reduce the cost of space travel. President Nixon said at the time that the program would "revolutionize transportation into near space, by routinizing it." It was projected that the shuttle would conduct an unprecedented fifty missions each year. Former air force secretary Sheila Widnall, who was a member of the Columbia Accident Investigation Board, later said that NASA pitched *Columbia* as "a 747 that you could simply land and turn around and operate again."

But as the HBS professors point out, "space travel, much like technological innovation, is a fundamentally experimental endeavor and should be managed that way. Each new flight should be an important test and source of data, rather than a routine application of past practices." Which is why Riesenfeld directed us to the study. Israeli war-fighting is also an "experimental endeavor," as we saw in the story of Israel's handling of the Saggers in 1973. The Israeli military and Israeli start-ups in many ways live by the *Apollo* culture, he told us.

Connected to this *Apollo* culture, certainly in Nava Swersky Sofer's estimation, is a can-do, responsible attitude that Israelis refer to as *rosh gadol*. In the Israeli army, soldiers are divided into those who think with a *rosh gadol*—literally, a "big head"—and those who operate with a *rosh katan*, or "little head." *Rosh katan* behavior, which is shunned, means interpreting orders as narrowly as possible to avoid taking on responsibility or extra work. *Rosh gadol* thinking means following orders but doing so in the best possible way, using judgment, and investing whatever effort is necessary. It emphasizes improvisation over discipline, and *challenging the chief* over respect for hierarchy. Indeed, "challenge the chief" is an injunction issued to junior Israeli soldiers, one that comes directly from a postwar military commission that we'll look at later. But everything about Singapore runs counter to a *rosh gadol* mentality.

Spend time in Singapore and it's immediately obvious that it is tidy. Extremely tidy. Perfectly manicured green lawns and lush trees are framed by a skyline of majestic new skyscrapers. Global financial institutions' outposts can be found on nearly every corner. The streets are free of trash; even innocuous litter is hard to spot. Singaporeans are specifically instructed on how to be polite, how to be less contentious and noisy, and not to chew gum in public.

Tidiness extends to the government, too. Lee Kuan Yew's People's Action Party has basically been in uninterrupted power since Singaporean independence. This is just the way Lee wants it. He has always believed that a vibrant political opposition would undermine his vision for an orderly and efficient Singapore. Public dissent has been discouraged, if not suppressed outright. This attitude is taken for granted in Singapore, but in Israel it's foreign.

Israeli air force pilot Tal Keinan is also a graduate of Harvard Business School. When it comes to "*Apollo* vs. *Columbia*," he believes that had NASA stuck to its exploratory roots, foam strikes would have been identified and seriously debated at the daily "debrief." In Israel's elite military units, each day is an experiment. And each day ends with a grueling session whereby everyone in the unit—of all ranks—sits down to deconstruct the day, no matter what else is happening on the battlefield or around the world. "The debrief is as important as the drill or live battle," he told us. Each flight exercise, simulation, and real operation is treated like laboratory work "to be examined and reexamined, and reexamined again, open to new information, and subjected to rich—and heated—debate. That's how we are trained."[12]

In these group debriefs, emphasis is put not only on unrestrained candor but on self-criticism as a means of having everyone—peers, subordinates, and superiors—learn from every mistake. "It's usually ninety minutes. It's with everybody. It's very personal. It's a very tough experience," Keinan said, recalling the most sweat-inducing debriefings of his military career. "The guys that got 'killed' [in the simulations], for them it's very tough. But for those who survive a battle—even a daily training exercise—the next-toughest part is the debriefing."

Keinan was an IAF formation commander flying F-16 fighter jets. "The way you communicate and deconstruct a disagreement between differing perspectives on an event or decision is a big part of our military culture. So much so that debriefing is an art that you get graded on. In flight school and all the way through the squadron ... there are numerous questions regarding a person's ability to debrief himself and to debrief others."

Explaining away a bad decision is unacceptable. "Defending stuff that you've done is just not popular. If you screwed up, your job is to show the lessons you've learned. Nobody learns from someone who is being defensive."

Nor is the purpose of debriefings simply to admit mistakes. Rather, the effect of the debriefing system is that pilots learn that mistakes are acceptable, provided they are used as opportunities to improve individual and group performance. This emphasis on useful, applicable lessons over creating new formal doctrines is typical of the IDF. The entire Israeli military tradition is to be tradition*less.* Commanders and soldiers are not to become wedded to any idea or solution just because it worked in the past.

The seeds of this feisty culture go back to the state's founding generation. In 1948, the Israeli army did not have any traditions, protocols, or doctrines of its own; nor did it import institutions from the British, whose military was in Palestine before Israel's independence. According to military historian Edward Luttwak, Israel's was unlike all postcolonial armies in this way. "Created in the midst of war out of an underground militia, many of whose men had been trained in cellars with wooden pistols, the Israeli army has evolved very rapidly under the relentless pressure of bitter and protracted conflict. Instead of the quiet acceptance of doctrine and tradition, witnessed in the case of most other armies, the growth of the Israeli army has been marked by a turmoil of innovation, controversy, and debate."

Furthermore, after each of its wars, the IDF engaged in far-reaching structural reforms based on the same process of rigorous debate.

While the army was still demobilizing after the 1948 War of Independence, Ben-Gurion appointed a British-trained officer named Haim Laskov to examine the structure of the IDF. Laskov was given a blank check to restructure the army from the ground up. "While such a total appraisal would not be surprising after a defeat," Luttwak explained to us, "the Israelis were able to innovate even after victory. The new was not always better than the old, but the flow of fresh ideas at least prevented the ossification of the military mind, which is so often the ultimate penalty of victory and the cause of future defeat."[13]

The victory in the 1967 Six-Day War was the most decisive one Israel has ever achieved. In the days before the war, the Arab states were openly boasting that they would be triumphant, and the lack of international support for Israel convinced many that the Jewish state was doomed. Israel launched a preemptive attack, destroying the entire Egyptian air force on the ground. Though the war was called the Six-Day War, it was essentially won on that first day, in a matter of hours. By the end, the Arab states had been pushed back on all fronts.

And yet, even in victory, the same thing happened: self-examination followed by an overhaul of the IDF. Senior officials have actually been fired after a successful war.

It should not be surprising, then, that after more controversial wars—such as the 1973 Yom Kippur War, the 1982 Lebanon war, and the 2006 Lebanon war, which most Israelis perceived as having been seriously botched—there were full-blown public commissions of inquiry that evaluated the country's military and civilian leaders.

"The American military does after-action reports inside the military," military historian and former top U.S. State Department official Eliot Cohen told us. "But they are classified. A completely internal, self-contained exercise. I've told senior officers in the U.S. military that they would well benefit from an Israeli-like national commission after each war, in which senior ranks are held accountable—and the entire country can access the debate."[14]

But that's not going to happen anytime soon, much to the frustration of U.S. Army Lieutenant Colonel Paul Yingling. "We've lost thousands of lives and spent hundreds of billions of dollars in the last seven years in efforts to bring stability to two medium-sized countries; we can't afford to adapt this slowly in the future,"[15] he said in a lecture at the marine base at Quantico, Virginia. The problem, he wrote in a controversial essay in 2007, is that "a private who loses a rifle suffers far greater consequences than a general who loses a war."[16]

The Israelis, on the other hand, have been so dogmatic about their commissions that one was even set up in the midst of an existential war. In July 1948, in what Eliot Cohen described as "one of the truly astonishing episodes" of Israel's War of Independence, the government established a commission staffed by leaders from across the political spectrum while the war was still going on. The commission stepped back for three days to hear testimony from angry army officers about the government and the military's conduct during the war and what they believed to be Ben-Gurion's micromanagement.[17] Setting up a commission amid the fighting of a war was a questionable decision, given the distraction it would impose on the leadership. But, as Tal Keinan told us earlier, in Israel the debrief is as important as the fighting itself.

This rigorous review and national debrief was in full public display as recently as the 2006 Lebanon war. Initially, there was almost unanimous public backing for the government's decision to respond massively to the attack by Hezbollah from across Israel's northern border on July 12, 2006. This public support continued even when civilians in northern Israel came under indiscriminate missile attack, forcing one out of seven Israelis to leave their homes during the war.

Support for continuing the offensive was even higher among those living under the missile barrage than in the rest of Israel. This support presumably came from an Israeli willingness to suffer in order to see Hezbollah destroyed for good.

But Israel failed to destroy Hezbollah in 2006, and was unable to weaken Hezbollah's position in Lebanon and to force the return of kidnapped soldiers. The reaction against the political and military leadership was harsh, with calls for the defense minister, IDF chief of staff, and prime minister to step down. Six companies of troops (roughly six hundred soldiers) were able to kill some four hundred Hezbollah fighters in face-to-face combat while suffering only thirty casualties, but the war was considered a failure of Israeli strategy and training, and seemed to signal to the public a dangerous departure from the IDF's core ethos.

Indeed, the 2006 Lebanon war was a case study in deviation from the Israeli entrepreneurial model that had succeeded in previous wars. According to retired general Giora Eiland, who has headed both the prestigious IDF Planning Branch and the National Security Council, the war underscored four principal IDF failures:

"Poor performance by the combat units, particularly on land; weakness in the high command; poor command and control processes; and problematic norms, including traditional values." In particular, Eiland said, "open-minded thought, necessary to reduce the risk of sticking to preconceived ideas and relying on unquestioned assumptions, was far too rare."

In other words, Israel suffered from a lack of organization *and* a lack of improvisation. Eiland also noted that soldiers were not sufficiently instilled with "the sense that 'the fate of the war is on our shoulders.'" Commanders "relied too much on technology, which created the impression that it was possible to wage a tactical land battle without actually being in the field."

Finally, Eiland leveled a criticism that is perhaps quintessentially Israeli and hardly imaginable within any other military apparatus: "One of the problems of the Second Lebanon War was the exaggerated adherence of senior officers to the chief of staff's decisions. There is no question that the final word rests with the chief of staff, and once decisions have been made, all must demonstrate complete commitment to their implementation. However, it is the senior officers' job to *argue with the chief of staff* when they feel he is wrong, and this should be done assertively on the basis of professional truth as they see it" (emphasis added).

Large organizations, whether military or corporate, must be constantly wary of kowtowing and groupthink, or the entire apparatus can rush headlong into terrible mistakes. Yet most militaries, and many corporations, seem willing to sacrifice flexibility for discipline, initiative for organization, and innovation for predictability. This, at least in principle, is not the Israeli way.

Eiland suggested that the IDF should consider drastic measures to reinforce its classic antihierarchical, innovative, and enterprising ethos. "Is it correct or even possible," he asked, "to allow lower-ranking officers to plan and lead current security operations *with less control from above* in order to prepare them better for a conventional war?" (emphasis added).[18]

The 2006 war was a very costly wake-up call for the IDF. It was suffering from an ossification and hollowing out that is common among militaries that have not been tested in battle in a long time. In Israel's case, the IDF had shifted its focus to commando-style warfare, which is appropriate when pursuing terrorist groups, but had neglected the skills and capabilities needed for conventional warfare.

Yet the Israeli reaction was not so much a call to tighten the ranks as it was to loosen them: to work harder at devolving authority and responsibility to lower levels and to do more to encourage junior officers to challenge their higher-ups. This radical push, moreover, was seen as one of restoring the "core values," not liberalizing them.

What does all this mean for a country like Singapore, trying not just to emulate Israel's military structure but to inject some of Israel's inventiveness into its economy, as well? As noted above, Singapore differs dramatically from Israel both in its *order* and in its insistence on *obedience*. Singapore's politeness, manicured lawns, and one-party rule have cleansed the fluidity from its economy.

Fluidity, according to a new school of economists studying key ingredients for entrepreneurialism, is produced when people can cross boundaries, turn societal norms upside down, and agitate in a free-market economy, all to catalyze radical ideas. Or as Harvard psychologist Howard Gardner puts it, different types of "asynchrony... [such as] a lack of fit, an unusual pattern, or an irregularity" have the power to stimulate economic creativity.[19]

Thus, the most formidable obstacle to fluidity is order. A bit of mayhem is not only healthy but critical. The leading thinkers in this area—economists William Baumol, Robert Litan, and Carl Schramm—argue that the ideal environment is best described by a concept in "complexity science" called the "edge of chaos." They define that edge as "the estuary region where rigid order and random chaos meet and generate high levels of adaptation, complexity, and creativity."[20]

This is precisely the environment in which Israeli entrepreneurs thrive. They benefit from the stable institutions and rule of law that exist in an advanced democracy. Yet they also benefit from Israel's nonhierarchical culture, where everyone in business belongs to overlapping networks produced by small communities, common army service, geographic proximity, and informality.

It is no coincidence that the military—particularly the elite units in the air force, infantry, intelligence, and information technology arenas—have served as incubators for thousands of Israeli high-tech start-ups. Other countries may generate them in small numbers, but the Israeli economy benefits from the phenomena of *rosh gadol* thinking and critical reassessment, undergirded by a doctrine of experimentation, rather than standardization, wide enough to have a national and even a global impact.

# PART III

**Beginnings**

# CHAPTER 6

# An Industrial Policy That Worked

*It was not simple to convince people that growing
fish in the desert makes sense.*

—PROFESSOR SAMUEL APPELBAUM

THE STORY OF HOW ISRAEL got to where it is—fiftyfold economic growth within sixty years—is more than the story of Israeli character idiosyncrasies, battle-tested entrepreneurship, or geopolitical happenstance. The story must include the effects of government policies, which had to be as adaptive as Israel's military and its citizens, and suffered as many turns of fortune.

The history of Israel's economy is one of two great leaps, separated by a period of stagnation and hyperinflation. The government's macroeconomic policies have played an important role in speeding the country's growth, then reversing it, and then unleashing it in ways that even the government never expected.

The first great leap occurred from 1948 to 1970, a period during which per capita GDP almost quadrupled and the population tripled, even amidst Israel's engagement in three major wars.[1] The second was from 1990 until today, during which time the country was transformed from a sleepy backwater into a leading center of global innovation. Dramatically different—almost opposite—means were employed: the first period of expansion was achieved through an entrepreneurial government that dominated a small, primitive private sector; the second period through a thriving entrepreneurial private sector that was initially catalyzed by government action.

The roots of the first period of economic growth can be traced to well before the country's founding—all the way back to the late nineteenth century. For example, in the 1880s, a group of Jewish settlers tried to build a farming community in a new town they had founded—Petach Tikva—a few miles from what is now Tel Aviv. After first living in tents, the pioneers hired local Arab villagers to build mud cabins for them. But when it rained the cabins leaked even more than the tents, and when the river swelled beyond its banks, the structures melted away. Some of the settlers were struck by malaria and dysentery. After just a few winters, the farmers' savings had been exhausted, their access to roads washed out, and their families reduced to near starvation.

In 1883, though, things began to look up. The French-Jewish banker and philanthropist Edmond de Rothschild provided desperately needed financial support. An agricultural expert advised the settlers to plant eucalyptus trees where the river's overflow created swamps; the roots of these trees quickly drained the swamps dry. The incidence of malaria dropped dramatically, and more families came to live in the growing community.[2]

Beginning in the 1920s and continuing through the decade, labor productivity in the Yishuv—the Jewish community of pre-state Palestine—increased by 80 percent, producing a fourfold increase in national product as the Jewish population doubled in size. Strikingly, as a global depression raged from 1931 to 1935, the average annual economic growth for Jews and Arabs in Palestine was 28 and 14 percent, respectively.[3]

The small communities established by settlers, like those of Petach Tikva, would never have been able to achieve such explosive growth on their own. They were joined by waves of new immigrants who contributed not only their numbers but a pioneering ethos that overturned the charity-based economy.

One of those immigrants was a twenty-year-old lawyer named David Gruen, who traveled from Poland in 1906. Upon arrival, he Hebraized his name to Ben-Gurion—naming himself after a Jewish general from the Roman period of 70 C.E.—and quickly rose to become the uncontested leader of the Yishuv. The Israeli author Amos Oz has written that "in the early years of the state, many Israelis saw him as a combination of Moses, George Washington, Garibaldi and God Almighty."[4]

Ben-Gurion was also Israel's first national entrepreneur. Theodore Herzl may have conceptualized a vision for Jewish sovereignty and begun to galvanize Diaspora Jews around a romantic notion of a sovereign state, but it was Ben-Gurion who organized this vision from an idea into a functioning nation-state. After World War II, Winston Churchill described the United States Army general George Marshall as the Allied Powers' "organizer of victory." To paraphrase Churchill, Ben-Gurion was the "organizer of Zionism." Or in business terms, Ben-Gurion was the "operations guy" who actually *built* the country.

The challenge facing Ben-Gurion in operational management and logistics planning was extremely complex. Consider just one issue: how to absorb waves of immigrants. From the 1930s through the end of the Holocaust, as millions of European Jews were being deported to concentration camps, some managed to flee to Palestine. Others who escaped, however, were denied asylum by different countries and forced to remain in hiding, often in horrendous conditions. After 1939 the British government, which was the colonial power in charge of Palestine, imposed draconian restrictions on immigration, a policy known as the "White Paper." British authorities turned away most of those trying to seek refuge in Palestine.

In response, Ben-Gurion launched two seemingly contradictory campaigns. First he inspired and organized some eighteen thousand Jews living in Palestine to return to Europe to join the British army in "Jewish battalions" fighting the Nazis. At the same time, he created an underground agency to secretly transport Jewish refugees from Europe to Palestine, in defiance of the United Kingdom's immigration policy. Ben-Gurion was at once fighting alongside the British in Europe and against the British in Palestine.

Most histories of this era focus on the political and military struggles that led to the founding of Israel in 1948. Along the way, a myth surrounding the economic dimension of this story has arisen: that Ben-Gurion was a socialist and that Israel was born as a thoroughly socialist state.

The sources of this myth are understandable. Ben-Gurion was steeped in the socialist milieu of his era and was heavily influenced by the rise of Marxism and the Russian Revolution of 1917. Many of the Jews arriving from the Soviet Union and Eastern Europe in pre-state Palestine were socialist, and they were highly influential.

But Ben-Gurion was singularly focused on building the state, by whatever means. He had no patience for experimenting with policies that he believed were simply designed to validate Marxist ideology. In his view, every policy—economic, political, military, or social—should serve the objective of nation building. Ben-Gurion was the classic *bitzu'ist,* a Hebrew word that loosely translates to "pragmatist," but with a much more activist quality. A *bitzu'ist* is someone who just gets things done.

*Bitzu'ism* is at the heart of the pioneering ethos and Israel's entrepreneurial drive. "To call someone a *bitzu'ist* is to pay him or her a high compliment," writes author and editor Leon Wieseltier. "The *bitzu'ist* is the builder, the irrigator, the pilot, the gunrunner, the settler. Israelis recognize the social type: crusty, resourceful, impatient, sardonic, effective, not much in need of thought but not much in need of sleep either."[5] While Wieseltier is describing the pioneering generation, his words fit those who risk all to found start-ups. *Bitzu'ism* is a thread that runs from those who braved marauders and drained the swamps to the entrepreneurs who believe they can defy the odds and barrel through to make their dreams happen.

For Ben-Gurion, the central task was the wide dispersion of the Jewish population over what would one day become Israel. He believed that an intensely focused settlement program was the only way to guarantee Israel's future sovereignty. Otherwise, unsettled or thinly settled areas could someday be reclaimed by adversaries, who would have an easier case to make to the international community if Jews were underrepresented in contested areas. Moreover, thick urban concentrations—in cities and towns like Jerusalem, Tiberias, and Safed—would make obvious targets for hostile air forces, which was another reason for dispersing the population widely.

Ben-Gurion also understood that people would not move to underdeveloped areas, far away from urban centers and basic infrastructure, if the government did not take the lead in settlement and provide incentives to relocate. Private capitalists, he knew, were unlikely to take on the risk of such efforts.

But this intense focus on development also produced a legacy of informal government meddling in the economy. The exploits of Pinchas Sapir were typical. During the 1960s and '70s Sapir served at different times as minister of finance and minister of trade and industry. His style of management was so *micro* that Sapir established different foreign currency exchange rates for different factories—called the "100 exchange rate method"—and kept track of it all by jotting each rate down in a little black notebook. According to Moshe Sanbar, the second governor of the Bank of Israel, Sapir famously had two notebooks. "One of them was his own personal central bureau of statistics: He had people in every large factory reporting back to him on how much they sold, to whom, how much electricity was consumed, etc. And this is how he knew, well before official statistics were kept, how the economy was doing."

Sanbar also believes that this system could have worked only in a small, striving, and idealistic nation: there was no government transparency, but "all the politicians then...died poor....They intervened in the market, and decided whatever they wanted, but at no point did anyone pocket even one cent."[6]

## *The Kibbutz and the Agriculture Revolution*

At the center of the first great leap was a radical and emblematic societal innovation whose local and global influence has been wildly disproportionate to its size: the kibbutz. Today, at less than 2 percent of Israel's population, kibbutzniks produce 12 percent of the nation's exports.

Historians have called the kibbutz "the world's most successful commune movement."[7] Yet in 1944, four years before Israel's founding, only sixteen thousand people lived on kibbutzim (*kibbutz* means "gathering" or "collective," *kibbutzim* is the plural, and members are called *kibbutzniks*). Created as agricultural settlements dedicated to abolishing private property and to complete equality, the movement grew over the following twenty years to eighty thousand people living in 250 communities, but this still amounted to only 4 percent of Israel's population. Yet by this time the kibbutzim had provided some 15 percent of the members of Knesset, Israel's parliament, and an even larger proportion of the IDF's officers and pilots. One-quarter of the eight hundred IDF soldiers killed in the 1967 Six-Day War were kibbutzniks—six times their proportion in the general population.[8]

Though the notion of a socialist commune might bring up images of a bohemian culture, the early kibbutzim were anything but. The kibbutzniks came to symbolize hardiness and informality, and their pursuit of radical equality produced a form of asceticism. A notable example of this was Abraham Herzfield, a kibbutz movement leader during the state's early years, who thought that flush toilets were unacceptably decadent. Even in the poor and beleaguered Israel of the 1950s, when many basic goods were rationed, flush toilets were considered a common necessity in most Israeli settlements and cities. Legend has it that when the first toilet was installed on a kibbutz, Herzfield personally destroyed it with an ax. By the 1960s, even Herzfield could not hold back progress, and most kibbutzim installed flush toilets.[9]

Kibbutzim were both hypercollective and hyperdemocratic. Every question of self-governance, from what crop to grow to whether members would have televisions, was endlessly debated. Shimon Peres told us, "In the kibbutzim, there were no police. There was no court. When I was a member, there was no private money. Before I came, there wasn't even private mail. The mail came and everyone could read it."

Perhaps most controversially, children were raised communally. While practices varied, almost all kibbutzim had "children's houses" where children lived and were tended to by kibbutz members. In most kibbutzim, children would see their parents for a few hours each day, but they would sleep with their peers, not in their parents' houses.

The rise of the kibbutz is partly a result of agricultural and technological breakthroughs made on Israeli kibbutzim and in Israeli universities. The transition from the extreme hardships and unbending ideologies of the founders' era, and from tilling the land to cutting-edge industry, can be seen in a kibbutz like Hatzerim. This kibbutz, along with ten other isolated and tiny outposts, was founded one night in October 1946 when the Haganah, the main pre-state Jewish militia, decided to establish a presence at strategic points in the southern Negev Desert. When daylight broke, the five women and twenty-five men who'd arrived to start the community found themselves on a barren hilltop surrounded by wilderness. A single acacia tree could be seen on the horizon.

It took a year before the group managed to lay a six-inch pipe that would supply water from an area forty miles away. During the 1948 War of Independence, the kibbutz was attacked and its water supply cut off. Even after the war, the soil proved so salty and difficult to cultivate that by 1959 the kibbutz members had begun to debate closing Hatzerim and moving to a more hospitable location.

But the community decided to stick it out since it became clear that the problems of soil salinity affected not only Hatzerim but also most of the lands in the Negev. Two years later, the Hatzerim kibbutzniks managed to flush the soil enough so that they were able to start growing crops. Yet this was just the beginning of Hatzerim's breakthroughs for itself and the country.

In 1965 a water engineer named Simcha Blass approached Hatzerim with an idea for an invention that he wanted to commercialize: drip irrigation. This was the beginning of what ultimately became Netafim, the global drip irrigation company.

Professor Ricardo Hausmann heads the Center for International Development at Harvard University and is a former minister of development in the Venezuelan government. He is also a world-renowned expert on national economic development models. All countries have problems and constraints, he told us, but what's striking about Israel is the penchant for taking problems—like the lack of water—and turning them into assets—in this case, by becoming leaders in the fields of desert agriculture, drip irrigation, and desalination. The kibbutz was at the forefront of this process early on. The environmental hardships the kibbutzim contended with were ultimately incredibly productive, much in the same way Israel's security threats were. The large amounts of R&D spending deployed to solve military problems through high technology—including in voice recognition, communications, optics, hardware, software, and so on—has helped the country jump-start, train, and maintain a civilian high-tech sector.

The country's disadvantage of having some of its area taken up by a desert was turned into an asset. Looking at Israel today, most visitors would be surprised to discover that 95 percent of the country is categorized as semi-arid, arid, or hyperarid, as quantified by levels of annual rainfall. Indeed, by the time Israel was founded, the Negev Desert had crept up almost all the way north to the road between Jerusalem and Tel Aviv. The Negev is still Israel's largest region, but its encroachment has been reversed as its northern reaches are now covered with agricultural fields and planted forests. Much of this was accomplished by innovative water policies since the days of Hatzerim. Israel now leads the world in recycling waste water; over 70 percent is recycled, which is three times the percentage recycled in Spain, the country in second place.[10]

Kibbutz Mashabbe Sade, in the Negev Desert, went even further: the kibbutzniks found a way to use water deemed useless not once, but twice. They dug a well as deep as ten football fields are long—almost half a mile—only to discover water that was warm and salty. This did not seem like a great find until they consulted Professor Samuel Appelbaum of nearby Ben-Gurion University of the Negev. He realized that the water would be perfect for raising warm-water fish.

"It was not simple to convince people that growing fish in the desert makes sense," said Appelbaum, a fish biologist. "But it's important to debunk the idea that arid land is infertile, useless land."[11] The kibbutzniks started pumping the ninety-eight-degree water into ponds, which were stocked with tilapia, barramundi, sea bass, and striped bass for commercial production. After use in the fishponds, the water, which now contained waste products that made excellent fertilizer, was then used to irrigate olive and date trees. The kibbutz also found ways to grow vegetables and fruits that were watered directly from the underground aquifer.

A century ago Israel was, as Mark Twain and other travelers described it, largely a barren wasteland. Now there are an estimated 240 million trees, millions of them planted one at a time. Forests have been planted all over the country, but the largest is perhaps the most improbable of all: the Yatir Forest.

In 1932, Yosef Weitz became the top forestry official in the Jewish National Fund, a pre-state organization dedicated to buying land and planting trees in what was to become the Jewish state. It took Weitz more than thirty years to convince his own organization and the government to start planting a forest on hills at the edge of the Negev Desert. Most thought it couldn't be done. Now there are about four million trees there. Satellite pictures show the forest sticking out like a visual typo, surrounded by desert and drylands in a place where it should not exist. FluxNet, a NASA-coordinated global environmental research project, collects data from over a hundred observation towers around the world. Only one tower is in a forest in a semi-arid zone: Yatir.

The Yatir Forest survives only on rain water, though only 280 millimeters (about eleven inches) of rain fall there each year—about a third of the precipitation that falls on Dallas, Texas. Yet researchers have found that the trees in the forest are naturally growing faster than expected, and that it soaks up about as much carbon dioxide from the atmosphere as lush forests growing in temperate climates.

Dan Yakir is a scientist at the Weizmann Institute who manages the FluxNet research station at Yatir. He says that the forest not only demonstrates that trees can thrive in areas that most people would call desert, but that planting forests on just 12 percent of the world's semi-arid lands could reduce atmospheric carbon by one gigaton a year—the annual $CO_2$ output of about one thousand 500-megawatt coal plants. A gigaton of carbon would also amount to one of seven "stabilization wedges" that scientists argue are necessary to stabilize atmospheric carbon at current levels.

In December 2008, Ben-Gurion University hosted a United Nations–sponsored conference on combating desertification, the world's largest ever. Experts from forty countries came, interested to see with their own eyes why Israel is the only country whose desert is receding.[12]

## The Israeli Leapfrog

The kibbutz story is just a part of the overall trajectory of the Israeli economic revolution. Whether it was socialist, developmentalist, or a hybrid, the economic track record of Israel's first twenty years was impressive. From 1950 through 1955, Israel's economy grew by about 13 percent each year; it hovered just below 10 percent growth annually into the 1960s. Not only did Israel's economy expand, it experienced what Hausmann calls a "leapfrog," which is when a developing country shrinks its per capita wealth gap with rich first-world countries.[13]

Whereas economic growth periods are common in most countries, leapfrogs are not. A third of the world's economies have experienced a growth period in the past fifty years, but fewer than 10 percent of them have had a leapfrog. The Israeli economy, however, increased its per capita income relative to the United States' from 25 percent in 1950 to 60 percent in 1970. That means Israel more than doubled its living standard relative to that of the United States within twenty years.[14]

During this period, the government made no effort to encourage private entrepreneurship and, if anything, was rhetorically hostile to the notion of private profit. Though some of the government's political opponents did begin to oppose its heavy economic hand and anti–free market attitudes, these critics were a small minority. If the government had valued and sought to ease the path for private initiative, the economy would have grown even faster.

In retrospect, however, it is clear that Israel's economic performance occurred in part because of the government's meddling, and not just in spite of it. During the early stages of development in any primitive economy, there are easily identifiable opportunities for large-scale investment: roads, water systems, factories, ports, electrical grids, and housing construction. Israel's massive investment in these projects—such as the National Water Carrier, which piped water from the Sea of Galilee in the north to the parched Negev in the south—stimulated high-velocity growth. Rapid housing development on kibbutzim, for example, generated growth in the construction and utilities industries. But it is important not to generalize: many developing countries engaged in large infrastructure projects waste vast amounts of government funds due to corruption and government inefficiencies. Israel was not a perfect exception.

Though infrastructure projects were perhaps the most visible element, even more striking was the deliberate creation of industries, as entrepreneurial projects, from *within* the government. Shimon Peres and Al Schwimmer, an American who helped smuggle airplanes and weapons to Israel during the War of Independence, together dreamed up the idea of creating an aeronautics industry in Israel. When they pitched the idea within the Israeli government, in the 1950s, reactions ranged from skepticism to ridicule. At the time, staples like milk and eggs were still scarce and thousands of just-arrived refugees were living in tents, so it is not surprising that most of the ministers thought that Israel could neither afford nor be capable of succeeding in such an endeavor.

But Peres had David Ben-Gurion's ear, and convinced him that Israel could start repairing surplus World War II aircraft. They launched an enterprise that at one point was Israel's largest employer. Bedek eventually became Israel Aircraft Industries, a global leader in its field.

During this stage of Israel's development, private entrepreneurs may not have been essential because the largest and most pressing needs of the economy were obvious. But the system broke down as the economy became more complex. According to Israeli economist Yakir Plessner, once the government saturated the economy with big infrastructure spending, only entrepreneurs could be counted on to drive growth; only they could find "the niches of relative advantage."[15]

The transition from central development to a private entrepreneurial economy should have occurred in the mid-1960s. The twenty-year period from 1946 through 1966, when most of the large-scale infrastructure investments had been made, was coming to an end. In 1966, with no more frothy investment targets, Israel experienced for the first time nearly zero economic growth. This should have convinced Israel's government to open the economy to private enterprise. But instead, needed reforms were staved off by the Six-Day War. Within one week of June 6, 1967, Israel had captured the West Bank, Gaza Strip, Sinai Peninsula, and Golan Heights. Collectively, the territory was equal to more than three times the size of Israel.

Suddenly the Israeli government was once again busy with new large-scale infrastructure projects. And since the IDF needed to establish positions in the new territories, massive spending was necessary for defense installations, border security, and other costly infrastructure. It was another giant economic "stimulus" program. As a result, from 1967 to 1968, investment in construction equipment alone increased by 725 percent. The timing of the war reinforced the worst instincts of Israel's central planners.

## Israel's "Lost Decade"

Still, Israel's economy was living on borrowed time. Another war six years later, the Yom Kippur War of 1973, did not yield the same economic boost. Israel suffered heavy casualties (three thousand fatalities and many more wounded) and enormous damage to its infrastructure. Forced to mobilize large numbers of reserves, the IDF pulled most of the labor force out of the economy for up to six months. The effect of such a massive and protracted call-up was jarring, paralyzing companies and even entire industries. Business activity came to a halt.

In any normal economic environment, private incomes among domestic workers would have experienced a corresponding decline. But in Israel they did not. Instead of allowing salaries to fall, the government artificially propped them up through a vehicle that resulted in extremely high levels of public debt. In order to try to offset the ballooning debt, every tax rate—including on capital investment—was raised. Short-term and high-priced debt was used to finance the deficit, which in turn increased interest payments.

All this coincided with a decline in net immigration. New immigrants have always been a key source of Israel's economic vitality. There had been a net gain of nearly one hundred thousand new Israelis between 1972 and 1973. But the number was down to fourteen thousand in 1974 and almost zero in 1975.

What made recovery especially unlikely—if not impossible—was the government's monopoly of the capital market. As the Bank of Israel itself described it at the time, "The government's involvement transcends anything that is known in politically free countries." The government set the terms and interest rate for every loan and debt instrument for consumer and business credit. Commercial banks and pensions were forced to use most of their deposits to purchase nonnegotiable government bonds or to finance private-sector loans for projects that had been earmarked by the government.[16]

This was the condition of Israel's economy during what is often described by economists as Israel's "lost decade," from the mid-1970s through the mid-1980s. Today, Intel's decision to search for scarce engineers in Israel seems like an obvious move. But the Israel that Intel found in 1974 was nothing like what it is today. While it may no longer have resembled an expanse of sand, swamps, and malaria, visitors during the 1970s might have been excused for thinking they had landed in a third-world country.

Israeli universities and Israel's engineering talent were by this time fairly advanced, but much of the country's infrastructure was antiquated. The airport was small, quaint, and shabby. It had a Soviet-style utilitarian feel as one arrived and entered immigration. There was no major road that could pass for a real highway. Television reception was shoddy, but it hardly mattered since there was only a single government-owned station broadcasting in Hebrew, along with a couple of Arabic channels that, with a powerful enough antenna, one could pick up from Jordan or Lebanon.

Not everyone had a telephone at home, and not because they all had cell phones, which didn't exist yet. The reason was that phone lines were still being slowly rationed out by a government ministry, and it took a long time to get one. Supermarkets, unlike the small food marts common in neighborhoods, were a novelty, and they did not carry many international products. Major international retail chains were nonexistent. If you needed something from abroad, you had to go yourself, or ask a visitor to bring it back for you. High customs duties—many of them protectionist attempts to coddle local producers—made most imports prohibitively expensive.

The cars on the road were a bland bunch—some produced in Israel (these became the butt of jokes, much like locally produced Russian cars did in Russia) and a motley assortment of the cheapest models of mostly Subaru and Citroën, the two companies brave or desperate enough to defy the Arab boycott. The banking system and the government's financial regulations were as antiquated as the auto industry. It was illegal to change dollars anywhere except at banks, which charged government-set exchange rates. Even holding an overseas bank account was illegal.

The overall mood was dour. The euphoria that had come with the stunning 1967 victory—which some likened to first receiving a death-row pardon and then winning the lottery—quickly dissipated after the 1973 Yom Kippur War and was replaced with a renewed sense of insecurity, isolation, and, perhaps worst of all, tragic blunder. The mighty Israeli army had been utterly surprised and badly bloodied. It was scarce consolation that, in military terms, Israel had won the war. Israelis felt that their political and military leadership had badly failed them.

A public commission of inquiry was appointed; this led to the removal of the IDF's chief of staff, its chief of intelligence, and other senior security officials. Though the commission exonerated her, Prime Minister Golda Meir took responsibility for what was seen as a fiasco and resigned a month after the release of the commission's report. But her successor, Yitzhak Rabin, was forced to resign from his first stint as prime minister when, in 1977, it was revealed that his wife had a foreign bank account.

As late as the early 1980s, Israel also suffered from hyperinflation: going to the supermarket meant spending thousands of almost worthless shekels. Inflation rose from 13 percent in 1971 to 111 percent in 1979. Some of this was due to rising oil prices at this time. But Israeli inflation continued to skyrocket beyond other countries', rising to 133 percent in 1980 and to 445 percent in 1984, and appeared to be on its way to a four-digit figure within a year or two.[17]

People would hoard phone tokens, since their value didn't change as their price rose sharply, and would rush to buy basic items in advance of expected price hikes. According to a joke of that time, it was better to take a taxi from Tel Aviv to Jerusalem than a bus, since you could pay the taxi at the end of the ride, when the shekel would be worth less.

A main reason for the hyperinflation was, ironically, one of the measures the government had taken for years to cope with inflation: indexing. Most of the economy—wages, prices, rents—were linked to the Consumer Price Index, a measure of inflation. Indexing seemed to protect the public from feeling the effects of inflation, since their incomes rose with their expenses. But indexing ultimately fed an inflationary spiral.

## *Path to Recovery?*

In this context, it is especially striking that Intel set up shop in Israel in the 1970s. An even greater mystery, however, is how Israel transformed itself from this somewhat provincial and isolated state to a thriving and technologically sophisticated country three decades later. Today, visitors to Israel arrive in an airport that is often far more slickly modern than the one they departed from. Unlimited numbers of new phone lines can be set up with only a few hours' notice, BlackBerrys never lose reception, and wireless Internet is as close as the nearest coffee shop. Wireless access is so abundant that during the 2006 Lebanon war, Israelis were busy comparing what kind of Internet service worked best in their bomb shelters. Israelis have more cell phones per capita than anywhere else in the world. Most kids above the age of ten have a cell phone, as well as a computer in their bedroom. The streets are full of late-model cars, ranging from Hummers to European Smart cars that take up less than half of a scarce parking spot.

"Looking for a few good programmers?" CNNMoney.com recently asked in a feature listing Tel Aviv among the "best places to do business in the wired world." "So are IBM, Intel, Texas Instruments, and other tech giants, which have flocked to Israel for its tech savvy....The best place to close a deal is at Yoezer Wine Bar, with its extensive selection of varietals and deliciously doused beef bourguignon."[18] In 1990, though, there wasn't a single chain of coffee shops, and probably not a single wine bar, decent sushi restaurant, McDonald's, Ikea, or major foreign fashion outlet in all of Israel. The first Israeli McDonald's opened in 1993, three years after the chain's largest restaurant opened in Moscow, and twenty-two years after the first McDonald's in Sydney, Australia. Now McDonald's has approximately 150 restaurants in Israel, about twice as many per capita as there are in Spain, Italy, or South Korea.[19]

The second-phase turnaround began after 1990. Up to that point, the economy had a limited capacity to capitalize on the entrepreneurial talent that the culture and the military had inculcated. And further stifling the private sector was the extended period of hyperinflation, which was not addressed until 1985, when then finance minister Shimon Peres led a stabilization plan developed by U.S. Secretary of State George Shultz, IMF economist Stanley Fischer, and the former chairman of president Nixon's Council of Economic Advisers, Herbert Stein. The plan dramatically cut public debt, limited spending, began privatizations, and reformed the government's role in the capital markets. But this didn't yet generate for Israel a private and dynamic entrepreneurial economy.

For the economy to truly take off, it required three additional factors: a new wave of immigration, a new war, and a new venture capital industry.

# CHAPTER 7

# Immigration

## The Google Guys' Challenge

*Immigrants are not averse to starting over. They are, by
definition, risk takers. A nation of immigrants
is a nation of entrepreneurs.*

—GIDI GRINSTEIN

IN 1984 SHLOMO (NEGUSE) MOLLA left his small village in northern Ethiopia with seventeen of his friends, determined to walk
to Israel. He was sixteen years old. Macha, the remote village where
Molla grew up, had virtually no connection to the modern
world—no running water, no electricity, and no phone lines. In
addition to the brutal famine that plagued the country, the Ethiopian Jews lived under a repressive anti-Semitic regime, a satellite of
the former Soviet Union.

"We always dreamed of coming to Israel," said Molla, who was
raised in a Jewish and Zionist home. He and his friends planned to
walk north—from Ethiopia to Sudan, Sudan to Egypt and through

the Sinai Desert, and from Sinai to Israel's southern metropolis, Beersheba; after that, they would continue on to Jerusalem.[1]

Molla's father sold a cow in order to pay a guide two dollars to show the boys the way on the first leg of their journey. They walked barefoot day and night, with few rest stops, trekking through the desert and into the jungle of northern Ethiopia. There they encountered wild tigers and snakes before being held up by a band of muggers, who took their food and money. Yet Molla and his friends continued, walking hundreds of miles in one week to Ethiopia's northern border.

When they crossed into Sudan, they were chased by Sudanese border guards. Molla's best friend was shot and killed, and the rest of the boys were bound, tortured, and thrown in jail. After ninety-one days, they were released to the Gedaref refugee camp in Sudan, where Molla was approached by a white man who spoke cryptically but clearly seemed well-informed. "I know who you are and I know where you want to go," he told the teenager. "I am here to help." This was only the second time in Molla's life that he had seen a white person. The man returned the next day, loaded the boys onto a truck, and drove across the desert for five hours, until they reached a remote airstrip.

There, they were pushed inside an airplane along with hundreds of other Ethiopians. This was part of a secret Israeli government effort; the 1984 airlift mission, called Operation Moses, brought more than eight thousand Ethiopian Jews to Israel.[2] Their average age was fourteen. The day after their arrival, they were all given full Israeli citizenship. The *New Republic*'s Leon Wieseltier wrote at the time that Operation Moses clarified "a classic meaning of Zionism: there must exist a state for which Jews need no visas."[3]

Today Molla is an elected member of Israel's parliament, the Knesset; he is only the second Ethiopian to be elected to this office. "While it was just a four-hour flight, it felt like there was a gap of four hundred years between Ethiopia and Israel," Molla told us.

Coming from an antiquated agrarian community, nearly all the Ethiopians who immigrated to Israel didn't know how to read or write, even in Amharic, their mother tongue. "We didn't have cars. We didn't have industry. We didn't have supermarkets. We didn't have banks," Molla recalled of his life in Ethiopia.

Operation Moses was followed seven years later by Operation Solomon, in which 14,500 Ethiopian Jews were airlifted to Israel. This effort involved thirty-four Israeli Air Force and El Al transport aircraft and one Ethiopian plane. The entire series of transport operations occurred over a thirty-six-hour period.

"Inside Flight 9, the armrests between the seats were raised," the *New York Times* reported at the time. "Five, six or seven Ethiopians including children crowded happily into each three-seat row. None of them had ever been on an airplane before and probably did not even know that the seating was unusual."[4]

Another flight from Ethiopia set a world record: 1,122 passengers on a single El Al 747. Planners had expected to fill the aircraft with 760 passengers, but because the passengers were so thin, hundreds more were squeezed in. Two babies were born during the flight. Many of the passengers arrived barefoot and with no belongings. By the end of the decade, Israel had absorbed some forty thousand Ethiopian immigrants.

The Ethiopian immigration wave has proven to be an enormous economic burden for Israel. Nearly half of Ethiopian adults age twenty-five to fifty-four are unemployed, and a majority of Ethiopian Israelis are on government welfare. Molla expects that even with Israel's robust and well-funded immigrant-absorption programs, the Ethiopian community will not be fully integrated and self-sufficient for at least a decade.

"Given the context of where they came from not so long ago, this will take time," Molla told us. The experience of Ethiopian immigrants contrasts sharply with that of immigrants from the former Soviet Union, most of whom arrived at roughly the same time as Operation Solomon, and who have been a boon to the Israeli economy. The success story of this wave can be found in places like the Shevach-Mofet high school.

The students had been waiting for some time, with the kind of anticipation usually reserved for rock stars. Then the moment arrived. The two Americans entered through a back door, shaking off the press and other groupies. This was their only stop in Israel, aside from the prime minister's office.

The Google founders strode into the hall, and the crowd roared. The students could not believe their eyes. "Sergey Brin and Larry Page...in *our* high school!" one of the students proudly recalled. What had brought the world's most famous tech duo to this Israeli high school, of all places?

The answer came as soon as Sergey Brin spoke. "Ladies and gentle-men, girls and boys," he said in Russian, his choice of language prompting spontaneous applause. "I emigrated from Russia when I was six," Brin continued. "I went to the United States. Similar to you, I have standard Russian-Jewish parents. My dad is a math professor. They have a certain attitude about studies. And I think I can relate that here, because I was told that your school recently got seven out of the top ten places in a math competition throughout all Israel."

This time the students clapped for their own achievement. "But what I have to say," Brin continued, cutting through the applause, "is what my father would say—'*What about the other three?*' "[5]

Most of the students at the Shevach-Mofet school were, like Brin, second-generation Russian Jews. Shevach-Mofet is located in an industrial area in south Tel Aviv, the poorer part of town, and was for years notoriously one of the roughest schools in the city.

We learned about the history of the school from Natan Sharan-sky, the most famous former Soviet Jewish immigrant in Israel. He spent fourteen years in Soviet prisons and labor camps while fighting for the right to emigrate and was the best-known "refusenik," as the Soviet Jews who were refused permission to emigrate were called. He rose to become Israel's deputy prime minister a few years after he was freed from the Soviet Union. He joked to us that in Israel's Russian immigrant party, which he founded soon after his arrival, politicians believe they should mirror his own experience: go to prison first and *then* get into politics, not the other way around.

"The name of the school—Shevach—means 'praise,'" Sharansky told us in his home in Jerusalem. It was the second high school to open in Tel Aviv, when the city was brand-new, in 1946. It was one of the schools where the new generation of native Israelis went. But in the early 1960s, "the authorities started to experiment with integration, a bit like in America," he explained. "The government said we can't have sabra schools, we must bring in the immigrants from Morocco, Yemen, Eastern Europe—let's have a mix."[6]

While the idea may have been a good one, its execution was poor. By the beginning of the 1990s, when large waves of Russian Jewish immigrants began to arrive following the collapse of the Soviet Union, the school was one of the worst in the city and known mainly for delinquency. At that time, Yakov Mozganov, a new immigrant who had been a professor of mathematics in the Soviet Union, was employed at the school as a security guard. This was typical in those years: Russians with PhDs and engineering degrees were arriving in such overwhelming numbers that they could not find jobs in their fields, especially while they were still learning Hebrew.

Mozganov decided that he would start a night school for students of all ages—including adults—who wanted to learn more science or math, using the Shevach classrooms. He recruited other unemployed or underemployed Russian immigrants with advanced degrees to teach with him. They called it Mofet, a Hebrew acronym of the words for "mathematics," "physics," and "culture" that also means "excellence." The Russian offshoot was such a success that it was eventually merged with the original school, which became Shevach-Mofet. The emphasis on hard sciences and on excellence was not in name only; it reflected the ethos that new arrivals from the former Soviet Union brought with them to Israel.

Israel's economic miracle is due as much to immigration as to anything. At Israel's founding in 1948, its population was 806,000. Today numbering 7.1 million people, the country has grown almost ninefold in sixty years. The population doubled in the first three years alone, completely overwhelming the new government. As one parliament member said at the time, if they had been working with a plan, they never would have absorbed so many people. Foreign-born citizens of Israel currently account for over one-third of the nation's population, almost three times the ratio of foreigners to natives in the United States. Nine out of ten Jewish Israelis are either immigrants or first- or second-generation descendants of immigrants.

David McWilliams, an Irish economist who lived and worked in Israel in 1994, has his own colorful, if less-than-academic, methodology to illustrate immigration data: "Worldwide, you can tell how diverse the population is by the food smells of the streets and the choice of menus. In Israel, you can eat almost any specialty, from Yemenite to Russian, from real Mediterranean to bagels. Immigrants cook and that is precisely what wave after wave of poor Jews did when they arrived having been kicked out of Baghdad, Berlin, and Bosnia."[7]

Israel is now home to more than seventy different nationalities and cultures. But the students Sergey Brin was addressing were from the single largest immigration wave in Israel's history. Between 1990 and 2000, eight hundred thousand citizens of the former Soviet Union immigrated to Israel; the first half million poured in over the course of just a three-year period. All together, it amounted to adding about a fifth of Israel's population by the end of the

1990s. The U.S. equivalent would be a flood of sixty-two million immigrants and refugees coming to America over the next decade.

"For us in the Soviet Union," Sharansky explained, "we received with our mothers' milk the knowledge that because you are a Jew— which had no positive meaning to us then, only that we were victims of anti-Semitism—you had to be exceptional in your profession, whether it was chess, music, mathematics, medicine, or ballet.... That was the only way to build some kind of protection for yourself, because you would always be starting from behind."

The result was that though Jews made up only about 2 percent of the Soviet population, they counted for "some thirty percent of the doctors, twenty percent of the engineers, and so on," Sharansky told us.

This was the ethos Sergey Brin absorbed from his Russian parents, and the source of the same competitive streak that Brin recognized in the young Israeli students. And it gives an inkling of the nature of the human resource that Israel received when the Soviet floodgates were opened in 1990.

It was a challenge to figure out what to do with an immigrant influx that, although talented, faced significant language and cultural barriers. Plus, the educated elite of a country the size of the Soviet Union would not easily fit into a country as small as Israel. Before this mass immigration, Israel already had among the highest number of doctors per capita in the world. Even if there had not been a glut, the Soviet doctors would have had a difficult adjustment to a new medical system, a new language, and an entirely new culture. The same was true in many other professions.

Though the Israeli government struggled to find jobs and build housing for the new arrivals, the Russians could not have arrived at a more opportune time. The international tech boom was picking up speed in the mid-1990s, and Israel's private technology sector became hungry for engineers.

Walk into an Israeli technology start-up or a big R&D center in Israel today and you'll likely overhear workers speaking Russian. The drive for excellence that pervades Shevach-Mofet, and that is so prevalent among this wave of immigrants, ripples throughout Israel's technology sector.

But it was not just an obsession with education that characterized the Jews who arrived in Israel, from wherever they came. If education was the only factor explaining Israel's orientation toward entrepreneurialism and technology, then other countries where students perform competitively on math and science standardized tests—such as Singapore—would be start-up incubators as well.

What the Soviet émigrés brought with them is symptomatic of what Israeli venture capitalist Erel Margalit believes can be found in a number of dynamic economies. "Ask yourself, why is it happening here?" he said of the Israeli tech boom. We were sitting in a trendy Jerusalem restaurant he owns, next to a complex he built that houses his venture fund and a stable of start-ups. "Why is it happening on the East Coast or the West Coast of the United States? A lot of it has to do with immigrant societies. In France, if you are from a very established family, and you work in an established pharmaceutical company, for example, and you have a big office and perks and a secretary and all that, would you get up and leave and risk everything to create something new? You wouldn't. You're too comfortable. But if you're an immigrant in a new place, and you're poor," Margalit continued, "or you were once rich and your family was stripped of its wealth—then you have drive. You don't see what you've got to lose; you see what you could win. That's the attitude we have here—across the entire population."[8]

Gidi Grinstein was an adviser to former prime minister Ehud Barak and was part of the Israeli negotiating team at the 2000 Camp David summit with Bill Clinton and Yasir Arafat. He went on to found his own think tank, the Reut Institute, which is focused on how Israel can become one of the top fifteen wealthiest nations by 2020. He makes the same point: "One or two generations back, someone in our family was packing very quickly and leaving. Immigrants are not averse to starting over. They are, by definition, risk takers. A nation of immigrants is a nation of entrepreneurs."

Shai Agassi, the founder of Better Place, is the son of an Iraqi immigrant. His father, Reuven Agassi, was forced to flee the southern Iraqi city of Basra, along with his family, when he was nine years old. The Iraqi government had fired all its Jewish employees, confiscated Jewish property, and arbitrarily arrested members of the community. In Baghdad, the government even carried out public hangings. "My father [Shai's grandfather], an accountant for the Basra port authority, was out of a job. We were very scared for our lives," Reuven told us.[9] With nowhere else to go, the Agassis joined a flood of 150,000 Iraqi refugees arriving in Israel in 1950.

In addition to the sheer numbers of immigrants in Israel, one other element makes the role of Israel's immigration waves unique: the policies the Israeli government has implemented to assimilate newcomers.

There is a direct connection between the history of immigration policies of Western countries and what would become the approach adopted by Israel's founders. During the seventeenth, eighteenth, and nineteenth centuries, immigration to the United States was essentially open, and, at times, immigrants were even recruited to come to America to help with the settlement of undeveloped areas of the country. Until the 1920s, no numerical limits on immigration existed in America, although health restrictions applied and a literacy test was administered.

But as racial theories started to influence U.S. immigration policy, this liberal approach began to tighten. The U.S. House Judiciary Committee employed a eugenics consultant, Dr. Harry H. Laughlin, who asserted that certain races were inferior. Another leader of the eugenics movement, author Madison Grant, argued in a widely selling book that Jews, Italians, and others were inferior because of their supposedly different skull size.

The Immigration Act of 1924 set new numerical limits on immigration based on "national origin." Taking effect in 1929, the law imposed annual immigration quotas that were specifically designed to prevent entrance of eastern and southern Europeans, such as Italians, Greeks, and Polish Jews. Generally no more than one hundred of the proscribed nationals were permitted to immigrate each year.[10]

When Franklin Roosevelt became president, he did little to change the policy. "Looking at Roosevelt's reactions over the full sweep of 1938 to 1945, one can trace a pattern of decreasing sensitivity toward the plight of the European Jews," says historian David Wyman. "In 1942, the year he learned that the extermination of the Jews was under way, Roosevelt completely abandoned the issue to the State Department. He never again dealt really positively with the problem, even though he knew the State Department's policy was one of avoidance—indeed, obstruction—of rescue."[11]

With the onset of World War II, America's gates remained barred to Jews. But the chief problem that faced Jews seeking refuge in the 1930s and the early 1940s was that America did not stand alone. Latin American countries opened their doors in only limited ways, while European countries, at best, tolerated only for a time the many thousands who arrived "in transit" as part of unrealized plans for permanent settlement elsewhere.[12]

Even after World War II ended and the Holocaust became widely known, Western countries were still unwilling to welcome surviving Jews. The Canadian government captured the mood of many governments when one of its officials declared, "*None* is too many!" British quotas on immigration to Palestine became increasingly tight during this period, as well. For many Jews, there literally was no place to go.[13]

Deeply aware of this history, when Britain's colonial term in Palestine expired, on May 14, 1948, "The Declaration of the Establishment of the State of Israel" was issued by the Jewish People's Council. It stated, "The catastrophe which recently befell the Jewish people—the massacre of millions of Jews in Europe—was another clear demonstration of the urgency of solving the problem of its homelessness....THE STATE OF ISRAEL will be open for Jewish immigration."[14]

Israel became the only nation in history to explicitly address in its founding documents the need for a liberal immigration policy. In 1950, Israel's new government made good on that declaration with the Law of Return, which to this day guarantees that "every Jew has the right to come to this country." There are no numerical quotas.

The law also defines as a Jew "a person who was born of a Jewish mother or has become converted to Judaism." Citizenship status is also granted to non-Jewish spouses of Jews, to non-Jewish children and grandchildren of Jews, and to their spouses, as well.

In the United States, an individual must wait five years before applying for naturalization (three years if a spouse of a U.S. citizen). U.S. law also requires that an immigrant seeking citizenship demonstrate an ability to understand English and pass a civics exam. Israeli citizenship becomes effective on the day of arrival, no matter what the language spoken by the immigrant, and there are no tests at all.

As David McWilliams describes it, most Israelis speak Hebrew plus another language, which was the only language they spoke upon arrival. In some Israeli towns, he says, "there is a Spanish-language paper published every day in Ladino, the medieval Spanish spoken by Sephardic Jews kicked out of Andalucia by Ferdinand and Isabella in 1492....In Tel Aviv's busy Dizengoff Street, old cafés hum with German. The older German immigrants still chat away in Hoch Deutsch—the language of Goethe, Schiller, and Bismarck.... Further down the street, you are in little Odessa. Russian signs, Russian food, Russian newspapers, even Russian-language television are now the norm."[15]

Like Shai and Reuven Agassi, there are also millions of Israelis with roots in the Arab Muslim world. At the time of Israeli independence, some five hundred thousand Jews had been living in Arab Muslim countries, with roots going back centuries. But a wave of Arab nationalism swept many of these countries after World War II, along with a wave of pogroms, forcing Jews to flee. Most wound up in Israel.

Crucially, Israel may be the only country that seeks to *increase* immigration, and not just of people of narrowly defined origins or economic status, as the Ethiopian immigration missions evidence. The job of welcoming and encouraging immigration is a cabinet position with a dedicated ministry behind it. Unlike the U.S. Citizenship and Immigration Service, which maintains as one of its primary responsibilities keeping immigrants out, the Israeli Immigration and Absorption Ministry is solely focused on bringing them in.

If Israelis hear on the radio at the end of the year that immigration was down, this is received as bad news, like reports that there was not enough rainfall that year. During election seasons, candidates for prime minister from different parties frequently pledge to bring in "another million immigrants" during their term.

In addition to the Ethiopian airlifts, this commitment has been repeatedly, and at times dramatically, demonstrated. One such example is Operation Magic Carpet, in which, between 1949 and 1950, the Israeli government secretly airlifted forty-nine thousand Yemenite Jews to Israel in surplus British and American transport planes. These were poverty-stricken Jews, with no means of making their way to Israel on their own. Thousands more did not survive the three-week trek to a British airstrip in Aden.

But perhaps the least-known immigration effort involves post–World War II Romania. About 350,000 Jews resided in Romania in the late 1940s, and although some escaped to Palestine, the Communist government held hostage others who wished to leave. Israel first provided drills and pipes for Romania's oil industry in exchange for 100,000 exit visas. But beginning in the 1960s, Romanian dictator Nicolae Ceauşescu demanded hard cash to allow Jews to leave the country. Between 1968 and 1989, the Israeli government paid Ceauşescu $112,498,800 for the freedom of 40,577 Jews. That comes out to $2,772 per person.

Against this backdrop, the Israeli government has made the chief mission of the Ministry of Immigrant Absorption the integration of immigrants into society. Language training is one of the most urgent and comprehensive priorities for the government. To this day, the ministry organizes free full-immersion Hebrew courses for new immigrants: five hours each day, for at least six months. The government even offers a stipend to help cover living expenses during language training, so newcomers can focus on learning their new language rather than being distracted with trying to make ends meet.

To accredit foreign education, the Ministry of Education maintains a Department for the Evaluation of Overseas Degrees. And the government conducts courses to help immigrants prepare for professional licensing exams. The Center for Absorption in Science helps match arriving scientists with Israeli employers, and the absorption ministry runs entrepreneurship centers, which provide assistance with obtaining start-up capital.[16]

There are also absorption programs supported by the government but launched by independent Israeli citizens. Asher Elias, for example, believes there is a future for Ethiopians in the vaunted high-tech industry in Israel. Elias's parents came to Israel in the 1960s from Ethiopia, nearly twenty years before the mass immigration of Ethiopian Jews. Asher's older sister, Rina, was the first Ethiopian-Israeli born in Israel.

After completing a degree in business administration at the College of Management in Jerusalem, Elias took a marketing job at a high-tech company and attended Selah University, then in Jerusalem, to study software engineering—he had always been a computer junkie. But Elias was shocked when he could find only four other Ethiopians working in Israel's high-tech sector.

"There was no opportunity for Ethiopians," he said. "The only paths to the high-tech sector were through the computer science departments at public universities or private technical colleges. Ethiopians were underperforming on the high school matriculation exams, which precluded them from the top universities; and private colleges were too expensive."

Elias envisioned a different path. Together with an American software engineer, in 2003 he established a not-for-profit organization called Tech Careers, a boot camp to prepare Ethiopians for jobs in high tech.

Ben-Gurion, both before and after the state's founding, had made immigration one of the nation's top priorities. Immigrants with no safe haven needed to be aided in their journey to the fledgling Jewish state, he believed; perhaps more importantly, immigrant Jews were needed to settle the land, to fight in Israel's wars, and to breathe life into the nascent state's economy. This is still seen as true today.

# CHAPTER 8

# The Diaspora

## Stealing Airplanes

*Like the Greeks who sailed with Jason in search of the
Golden Fleece, the new Argonauts [are] foreign-born,
technically skilled entrepreneurs who travel back and forth
between Silicon Valley and their home countries.*

—ANNALEE SAXENIAN

TODAY," JOHN CHAMBERS SAID AS HE TOOK LARGE sideways steps across the stage to illustrate his point, "we're making the biggest jump in innovation since the router was first introduced twenty years ago." He was speaking into a cordless microphone at a 2004 Cisco conference.[1] Though he was in a business suit, the fifty-four-year-old chief executive of Cisco—which during the tech boom had a market value higher than General Electric's—looked like he might break into a dance routine.

After properly building the drama, Chambers walked over to a large closetlike enclosure and opened the doors to reveal three complicated-looking boxes, each about the size and shape of a refrigerator. It was the CRS-1, in all its glory.

Most people do not know what a router is, and so might have trouble relating to Chambers's excitement. A router is something like the old modems we used to use to connect our computers to the Internet. If the Internet is like a mighty river of information that all of our computers connect into, then routers are at all the junctions of the tributaries that feed in, and are the main bottleneck that determines the capacity of the Internet as a whole.

Only a few companies can build the highest-end routers, and Cisco—like Microsoft for operating systems, Intel for chips, and Google for Internet searches—dominates this market. Upon its unveiling, the CRS-1, which took four years and $500 million to develop, earned a place in the current volume of *Guinness World Records* as the fastest router in the world. "We liked this entry, because the numbers are so huge," said David Hawksett, science and technology editor at Guinness World Records. "I just installed a wireless network at home and was quite pleased with 54 megabits per second of throughput, but 92 terabits is just incredible."[2]

The *tera* in *terabit* means "trillion," so one terabit is a million megabits. According to Cisco, the CRS-1 has the capacity to download the entire printed collection of the U.S. Library of Congress in 4.6 seconds. Doing this with a dial-up modem would take about eighty-two years.

A chief proponent of the CRS-1 was an Israeli named Michael Laor. After earning an engineering degree at Ben-Gurion University in Beersheba, Israel, Laor went to work for Cisco in California for eleven years, where he became director of engineering and architecture. In 1997, he decided he wanted to return to Israel, and Cisco, rather than lose one of its leading engineers, agreed that he would open an R&D center for the company in Israel—its first outside the United States.

At around this time, Laor started to argue for the need for a massive router like the CRS-1. Back then the Internet was still quite young and the idea that there might be a market for a router this big seemed far-fetched. "People thought we were a little nuts to be developing this product four years ago," Cisco's Tony Bates said at the time. "They said, 'You're biting off more than you can chew,' and they asked, 'Who is going to need all that capacity?'"[3]

Laor argued that, to paraphrase the movie *Field of Dreams*, if Cisco built it, the Internet would come. It was hard to see back then that the Internet, which was just starting off with e-mail and the first Web sites, would in a few years balloon exponentially with an insatiable need to move the massive data flows produced by pictures, videos, and games.

Though the CRS-1 was the company's biggest ever and thus a company-wide project, Laor's team in Israel was pivotal in designing both the chips and the architecture needed to bring the technology to a new level. In the end, when Chambers unveiled the CRS-1 at the 2004 conference, he was right to be enthusiastic. Fully configured, the routers sold for about $2 million each. Yet by the end of 2004, the company had sold the first six machines. And in April 2008, the company announced that CRS-1 sales had doubled in less than nine months.[4]

By 2008, the center opened by Laor a decade earlier had seven hundred employees. It had swelled quickly with Cisco's acquisition of nine Israeli start-ups, more companies than Cisco had bought anywhere else in the world. In addition, Cisco's investment arm made another $150 million in direct investments in other Israeli start-ups, and also put $45 million into Israel-focused venture capital funds. All told, Cisco has spent about $1.2 billion to buy and invest in Israeli companies.[5]

Yoav Samet, a graduate of the IDF's elite 8200 intelligence technology unit who now runs Cisco's acquisitions department for

Israel, the former Soviet Union, and central Europe, says that Cisco Israel is among the company's largest overseas centers, along with those in India and China. "But," he notes, "whereas in China and in India there is quite a bit of engineering work done, when it comes to pure innovation and acquisition activity, Israel is still holding the front line."[6]

It is unlikely that Cisco would have become so deeply invested in Israel, and that its Israeli team would have almost immediately become central to the company's core business, if Michael Laor had not decided it was time to come home. As with Dov Frohman of Intel and many others, Laor's decision to gain knowledge and experience in the United States or elsewhere ultimately redounded to the benefit of both the multinational company he worked for and the Israeli economy.

While many countries, including Israel, bemoan the fact that some of their brightest academics and entrepreneurs go abroad, people like Michael Laor show that the "brain drain" is not a one-way street. In fact, international-migration researchers are increasingly noting a phenomenon they call "brain circulation," whereby talented people leave, settle down abroad, and then return to their home countries, and yet are not fully "lost" to either place. As Richard Devane writes in a study issued by the World Bank, "China, India, and Israel enjoyed investment or technology booms over the past decade, and these booms are linked...by expatriate leadership in all three countries."[7]

AnnaLee Saxenian is an economic geographer at U.C. Berkeley and author of *The New Argonauts*. "Like the Greeks who sailed with Jason in search of the Golden Fleece," Saxenian writes, "the new Argonauts [are] foreign-born, technically skilled entrepreneurs who travel back and forth between Silicon Valley and their home countries." She points out that the growing tech sectors in China, India, Taiwan, and Israel—particularly the last two countries—

have emerged as "important global centers of innovation" whose output "exceeded that of larger and wealthier nations like Germany and France." She contends that the pioneers of these profound transformations are people who "marinated in the Silicon Valley culture and learned it. This really began in the late '80s for the Israelis and Taiwanese, and not until the late '90s or even the beginning of the '00s for the Indians and Chinese."[8]

Michael Laor at Cisco and Dov Frohman at Intel were classic new Argonauts. Even while gaining knowledge and status within their major international companies, they always intended to return to Israel. When they did, they not only became catalysts for Israel's technological development but founded Israeli operations that provided critical breakthroughs for the companies they worked for.

The new Argonaut, or "brain circulation," model of Israelis going abroad and returning to Israel is one important part of the innovation ecosystem linking Israel and the Diaspora. Another Diaspora network is a non-Israeli Jewish Diaspora.

Israel owes much of its success to a deep Diaspora network that other countries, from Ireland to India and China, have also developed. Yet the non-Israeli Jewish Diaspora ties are not automatic, nor are they the key catalysts to the development of the tech sector in Israel. In fact, whereas China's Diaspora is the source of 70 percent of foreign direct investment (FDI) into China and India's Diaspora did much to help build its homeland's high-tech infrastructure when the country's economy and legal system were both underdeveloped, Israel's experience has been different. The vast majority of American Jewish investors historically would not touch the Israeli economy. It was not until much later, when Israel became more successful, that many Diaspora Jews started looking at Israel as a place to do business, not just as a draw for their sympathy and philanthropy.

So it has required creativity for Israel to learn how to use its Diaspora community in order to catalyze its economy. The tradition of Israelis' tapping into a very small but passionate subset of the Jewish Diaspora to help build the state has its roots in institutions like Israel's start-up air force.

The fantasy of an Israeli aircraft industry took shape on a bumpy flight over the North Pole in 1951, inside what was to become the first aircraft in Israel's new national airline. The conversation was between a pair of opposites: Shimon Peres, the erudite future president of Israel, who in 1951 was the chief arms buyer for the new Jewish state, and Al Schwimmer, a swashbuckling American aviation engineer from Los Angeles, whose pals included Howard Hughes and Kirk Kerkorian. Schwimmer's first name was Adolph, but against the backdrop of World War II, he'd opted for Al.[9]

Peres and Schwimmer were on one of their many flights over the Arctic tundra in used planes purchased for Israel's fledgling air force. Flying over the North Pole was dangerous, but they took the risk because the route was shorter—no small consideration when piloting planes that were falling apart.

Al Schwimmer was a raconteur who'd been captivated by the airline business in its earliest days, when flying machines were an exotic novelty. He was working for TWA when the United States entered World War II and the entire airline was drafted into the war effort. Though not officially in the U.S. Air Force, Schwimmer and his fellow fliers were given military ranks and uniforms and spent the war ferrying troops, equipment, and the occasional movie star all over the world.

During the war, Schwimmer's identity as a Jew meant little to him and had almost no influence on his thinking or way of life. But seeing a liberated concentration camp and the newsreel footage of countless bodies and speaking with Jewish refugees in Europe trying to reach Palestine transformed him. Almost overnight, Schwimmer became a committed Zionist.

When he heard that the British in Palestine were turning back ships full of European Jewish refugees, Schwimmer came up with what he was convinced was a better way: fly over the British navy patrols and smuggle the Jews in by landing them at hidden airfields. He tracked down Ben-Gurion's secret emissary in New York and pitched him the idea. For months, the representative of the Haganah, the main underground Jewish army in Palestine, sat on the idea. But when it became clear that the British would soon withdraw and a full-scale Arab-Jewish war over Israel's independence would ensue, the Haganah contacted Schwimmer.

By this time they had an even more urgent need than smuggling refugees: building an air force. The Haganah did not have a single aircraft and would be completely exposed to the Egyptian air force. Could Schwimmer buy and repair fighter planes and smuggle them into Israel?

Schwimmer told Ben-Gurion's agents that he'd start immediately, even though he knew he would be violating the 1935 Neutrality Act, which prohibited U.S. citizens from exporting weaponry without government authorization. This wasn't just *chutzpah*. This was criminal.

Within days, Schwimmer had tracked down a handful of Jewish pilots and mechanics from the United States and the United Kingdom for what he told them would be the first civilian Jewish airline. He was obsessed with secrecy, and did not even want to bring them into the fold about the idea of building fighter planes. Few were even informed that the planes were destined for Israel. When outsiders inquired, the cover story was that they were building a national airline for Panama and would ferry cattle to Europe.

Though the FBI impounded the largest aircraft he bought—three Constellations—Schwimmer and his gang succeeded in smuggling out other aircraft, some by literally flying over the heads of the FBI agents who'd demanded that the planes be grounded. At the last minute, the Haganah cut a separate deal to buy German

Messerschmitts from Czechoslovakia, which Schwimmer was also drafted to fly to Israel.

When the 1948 War of Independence came, Schwimmer's aircraft fought off Egyptian planes that were bombing Tel Aviv. In certain battles, the barely trained Israeli pilots were instrumental in ensuring that the Negev Desert—a relatively large triangular swath of land starting a few miles south of Jerusalem and Tel Aviv, between the Egyptian Sinai and Jordan—became part of Israel.

After Israel prevailed in the War of Independence, Schwimmer returned to the United States, despite being a wanted man. The FBI had figured out the smuggling scheme, and the U.S. Justice Department had built a criminal case against him. His trial, along with those of a number of the pilots he had recruited, was a public sensation. The defendants pleaded not guilty, on the grounds that the law itself was unjust. Schwimmer got off with paying a fine, which was widely seen as exoneration.

Once Schwimmer was cleared, it didn't take him long to get back into the smuggling game. By 1950, Schwimmer had joined forces with Shimon Peres, then a young Ben-Gurion protégé working for the new Israeli Defense Ministry. Peres had tried to buy thirty surplus Mustang aircraft for the Israeli Air Force, but the United States had decided to destroy the planes instead. Their wings were sliced off and their fuselages cut in two.

So Schwimmer's team bought the cut-up planes at cost from a Texas junk dealer, reconstructed them, and made sure they had all their parts and were operational. Then the team disassembled the planes again, packed them in crates marked "Irrigation Equipment," and shipped them to Israel.

But because of the urgency with which they had to get the aircraft to Israel, a few of the planes were left assembled, and Schwimmer and Peres flew these to Tel Aviv. And that is how they found themselves in 1951 talking about a future Israeli aviation industry.

Peres became captivated by Schwimmer's ideas for creating an air-craft industry in Israel that would serve a purpose beyond short-term military strategy. It was part of Peres's fascination with creating industries in Israel.

Schwimmer insisted that in a world flooded with surplus aircraft from the war, there was no reason why Israel could not buy planes cheaply, repair and improve them, and sell them to militaries and airlines in many countries, while building Israel's own commercial industry. Shortly after they returned to the United States, Peres took Schwimmer to meet Ben-Gurion, who was on his first visit to America as Israel's prime minister.

"You learning Hebrew now?" was Ben-Gurion's first question when Schwimmer reached out his hand to greet him; they had met repeatedly during the War of Independence. Schwimmer laughed and changed the subject: "Nice girls here in California, don't ya think, Mr. Prime Minister?"

Ben-Gurion wanted to know what Schwimmer was working on. Schwimmer told him about the renovations he was carrying out.

"What? With this tiny collection of machines you can renovate planes?"

Schwimmer nodded.

"We need something like this in Israel. Even more. We need a real aviation industry. We need to be independent," Ben-Gurion said. This was exactly what Schwimmer had discussed with Peres, while flying over the tundra. "So, what do you think?"

Unbeknownst to Schwimmer, Ben-Gurion had recently instructed the Technion to build an aeronautical engineering department. In giving the order, he'd said, "A high standard of liv-ing; a rich culture; spiritual, political and economic indepen-dence...are not possible without aerial control."

"Sure, I think you're right," said Schwimmer, falling into the prime minister's trap.

"I'm glad you think so. We'll expect you to come back to Israel to build one for us."

Schwimmer stared dumbfounded at Peres.

"Just do it, Al," said Peres. Schwimmer resisted. He immediately began thinking of the run-ins he would have with the Israeli Air Force chiefs and the small but powerful Israeli establishment. Plus, he didn't speak Hebrew. He wasn't a party insider. He hated politics and bureaucracy. And the Israeli combination of socialist economic planning and cronyist politics could be stifling for anyone, let alone someone trying to build an aviation industry.

He told Ben-Gurion that he could build the company only if it would be free from cronyism—no political hacks getting jobs. A private company, organized along commercial lines, he told Ben-Gurion.

"You're just right for Israel. Come," Ben-Gurion responded.

Schwimmer did go to Israel. Within five years, Bedek, the airplane-maintenance company he founded with two Israelis, became the largest private employer in the country.

By 1960, Bedek was producing a modified version of the French Fouga fighter plane. At an official unveiling and test flight of the plane, dubbed Tzukit ("swallow" in Hebrew), Ben-Gurion told Schwimmer, "This place isn't just Bedek anymore. You've gone beyond repairs. You guys have built a jet. The new name should be Israel Aircraft Industries." Peres, who by now was deputy defense minister, translated the new company name.

Peres and Ben-Gurion had managed to recruit an American Jew to help provide one of the biggest long-term jolts to Israel's economy, all without asking anyone for one investment dollar.

# CHAPTER 9

# The Buffett Test

*For our customers around the world, there was no war.*

—Eitan Wertheimer

W E'RE NOT HERE TO STEAL WORKERS FROM MICROSOFT," said Google's Yoelle Maarek. "But," she continued, grinning mischievously, "if they think they'll be happier with us, they're welcome."[1] Only ten weeks earlier, Hezbollah missiles had been raining down on Haifa, home to the Google R&D center she headed. A few months later, Google opened a second research center about an hour's drive south, in Tel Aviv.

Yoelle Maarek grew up in France, where she studied engineering, then earned her PhD in computer science at Columbia University and the Technion in Haifa. Before being tapped to head Google Israel's first R&D center, she worked at IBM Research for seventeen years, specializing in a field called "search" before Google existed and when the Internet was in its infancy.

To Maarek, the roots of search go deep into history. Scholars in the sixteenth century would consult a Bible concordance to see where Moses was mentioned and in which context. A concordance is "basically an index, which is the data structure that every search engine is using. Five centuries ago, people would do that manually.... As Israelis and as Jews, we are the people of the Book. We like to consult texts. We like to search," Maarek said.

In 2008 Google Israel sold $100 million in advertising, about double the previous year and 10 percent of the total advertising market in Israel—a higher market share than Google has in most countries.

While Google has become a growing empire of products and technologies—from search, to Gmail, to YouTube, to cell phone software, and much more—the heart of the company remains its ubiquitous home page. And if the most trafficked home page in the world is Google's temple, the search box on it is the holy of holies.

It was somewhat ambitious, then, for Google Israel to take on a project that went right to the heart of the company, to the search box. The Israeli team took a small experimental idea that had been sitting untouched for two years—Google Suggest—and made it something that millions of people see and use every day.

For those who have not noticed it, Google Suggest is that list of suggestions that pop down as you type in a search request. The suggestions update as you type in each letter of the request, just about as fast as you can type.

Google is famous for delivering results almost instantaneously. But Google Suggest had to achieve this feat with each *letter*. Information had to go to Google's servers and send back a list of relevant suggestions, all in the split second before the next letter was typed.

Two months into the project, the team got its first break. Kai-Fu Lee, who was the president of Google China, said that he was willing to take the risk that queries would be slowed down. Chinese is very hard to type, so having Suggest to fill words in was particularly valuable in China. Suggest worked, and it expanded quickly to Google's sites in Hong Kong, Taiwan, Russia, and Western Europe, and soon to Google around the world.

Microsoft was not far behind in capitalizing on Israel. While the damage from two thousand missile strikes during the 2006 Lebanon war was still being repaired, a defiant Bill Gates visited Israel. He came with a clear message: "We are not afraid of Google," he told an Israeli news agency. While he couldn't resist getting in a dig about Internet search engines being "in a terrible state compared to where they could be," he also conceded that Google and Microsoft were in fierce competition. And the new battlefront was Israel. Earlier Gates had said that the "innovation going on in Israel is critical to the future of the technology business."[2]

No sooner did the richest man in the world leave Israel than the second-richest, Warren Buffett, showed up. The most revered investor in America had arrived to visit the first company he'd bought outside the United States. Buffett spent fifty-two hours touring Iscar, the machine-tool company he'd purchased for $4.5 billion, and Israel, the country he had heard so much about. "You think of people walking those steps 2,000 years ago," he said of his visit to Jerusalem, "and then you look at the Iscar factory on a mountaintop, supplying 61 countries—whether it's Korea or the United States or Europe or you name it. It's pretty remarkable. I don't think you can really find that kind of combination of the past and the future, in such close proximity, virtually any place in the world."[3]

But it seems unlikely that it was an appreciation of history that convinced Warren Buffett to choose Israel as the place to change his decades-long policy of not making acquisitions outside the United States. And nor was it, for this apostle of risk aversion, an indifference to Israel's vulnerabilities.

You do not have to be Warren Buffett to worry about risk. Every company carefully considers the risks of doing business anywhere far from headquarters, let alone somewhere perceived as a war zone. The question, according to Buffett, is *how* you think about risk.

We sat in Jon Medved's office—at the Vringo headquarters, in

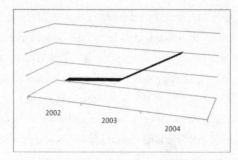

**FIGURE 9.1**

Beit Shemesh, a neighborhood between Jerusalem and Tel Aviv—to discuss the risks of investing in Israel.[4] But before he would answer our questions, Medved posed one of his own. He pulled out one of the slides from a PowerPoint presentation, the "Israel Inside" presentation he often gives in his role as unofficial economic ambassador.

"Look at this graph," he told us (figure 9.1).

"What do you see here?" Medved probed. The horizontal $x$-axis showed the years 2002 through 2004; the vertical $y$-axis was unlabeled. And there was a line heading—in a relatively linear, diagonal direction—up into the upper-right corner of the graph. But with no $y$-axis label, the graph was incomplete. We figured Medved had posed a trick question.

"Well, there is something increasing over the 2002-to-2004 time frame," we hazarded. "But the vertical $y$-axis doesn't tell us what the 'it' is."

"Exactly," he quickly responded. "The 'it' could be a number of things. For one: violence. It was, tragically, one of Israel's most violent periods in our history, during the second intifada and leading up to the second Lebanon war. The graph illustrates the number of rockets that hit Israel over those years."

But, Medved told us, the graph also illustrates the performance of Israel's economy, which also rose steeply in the first half of the

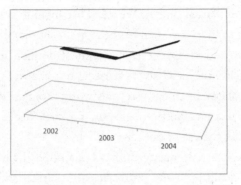

**FIGURE 9.2**

decade. He then pulled out another slide that was virtually identical to the first (figure 9.2).

The vertical *y*-axis on this next slide was labeled "Foreign Investment in Israeli High Tech." Remarkably, during the same period, there was an increase in investments coming in as the rocket attacks were increasing.

In fact, as we researched other economic metrics, we found that a number of sets of data would fit roughly along this generic graph structure. For example, foreign direct investment (FDI)—another macroeconomic metric—measures the total amount of overseas direct investment in any form that comes into a country. During the period from 2000 to 2005, Israel's FDI tripled, and Israel's share of the global venture dollars invested inside Israel doubled.

Medved was not suggesting that there was a correlation between violence in Israel and its attractiveness to investors. Rather, he believes that Israel has managed to divorce the security threat from its economic growth opportunities. In other words, Israelis are confident that their start-ups will survive during war and turbulence. And Israeli entrepreneurs have managed to convince investors of this, too.

Alice Schroeder, the author of *The Snowball*, is the only authorized biographer of Warren Buffett. We asked her about the perceived risk of investing in Israel. "Warren has been in the insurance business for a long time, and looks at every investment decision through that lens," she told us. "It's all about assessing risk like you would in an insurance policy. The things you really worry about are the potential for earthquakes and hurricanes. Warren asks: What kind of catastrophic risk is there, and can I live with it?"[5]

Iscar, the Israeli company Buffett bought, has its main factory and R&D facilities in the northern part of Israel and was twice threatened by missile attacks—in 1991, when the whole country was targeted by Iraq's Saddam Hussein during the Gulf War, and during the 2006 Lebanon war, when Hezbollah fired thousands of missiles at Israel's northern towns. "Doesn't this constitute catastrophic risk?" we asked her.

Buffett's view, she told us, is that if Iscar's facilities are bombed, it can go build another plant. The plant does not represent the value of the company. It is the talent of the employees and management, the international base of loyal customers, and the brand that constitute Iscar's value. So missiles, even if they can destroy factories, do not, in Buffett's eyes, represent catastrophic risk.

During the 2006 Lebanon war, just two months after Buffett acquired Iscar, 4,228 missiles landed in Israel's north.[6] Located less than eight miles from the Lebanese border, Iscar was a prime target for rocket fire.

Eitan Wertheimer, chairman of Iscar, who'd made the sale to Buffett, told us that he called his new boss on the first day of the war. "Our sole concern was for the welfare of our people, since wrecked machines and shattered windows can always be replaced," Wertheimer recalled of his conversation with Buffett. "'But I am not sure that you understand our mind-set,' I told him. 'We're going to carry on with half the workforce, but we will ensure that all the customers get their orders on time or even earlier."[7]

One rocket did slam into Tefen Industrial Park, which was founded by the Wertheimer family and centered around Iscar, and a slew of rockets landed nearby. And though, during the war, many workers did temporarily relocate, with their families, to the southern part of the country, Iscar's customers would never have known it. "It took us a brief time to adjust, but we didn't miss a single shipment," Wertheimer said. "For our customers around the world, there was no war."

By responding to the threat this way, Wertheimer and others have transformed the very dangers that may make Israel seem risky into evidence of Israel's inviolable assets—the same assets that attracted Buffett, Google, Microsoft, and so many others in the first place.

Few illustrate Israeli grit better than Dov Frohman, who was born in Amsterdam just months before the onset of World War II. As the Nazis' grip on Holland tightened, his parents decided to hide Dov with the Van Tilborgh family, devout Christian farmers they found through the Dutch underground. Dov was only three years old when he arrived at their farmhouse in the Dutch countryside, but he remembers having to cover his dark hair with a hat, since the rest of his adopted family was blond. When the Germans periodically searched the house, he would hide under a bed, in a cellar, or in the woods with his adopted brothers. Years later, Dov learned that his father died at Auschwitz; he never knew for sure where his mother was murdered.[8]

After the war, Frohman's aunt, who had escaped to Palestine in the 1930s, tracked down Frohman's Dutch family and convinced them to put him in a Jewish orphanage, so that he could emigrate to Palestine. In 1949, ten-year-old Dov landed in the brand-new State of Israel.

In 1963, as Dov Frohman was about to graduate from the Technion (Israel Institute of Technology), he decided to pursue graduate studies in the United States in order to "bring a new field of technical expertise back to Israel." He was admitted to MIT but instead went to the University of California at Berkeley, which offered him a stipend. It was a fortuitous choice.

While still a graduate student, Frohman was hired by Andy Grove to work at Fairchild Semiconductor. A few years later, Grove joined Gordon Moore and Robert Noyce to found Intel. Frohman became one of the new start-up's first employees. He quickly made his mark by inventing what would become one of Intel's most legendary and profitable products, a new kind of reprogrammable memory chip. Then, with a senior management position within reach, Frohman announced that he was leaving Intel to teach electrical engineering in Ghana. In his words, he was "looking for adventure, personal freedom, and self-development"—another "person of the Book."

Colleagues at Intel thought Frohman was crazy to leave just as the company was about to go public and shower its employees with lucrative stock options. But Frohman knew what he wanted: to start an enterprise, not just work for one. He also knew that if he stayed on the management track he might never be able to return to Israel, where he had a revolutionary idea for the local economy: he wanted Israel to become a leader in the chip design industry.

By 1973, the time to realize his idea had arrived. Intel was facing an acute shortage of engineers. Frohman returned to Intel, pitched the idea of an Israeli design center to Grove, and quickly organized an exploratory mission to Israel. Delayed by the Yom Kippur War, the Intel team arrived in Israel in April 1974 and quickly hired five engineers for its new design center in Haifa. Intel had never before established a major research and development center in a foreign country. "At the end of the day, we are in the R&D business. We could not risk the company's future by putting our core mission and operations overseas—out of our control," recalled one former

Intel employee from California. "Israel was the first place we did that. A lot of people thought we were nuts."[9]

The Israel team began with an investment of $300,000 and five full-time employees. But it would become Israel's largest private employer, with fifty-four hundred workers, by the nation's thirtieth anniversary. Intel's investment in Israel, while seemingly a gamble at the time, would go on to become central to the company's success. Intel Israel was responsible for designing the chip in the first IBM personal computers, the first Pentium chips, and a new architecture that analysts agree saved Intel from a downward spiral during the 1990s, as we chronicled in chapter 1. In the southern Israeli town of Qiryat Gat, Intel built a $3.5 billion plant where Israelis designed chips with transistors so small that thirty million of them can fit on the head of a pin. As remarkably, Israel's emergence as a critical manufacturing center for Intel proved that nothing could stop its production, even a war.

"We will trust your judgment, Dov. Do whatever you must do." That was the message of Intel's management days after the January 1991 start of the Gulf War.

Iraq had invaded Kuwait five months earlier. From the moment Frohman heard the news, the worry that he might have to send all his workers home began to creep into his thoughts—during quiet moments driving into work, waiting on the tarmac for takeoff, or before bed at night. He knew that to *shut everything down* would be devastating for Intel Israel. So he tried to put it out of his mind.

While hundreds of thousands of U.S. troops deployed to Saudi Arabia in preparation for war, Frohman was distracted by the risk Intel was undertaking. That gamble was a product of IBM's decision, in 1980, to give Intel its big break, choosing the 8088 chip to power the IBM PC. But the computer giant had forced Intel to license its technology to a dozen manufacturers; even though Intel had designed the 8088, IBM thought it was risky to rely on Intel alone to manufacture the chip. So Intel was able to earn only 30 percent of the total revenues. Security and price leverage for IBM meant lower profits for Intel.

In 1983, with the 286, its next-generation chip, Intel had managed to convince IBM to cut the number of manufacturers to four, thereby increasing Intel's own share of the work. And by 1985, after investing $200 million and four years of development in its even faster 386 chips, Intel had been prepared for a gamble. This time, IBM had acquiesced to Intel's request to become the sole manufacturer of the chip that would power most of the world's new desktops. This strategy would maximize Intel's profits, but also its risk. What if Intel could not ramp up its manufacturing capability in time? And the bigger risk was the decision made by Intel's management in Santa Clara to center much of this new responsibility in Israel.

The main burden fell on Intel's Israeli chip plant in Jerusalem, which produced about three-quarters of Intel's global output by running two twelve-hour shifts, seven days a week.

But now that output was under threat. Saddam Hussein had declared that if the United States launched an offensive, he would respond with missile strikes against Israel.

The Israeli government took Saddam at his word. Iraq had Scud missiles that could reach Tel Aviv in under ten minutes, and those missiles might be armed with chemical warheads. In October 1990, the Israeli government ordered the largest distribution of gas masks anywhere since World War II.

It was a surreal time in Israel. In kindergartens, teachers showed five-year-olds how to put on their gas masks in case of attack, and everyone practiced rushing to specially prepared "sealed rooms" if the sirens went off. The distribution system for the masks was elaborate, with every household receiving a note in the mail telling them where they could pick up the equipment. The IDF placed its Home Front Command offices in malls, so it was not uncommon to pick up some new shoes and a cup of coffee along with a set of gas masks for the whole family.

Frohman did what every Israeli manager does during or in advance of war: he drew up contingency plans for the "standard" war scenario, in which employees would be called up for reserve duty. Most Israeli men under forty-five serve in the reserves for one month every year. During an extended war, these civilian-soldiers can be called up for as long as the government deems necessary. This exacts a huge economic toll on businesses in Israel—including lost work days and less productivity—even during peaceful times. During a war, employees can be absent for weeks or even months. As a result, some Israeli businesses go bankrupt during war.

In early January 1991, U.S. and European commercial airlines suspended or curtailed their flights to the region. On January 11, four days before the United Nations deadline for Iraq to withdraw from Kuwait, the U.S. government advised its nationals to leave Israel. On January 16, the Israeli government announced that all schools and businesses, except for certain essential enterprises (the electric utility, for example), must close for the week and maybe longer. The government wanted people at home, off the roads, and poised to hop into their sealed rooms at the sound of air-raid sirens.

For Frohman, compliance with the government's directive would mean suspending the production of Intel's 386 microchip at a critical moment for the company. Frohman expected to have management's full support for a shutdown, but he also knew that just because an employer is willing to grant an employee sick leave, it does not mean that their relationship will go on unaffected. Especially when the "ailment" is one that could conceivably repeat itself in the future.

"We already had a number of struggles inside the company over the transfer of strategic technologies and critical products to the Israeli operation," recalled Frohman. "I was convinced that if we had to interrupt production, even for a brief period of time, we would pay a serious price over the long term." Frohman had expended time and political capital to persuade Intel's management to put the future of the company in the hands of an overseas out-post, a dream of his since he'd first left Intel. And it was this outpost that was about to find itself on the receiving end of Scud missiles.

But Frohman had another—surprisingly far greater—concern: "I kept thinking about the survival of Israel's . . . still small high-tech economy." The key stumbling block to further investment in Israel was the lingering impression of geopolitical instability in the region. If Intel couldn't operate in an emergency situation, then any confi-dence that multinationals, investors, or the markets had in Israel's stability would instantly crumble.

Frohman had spent enough time abroad to be familiar with the rap against investing in Israel. Almost every day a bad headline about Israel ricocheted around the world: another terrorist attack . . . another provocation on its border . . . more bloodshed. Intifada. Violence, terror, war. It was the only narrative people knew.

He believed that both Israel and its economy needed a counter-narrative. As the January 15 deadline approached, he became fix-ated on an imaginary boardroom debate—taking place somewhere in the United States—between an executive who was enthusiastic about investing in Israel and a cautious board that thought he was reckless. What would the enthusiast need in his back pocket? *I understand your skepticism. I saw the news, too. But let's not forget that Intel was producing the 386 chip—one of Intel's most important microchips—in Israel during the Gulf War, and the Israelis never missed a beat. They stayed on schedule. They were not late . . . not even once . . . not even when missiles were falling on them.*

On January 17, Frohman informed his employees of his unilat-eral decision to keep Intel Israel open during the war, in defiance of government orders, but on a voluntary basis: no worker would be punished for not showing up.

At 2:00 A.M. on January 18, Frohman, like most Israelis, was awoken by air-raid sirens. He and his family quickly put on their gas masks and sealed themselves into their home's safe room. When the all clear sounded, they learned that eight missiles had struck Tel Aviv and Haifa—near Intel's main R&D facility—but they had not been armed with chemical warheads. More missiles were expected in the days ahead. Whether Saddam would arm future Scuds with chemical capabilities was still unclear.

At 3:30 A.M., when Frohman arrived at the plant with his gas mask, he went straight to the clean room—the heart of the chip factory, where, to maintain a dust-free environment, technicians worked in sealed suits that made them look like astronauts. Work there had already resumed. He was told that when the sirens had sounded earlier, the employees had gone to a sealed room in the plant, but after quick calls home, they had returned to their work stations. When the first postattack morning shift began, Frohman expected to see—best-case scenario—half of the shift; 75 percent showed up. Following a second Iraqi missile attack the next night, turnout at Intel's Haifa design center increased to 80 percent. The more brazen the attacks, the larger the turnout. Welcome to Israel's "new normal."

The executives in Intel's Santa Clara headquarters could not get their heads around this. During a conference call with Santa Clara two days later, air-raid sirens went off again. The Israeli team members asked for a moment to relocate, put on their gas masks, and continued the call from their sealed room. A group of Intel workers even set up a wartime kindergarten on the premises, since schools were still closed and if employees wanted to be part of Frohman's defiant mission, they had no choice but to bring their children to work. On top of their regular jobs, the workers volunteered to serve shifts on kindergarten duty.

The legacy of Frohman's commitment is still seen in the decisions of new multinational companies to set up critical operations in Israel. And some of these facilities, such as Google's, were being built around the time of the 2006 Lebanon war.

The explanation for this concerns more than just engineering talent. It is also a matter of less tangible factors, such as a drive to succeed that is both personal and national. Israelis have a term for this: *davka*, an untranslatable Hebrew word that means "despite" with a "rub their nose in it" twist. As if to say, "The more they attack us, the more we will succeed."

As Eitan Wertheimer told Warren Buffett at the start of the 2006 Lebanon war, "We're going to determine which side has won this war by ramping up factory production to an all-time high, while the missiles are falling on us."[10] Israelis, by making their economy and their business reputation both a matter of national pride and a measure of national steadfastness, have created for foreign investors a confidence in Israel's ability to honor, or even surpass, its commitments. Thanks to Dov Frohman, Eitan Wertheimer, and many others, the question of catastrophic risk, for investors and multinationals looking to do business in Israel, is virtually irrelevant.

# CHAPTER 10

# Yozma

## The Match

*John Lennon once said about the early years of rock and roll, "Before Elvis, there was nothing." On the success of venture capital and high-tech entrepreneurship in Israel, to paraphrase Lennon, before Yozma, there was nothing.*

—ORNA BERRY

ORNA BERRY'S SON, Amit, delivered what would be the $32 million message. Amit had retrieved the voice-mail message for his mom. A vice president from Siemens, the German telecommunications conglomerate, had called. Orna Berry, away on yet another trip abroad to pitch her start-up to bigger companies looking to buy, had missed the call. The message from Siemens marked the beginning of a process that culminated in the first acquisition of an Israeli start-up by a European company. The transaction was finalized in 1995.

Though today it's a pretty commonplace event—Europeans have invested hundreds of millions of euros in Israeli companies—in 1995, for an Israeli start-up to be acquired by a European company was unheard-of. Orna Berry believes a new Israeli government program at the time, called Yozma, was what made it possible. She also believes that hundreds of other start-ups have had similar experiences because of the government's initiative.

Berry is hailed as one of Israel's leading business leaders.[1] In 1997, she was named Israel's chief scientist in the Ministry of Industry, Trade, and Labor—Israel's innovation czar; in 2007, she became chair of the Israel Venture Association. She earned a PhD in computer science from the University of Southern California, worked for the technology consulting company Unisys in the United States, and then returned to Israel to work for IBM and, later, for Intel.

But in 1992, she was a first-time entrepreneur. She founded Ornet Data Communications with five colleagues from Fibronics, one of Israel's early tech companies. Ornet Data developed software and equipment for local area networks (LANs), to double the speed of data transmission.

While most users were dialing into the World Wide Web through telephone lines, the Ethernet networking technology was growing as a way to connect LANs—groups of computers that were close together in homes and offices. LANs could move more information, faster, between computers in the network, but bandwidth was still quite limited. Ornet Data's solution created a switch for these networked computers that, Berry estimated, multiplied the bandwidth fifty times.

Ornet Data had just a handful of employees in Karmiel, a city in northern Israel, and an office in Boston that Berry used when she came through town. In the early days of the company, she flew to the United States repeatedly to try to raise money, but she soon realized there was none available.

"There was no mechanism for early-stage high-risk funding in the absence of local venture capital," she told us.[2]

Venture capital is investment funding that is usually put to work in high-growth technology companies. But for most foreign investors, putting money into Israel seemed absurd. To them, Israel was synonymous with ancient religions, archaeological digs, and deadly conflict. Even those investors who had marveled at Israel's R&D capabilities were spooked by the surge in violence that came with the Palestinian uprising—or intifada—in the late 1980s. This was before Dov Frohman's decision to keep Intel open during the 1991 Gulf War.

According to Jon Medved, founder of Israel Seed Partners, "You could talk to an American fund until you were blue in the face and say, 'Hey, come invest in Israel,' and they would laugh at you."[3]

Israel's dearth of venture capital through the 1980s was also creating other problems. In the West, the role of the venture capitalist is not simply to provide cash. It's mentoring, plus introductions to a network of other investors, prospective acquirers, and new customers and partners, that makes the venture industry so valuable to a budding start-up. A good VC will help entrepreneurs build their companies.

"It was very clear that something was missing in Israel at the time," said Yigal Erlich, another chief scientist, who was serving in the government in the late 1980s. "While Israel was very good at developing technologies, Israelis didn't know how to manage companies or market products."[4]

Israeli entrepreneurs had to think globally from the start, creating products for markets thousands of miles and several time zones away. But serious questions loomed: How to customize the product for the market? How to manufacture, market, and ultimately distribute the product to customers so far from the shores of the Mediterranean?

Before the introduction of venture capital in Israel, there were only two sources of funding. First, Israeli start-ups could apply to the Office of the Chief Scientist (OCS) for matching grants. These grants, however, didn't provide anywhere near the amount of money start-ups actually needed, and as a result, most failed. A government report published in the late 1980s claimed that 60 percent of the technology companies deemed worthy of OCS grants were unable to raise follow-on capital to market their products. They may have created great products, but they couldn't sell them.[5]

Second, Israeli companies could apply for what are called BIRD grants. Created from $110 million put up by the U.S. and Israeli governments, the Binational Industrial Research and Development (BIRD) Foundation created an endowment to support U.S.-Israeli joint business ventures. BIRD gave modest grants of $500,000 to $1 million, infused over two to three years, and would recoup funds through small royalties earned from successful projects.[6]

Ed Mlavsky became the executive director of BIRD when, in 1978, he made an offhand comment at a meeting of the U.S.-Israel Advisory Council on Industrial R&D. BIRD had been established two years earlier, but the foundation had not funded a single project. The council was meeting to choose a successor to run the foundation, and members were disappointed with the flock of candidates. Mlavsky, born in England but by now an American citizen, said, "Gentlemen, this is horrible; even I can do a better job than any of [the candidates]." The committee thought this was a great idea and tried to convince Mlavsky to quit his job as executive vice president of Tyco International and move his family to Israel. Mlavsky's wife wasn't Jewish and he didn't have a strong emotional connection to Israel, but at the urging of Jordan Baruch, the U.S. assistant secretary of commerce for science and technology, Mlavsky went to Israel to, as he says, "interview for a job I did not want in a country in which I had no wish to live." His wife was supportive; she had visited Israel in 1979 and fallen in love with the pioneering culture of the still young country. So Mlavsky took a sabbatical from Tyco, put their furniture in storage, and went to Israel. He would end up staying in the position for thirteen years, until he cofounded Gemini, one of Israel's first government-funded venture capital firms. Part of what appealed to Mlavsky was an openness in Israel to experiment with any idea, which he didn't fully appreciate until he was on the ground and immersed in Israeli life.

Mlavsky called BIRD a kind of "dating service," because he and his team played matchmaker between an Israeli company with a technology and an American company that could market and distribute the product in the United States. Not only that, but this matchmaker would subsidize the cost of the date.

Most of the U.S. tech companies BIRD pursued had limited R&D budgets. Because they were midsized to large publicly traded companies, they were skittish about dipping into the quarterly revenues to pay for costly research.

Mlavsky recalls, "We came to [U.S. companies] and said, 'There is this place called Israel, which you may or may not have heard of. We can put you in touch with smart, creative, and well-trained engineers there. You don't have to pay to hire them, relocate them, and you don't have to worry about what happens after the project is over. We will not only introduce you to such a group—we'll give you half the money for your part of the project and half the money the Israelis will need for their part.'"

To date, BIRD has invested over $250 million in 780 projects, which has resulted in $8 billion in direct and indirect sales.[7]

The impact of the BIRD program far surpassed mere revenues: it helped teach burgeoning Israeli tech companies how to do business in the United States. The companies worked closely with their

American partners. Many rented office space in the United States and sent employees overseas, where they could learn about the market and their customers.

In the absence of equity financing, BIRD provided a shortcut to American markets. Even when the venture failed, there was tremendous learning about how to create products designed for markets, as opposed to simply developing technologies.

By 1992, nearly 60 percent of the Israeli companies that went public on the New York Stock Exchange and 75 percent of those listed on the NASDAQ had been supported by BIRD.[8] American venture capitalists and investors were beginning to take notice. And yet 74 percent of high-tech exports out of Israel were generated by just 4 percent of high-tech companies.[9] The benefits were not being widely dispersed. If new tech companies couldn't get BIRD or government grants, they had to master the art of "bootstrapping": using personal resources, connections, or any other means to cobble together funds.

Jon Medved tried bootstrapping when he went door-to-door to sell his father's optical transceivers in 1982. At the time, the company consisted of just ten people working out of an actual garage, building optical transmitters and receivers. Medved admitted that he had not taken a single math or physics class in college and knew nothing about the nuances of the business that his father had put together. He also didn't know Hebrew.

"I would speak before groups of Israeli engineers who knew nothing about fiber," Medved recalls, "and give them a lecture about fiber optics. If they ever asked a tough technical question, I'd hide behind their Hebrew—'I can't understand you, sorry!' "[10] Medved did write a business plan for the company, and he developed revenue projections on the first spreadsheet software available on his suitcase-sized computer; but, like Orna Berry, he found fund-raising to be impossible.

Chief scientist Erlich became fixated on ways to overcome the funding challenges facing entrepreneurs. But there was some opposition: "Don't waste your time and money on new, small companies. They're a losing proposition," detractors told him.[11] Instead, government economists called for increased funding and partnerships between Israel and the big multinational companies, which at this point were employing thousands of Israelis.

There was also another challenge bearing down on Israel at the time: how to deal with the nearly one million Soviet Jewish immigrants beginning to flood the country. The government believed that to absorb these immigrants, the Israeli economy would have to create half a million new jobs. With one out of every three Soviet immigrants a scientist, engineer, or technician, Israel's high-tech sector seemed to be the best solution. But existing R&D centers alone would never be able to handle that many new employees.

In 1991, the government created technology incubators—twenty-four of them. These incubators gave most Russian scientists the resources and financing they needed in the early stage of R&D for their innovations. The goal was not only to develop the technology but to determine whether or not that product could be commercialized and sold. The government funded hundreds of companies through payments of up to $300,000. This got many of the new Russian immigrants working at their craft, but those doling out the money had little, if any, experience with start-up ventures. The government financiers were unable to give these entrepreneurs the support and management they needed to turn these R&D successes into commercially viable products.

"Every year when I tried to review the success of these small companies, it was disappointing," said Erlich. "While they may have succeeded in R&D, we didn't see them succeed in growing companies."[12] He became convinced that a private venture capital industry was the only antidote. But he also knew that in order to succeed, an Israeli VC industry would need strong ties with foreign financial markets. The international connections were not just about raising funds; aspiring Israeli VCs needed to be mentored in the art of business mentoring. There were thousands of venture capital firms in the United States that were involved in the nuts and bolts of successful tech start-ups in Silicon Valley. They had experience building companies, understood the technology and the funding process, and could guide first-time entrepreneurs. That's what Erlich wanted to bring to Israel.

That's when a band of young bureaucrats at the Ministry of Finance came up with the idea for a program they called Yozma, which in Hebrew means "initiative."

As Orna Berry told us, "John Lennon once said about the early years of rock and roll, 'Before Elvis, there was nothing.' On the success of venture capital and high-tech entrepreneurship in Israel, to paraphrase Lennon, before Yozma, there was nothing."[13]

The idea was for the government to invest $100 million to create ten new venture capital funds. Each fund had to be represented by three parties: Israeli venture capitalists in training, a foreign venture capital firm, and an Israeli investment company or bank. There was also one Yozma fund of $20 million that would invest directly in technology companies.

The Yozma program initially offered an almost one-and-a-half-to-one match. If the Israeli partners could raise $12 million to invest in new Israeli technologies, the government would give the fund $8 million. There was a line around the corner. So the government raised the bar. It required VC firms to raise $16 million in order to get the government's $8 million.

The real allure for foreign VCs, however, was the potential upside built into this program. The government would retain a 40 percent equity stake in the new fund but would offer the partners the option to cheaply buy out that equity stake—plus annual interest—after five years, if the fund was successful. This meant that while the government shared the risk, it offered investors all of the reward. From an investor's perspective, it was an unusually good deal.

"This was a rare government program that had a built-in get in and get out," said Jon Medved. "This was key to its success." And it was also rare for a government program to actually disappear once it had served its initial purpose, rather than continue indefinitely.

At the time, most business-savvy Diaspora Jews were not investing in Israel. They viewed philanthropy and business as two distinct activities. While they would make huge donations to not-for-profit organizations that benefited Israel, for the most part they were reluctant to invest in Israel's high-tech endeavors.

There were exceptions, of course.

Stanley Chais, a money manager in California, helped raise money for the first round of Yozma funds by setting up parlor meetings in California with wealthy Jews. He raised millions of dollars for the funds. Erel Margalit, who left the Jerusalem Development Authority to manage one of the first funds, said that most of the first round of funding was raised from people who had a "warm place in their heart for Jerusalem or Israel." Margalit's first institutional investor was the French insurance giant GAN, whose chairman was a French Jew Margalit met by chance on a flight to Paris.

"The government was used as the catalyst," said Erlich. The first Yozma fund was created in partnership with the Discount Israel Corporation, an investment bank, and Advent Venture Partners, a premier VC firm from Boston. It was led by Ed Mlavsky, the long-time director of the BIRD Foundation, and Yossi Sela.

Clint Harris, a partner at Advent, said he knew something was different about Israel on his first trip. In the taxicab on the way from the airport to his Tel Aviv hotel, the driver asked him why he was visiting Israel. Harris replied that he was there to get a sense of the venture capital industry. The driver then proceeded to give Harris a briefing on the state of VC in Israel.

The Advent-sponsored fund would be called Gemini Israel Funds. One of its first investments was in November 1993, when it allocated $1 million to Ornet Data Communications. This investment, as well as the managerial help, was just what Ornet needed to succeed. Recognizing the company management's lack of business experience, Mlavsky and Sela helped recruit Meir Burstin to serve as chairman of the board for the new company. Burstin was an old hand in the high-tech entrepreneurial world, having founded and led Tekem, one of Israel's first software companies, and then served as president of Tadiran, one of Israel's big defense-technology companies. Burstin brought instant credibility and experience to Ornet.

When the company was teetering on the brink of closing down after wasting the first big financing round, Yossi Sela from Gemini took over as interim CEO of the company and commuted from Ramat Hasharon to Karmiel, a two-hour drive, four days a week. "It took six months of single-minded determination," Sela recalled, "from both Gemini and the Ornet founding team, to sell the company and keep the management team from splintering—not to mention more hours driving from Ramat Hasharon to Karmiel than I'd like to remember—but we did it."[14]

The other piece that was critical to the company's success was Gemini's ability to bring Walden Venture Capital in as an investor. Walden, an established firm in Silicon Valley, had experience in the kind of technology Ornet had developed. Returning over three times its investment in about two years made Ornet Gemini's first success story.

The ten Yozma funds created between 1992 and 1997 raised just over $200 million with the help of government funding. Those funds were bought out or privatized within five years, and today they manage nearly $3 billion of capital and support hundreds of new Israeli companies. The results were clear. As Erel Margalit put it, "Venture capital was the match that sparked the fire."[15]

Several of the Yozma funds had high-profile successes early on, with investments in companies such as ESC Medical, which designed and built light-based medical solutions like lasers; Galileo, a high-end semiconductor firm; Commontouch, an enterprise e-mail and messaging provider; and Jacada, which builds online work spaces for customer-service employees at leading companies.

Along the way, others jumped into the venture capital world—even without the government's Yozma backing. Jon Medved just missed the Yozma financing. Years after he sold the company he and his father had built, he heard that there was a $5 million Yozma allotment available to invest in very-early-stage companies. Known as seed funds, these investments tend to be considered the riskiest, so Yozma offered a one-to-one match: investors had to bring $2.5 million to the table to get the government's $2.5 million.

Medved went to Yigal Erlich with investors ready to write checks and asked for the grant. Unfortunately, it was too late. But it didn't matter. The Yozma program was generating the buzz in the U.S. venture community to overcome investors' reticence about doing business in Israel. "Israel had excited investors enough that we were able to bring in the $2.5 million and start Israel Seed Partners in 1994," even without the government's matching grant, Medved said. The fund would quickly grow to $6 million, and Israel Seed would go on to raise $40 million in 1999 and $200 million in 2000.

According to the Israel Venture Association, there are now forty-five Israeli venture capital funds. Ed Mlavsky said that over the period from 1992 to early 2009, there have been as many as 240 VCs in Israel, defined as companies both foreign and domestic investing in Israeli start-ups.

Soon other governments around the world were taking notice of Yozma's success. Chief scientist Erlich got calls from foreign governments, including Japan, South Korea, Canada, Ireland, Australia, New Zealand, Singapore, and Russia, all wanting to come to Israel and meet the founders of Yozma.

In December 2008, Ireland launched a €500 million "innovation fund" designed to attract cofinancing from foreign venture capitalists. "The Irish state—ironically for a country that didn't have diplomatic relations with Israel for the first 40 years of its existence—has copied the Jewish state," wrote Irish economist David McWilliams.

Like Yozma, the Irish innovation fund lures foreign VCs to Ireland through a series of state-backed venture capital funds that partner up with private-sector funds.

McWilliams said, "The big idea is not to attract only U.S. capital and commercial know-how, but to suck in entrepreneurs from all over Europe. At the moment, Europe has huge reservoirs of scientific talent, but a very poor record at creating start-ups. The question many investors ask is: Where is the European Google? It's a fair question. In the next ten years, what if that European Google was set up here using Irish and European brains and U.S. capital? That is the prize."[16]

Yozma provided the critical missing component that allowed the Israeli tech scene to join in the tech boom of the 1990s. But in 2000, the Israeli tech sector was hit by multiple blows at once: the global tech bubble burst, the Oslo peace process blew up into a wave of terrorism, and the economy went into a recession.

Yet Israel's start-ups quickly adapted and rebounded. During this period, Israel doubled its share of the global venture capital pie with respect to Europe, growing from 15 to 31 percent. This growth occurred, however, within a tax and regulatory environment that, while favoring technology start-ups and foreign investors, did not offer the same support to the rest of the economy.

For example, while a technology start-up could attract financing from numerous sources, anyone trying to launch a more conventional business would have a lot of trouble getting a simple small business loan. Israel's capital markets were highly concentrated and constrained. And a particular industry that would seem to be a natural for Israel—financial services—was prevented from ever getting off the ground.

In 2001, Tal Keinan graduated from Harvard Business School. "Many of my friends who were going off to work on Wall Street were Jewish, and it struck me that the Jewish state doesn't have such an industry. When it came to managing investments, Israel was not even on the map," Keinan said.

The reason was government regulations. In venture capital, Keinan discovered, "the way the regulatory and tax regime was set up here, you could essentially operate as though you weren't in Israel, which was great, and it created a wonderful industry. The government basically kept its hands off of venture capital." But, he adds, "you couldn't do anything outside of venture capital in any meaningful way. You weren't allowed to take the performance fees on any money you managed, so you could forget that entire industry. It was a nonstarter."[17]

The asset-management business has a simple model: firms receive a flat management fee of about 1 to 2 percent of the money they manage. But the real upside is in performance fees, which are typically 5 to 20 percent of the return on the investment, depending on the firm.

Until January 2005, it was illegal for Israeli money-management firms to charge performance fees. So not surprisingly, there was no industry to speak of.

The change came from then finance minister Benjamin "Bibi" Netanyahu.

With Prime Minister Ariel Sharon's backing in 2003, Netanyahu cut tax rates, transfer payments, public employee wages, and four thousand government jobs. He also privatized major symbols of the remaining government influence on the economy—such as the national airline, El Al, and the national telecommunications company, Bezeq—and instituted financial-sector reforms.

"In the sense that he tackled the stifling role of government in our economy, Bibi was not a reformer but a revolutionary. A reform happens when you change the policy of the government; a revolution happens when you change the mind-set of a country. I think that Bibi was able to change the mind-set," said Ron Dermer, who served as an adviser to four Israeli ministers of finance, including Netanyahu.[18]

Netanyahu told us, "I explained to people that the private economy was like a thin man carrying a fat man—the government—on its back. While my reforms sparked massive nationwide strikes by labor unions, my characterization of the economy struck a chord. Anyone who had tried to start a [nontech] business in Israel could relate."[19] Netanyahu's reforms gained increasing public support as the economy began to pull out of its rut.

At the same time, a package of banking-sector reforms pushed through by Netanyahu began to take effect. These reforms launched the phaseout of the government's bonds that had guaranteed about 6 percent annual return. Up until that point, asset managers for Israeli pensions and life insurance funds simply invested in the Israeli guaranteed bonds. The pension and life insurance funds "could meet their commitments to beneficiaries just by buying the earmarked bonds. So that's exactly what they did—they didn't invest in anything else," Keinan told us. "Because of these bonds, there was no incentive for Israeli institutional investors to invest in any private investment fund."

But as the government bonds began to mature and could not be renewed, they released some $300 million a month that needed to be invested elsewhere. "So all of a sudden, boom, you've got a local pool of capital to spark an investment industry," noted Keinan, as we sat, looking out at the Mediterranean, in his thirtieth-floor office in Tel Aviv, which is where his new investment fund is head-quartered. "As a result, there are very few large international money managers that don't have some exposure in Israel now, either in equities or the new corporate bond market, which didn't exist three years ago, or in the shekel."

Because of Netanyahu's financial-sector reforms, it also became legal for investment managers to charge performance fees. Keinan didn't waste any time; he founded KCPS, Israel's first full-spectrum financial-asset-management firm, in Tel Aviv and New York. "The moment I read the draft law of Bibi's reforms, my wheels started turning," Keinan said. "It was clear that this truly could liberate our non-high-tech economy."

Keinan argues that a ton of local talent was untapped. "If you think about what young Israelis learn in some of the army intelligence units, for example . . . often highly sophisticated quantitative analytical skills—algorithms, modeling out macroeconomic trends. If they wanted to go into high tech, there were plenty of start-ups that would gobble them up after their army service. But if they wanted to go into finance, they'd have to leave the country. That's now changed. Just think about this," he continued. "There are Israelis working on Fleet Street in London because there was no place for them here. Now, since 2003, there is a place for them in Israel."

# PART IV

## Country with a Motive

# CHAPTER 11

# Betrayal and Opportunity

*The two real fathers of Israeli hi-tech are the Arab*
*boycott and Charles de Gaulle, because they forced on*
*us the need to go and develop an industry.*

—Yossi Vardi

THROUGHOUT THIS BOOK, we've pointed to the ways the IDF's improvisational and antihierarchical culture follows Israelis into their start-ups and has shaped Israel's economy. This culture, when combined with the technological wizardry Israelis acquire in elite military units and from the state-run defense industry, forms a potent mixture. But there was nothing normal about the birth of Israel's defense industry. It was unheard-of for a country so small to have its own indigenous military-industrial complex. Its origins are rooted in a dramatic, overnight betrayal by a close ally.

The best way to understand Israel's watershed moment is through a shock to Americans that had a similar effect. During the postwar boom years, America's global status was suddenly punctured when the Soviet Union upstaged the United States by launching the first space satellite—*Sputnik 1*. That the Soviets could pull ahead in the space race stunned most Americans. But in retrospect, it was a boon for the U.S. economy.

Innovation economist John Kao says that *Sputnik* "was a wake-up call, and America answered it. We revised school curricula to emphasize the teaching of science and math. We passed the $900 million National Defense Education Act (about $6 billion in today's dollars), providing scholarships, student loans, and scientific equipment for schools."[1] NASA and the Apollo program were created, as was a powerful new Pentagon agency dedicated to galvanizing the civilian R&D community.

A little over a decade later, Neil Armstrong stepped onto the moon. The Apollo program and the Pentagon's related defense investments spurred a generation of new discoveries that were ultimately commercialized, with a transformative impact on the economy. This concerted research and development campaign gave birth to entirely new business sectors within avionics and telecommunications, as well as the Internet itself, and became a legacy of America's response to *Sputnik*.

Israel had its own *Sputnik* moment, ten years after America's. On the eve of the 1967 Six-Day War, Charles de Gaulle taught Israel an invaluable lesson about the price of dependence.

De Gaulle, a founder of France's Fifth Republic, had been in and out of senior military and government positions since World War II and served as president from 1959 to 1969. After Israel's independence, de Gaulle had forged an alliance with the Jewish state and nurtured what Israeli leaders believed to be a deep personal friendship. The alliance included a French supply of critical military equipment and fighter aircraft, and even a secret agreement to cooperate in the development of nuclear weapons.[2]

Like many small states, Israel preferred to buy large weapon systems from other countries, rather than devote the tremendous resources needed to produce them. But in May 1950, the United States, Britain, and France jointly issued the Tripartite Declaration to limit arms sales to the Middle East.

With no ready supply from abroad, Israel had already begun its arms industry with underground bullet and gun factories. One factory was literally hidden underground, beneath a kibbutz laundry; the machines were kept running to mask the banging noise from below. This factory, built with war-surplus tools smuggled from the United States, was producing hundreds of machine guns daily by 1948. Makeshift factories were supplemented by scattershot gun-running across the globe. David Ben-Gurion had sent emissaries abroad to collect weapons as far back as the 1930s. In 1936, for example, Yehuda Arazi managed to stuff rifles into a steam boiler headed from Poland to the port of Haifa. In 1948, he posed as an ambassador from Nicaragua to negotiate the purchase of five old French mounted guns.

The Israelis got by on these banana republic schemes until 1955, when the Soviet Union, via Czechoslovakia, ignored the leaky Tripartite Declaration and made a massive $250 million arms sale to Egypt. In response, de Gaulle took the other side. In April 1956, he began to transfer large quantities of modern arms to Israel. The tiny state finally had a reliable and first-rate national arms supplier.

After Egypt nationalized the Suez Canal in 1956, the relationship only deepened. France relied on the Suez for sea transport from the region to Europe. The IDF helped guarantee French access to the Suez, and France in return showered Israel with more arms. The supply only grew as the French and the Israelis colluded on more and more operations. De Gaulle's spy agency enlisted Israel's help in undermining anti-French resistance in Algeria, one of France's colonial strongholds. In 1960, France promised to supply Israel with two hundred AMX-13 tanks and seventy-two Mystère fighter jets over the next ten years.[3]

But on June 2, 1967, three days before Israel was to launch a preemptive attack against Egypt and Syria, de Gaulle cut Israel off cold. "France will not give its approval to—and still less, support—the first nation to use weapons," he told his cabinet.[4]

But there was more to de Gaulle's decision than trying to defuse a Middle East war. New circumstances called for new French alliances. By 1967, France had withdrawn from Algeria. With his long and bitter North African war behind him, de Gaulle's priority was now rapprochement with the Arab world. It was no longer in France's interest to side with Israel. "Gaullist France does not have friends, only interests," the French weekly *Le Nouvel Observateur* remarked at the time.[5]

De Gaulle's successor, Georges Pompidou, continued the new policy after his own election in 1969. The two hundred AMX tanks France had originally committed to Israel were to be rerouted to Libya, and France even sent fifty Mirage jet fighters Israel had already paid for to Syria, one of Israel's fiercest enemies.

The Israelis quickly pursued stopgap measures. Israeli Air Force founder Al Schwimmer personally recruited a sympathetic Swiss engineer to give him the blueprints to the Mirage engine, so Israel could copy the French fighter. Israel also returned to its pre-state smuggling exploits. In one mission in 1969, five Israeli-manned gunboats battled twenty-foot waves on a three-thousand-mile race from France to Israel; these naval vessels, worth millions of dollars, had been promised to Israel before the new embargo. As *Time* magazine colorfully described it in 1970: "Not since Bismarck has there been such a sea hunt....At various points, [the Israelis] were tracked by French reconnaissance planes, an R.A.F. Canberra from Malta, Soviet tankers, the radar forests of the U.S. Sixth Fleet, television cameramen and even Italian fishermen."[6]

These shenanigans, however, could not compensate for the hard truth: the Middle East arms race was accelerating just at the moment that Israel had lost its most indispensable arms and aircraft supplier. The 1967 French embargo put Israel in an extremely vulnerable position.

Prior to the 1967 war, the United States had already begun to sell weapons systems to Israel, starting with the transfer of Hawk surface-to-air missiles by the Kennedy administration in 1962. Jerusalem's first choice, then, was for the United States to take France's place as Israel's main arms supplier. But the French betrayal had built a consensus in Israel that it could no longer rely so heavily on foreign arms suppliers. Israel decided that it must move quickly to produce major weapons systems, such as tanks and fighter aircraft, even though no other small country had successfully done so.

This drive for independence produced the Merkava tank, first released in 1978 and now in its fourth generation. It also led to the Nesher—Israel's version of the Mirage aircraft—and then to the Kfir, first flown in 1973.[7]

The most ambitious project of all, however, was to produce the Lavi fighter jet, using American-made engines. The program was jointly funded by Israel and the United States. The Lavi was designed not only to replace the Kfir but to become one of the top-line fighters in the world.

The Lavi went into full-scale development in 1982; on the last day of 1986, the first plane took its inaugural test flight. But in August 1987, after billions of dollars had been spent to build five planes, mounting pressure in both Israel and the United States led to the program's cancellation, first by the U.S. Congress and then by a 12–11 vote in the Israeli cabinet.

Many years later, the project and its cancellation still remain controversial: some people believe that it was an impossibly ambitious boondoggle from the beginning, while others claim that it was a great opportunity missed. In a 1991 article in *Flight International* magazine, published during Operation Desert Storm, an editor wrote about his experience flying the Lavi back in 1989: "Now when the coalition forces fight in the Gulf they miss the aircraft they really need. It's a real shame that I had to fly the world's best fighter knowing it would never get into service."[8]

Even though the program was canceled, the Lavi's development had significant military reverberations. First, the Israelis had made an important psychological breakthrough: they had demonstrated to themselves, their allies, and their adversaries that they were not dependent on anyone else to provide one of the most basic elements for national survival—an advanced fighter aircraft program. Second, in 1988 Israel joined a club of only about a dozen nations that had launched satellites into space—an achievement that would have been unlikely without the technological know-how accumulated during the Lavi's development. And third, although the Lavi was canceled, the billions invested in the program brought Israel to a new level in avionic systems and, in some ways, helped jump-start the high-tech boom to come. When the program shut down, its fifteen hundred engineers were suddenly out of jobs. Some of them left the country, but most did not, resulting in a large infusion of engineering talent from the military industries into the private sector. The tremendous technological talent that had been concentrated on one aircraft was suddenly unleashed into the economy.[9]

Yossi Gross, one of the Lavi's engineers, was born in Israel. His mother, who'd survived Auschwitz, emigrated from Europe after the Holocaust. As a student in Israel, Gross trained in aeronautical engineering at the Technion and then worked at Israel Aircraft Industries (IAI) for seven years.

Gross, a test-flight engineer at IAI, began in the design department. When he came up with a new idea for the landing gear, he was told by his supervisors to not bother them with innovations but to simply copy the American F-16. "I was working in a large company with twenty-three thousand employees, where you can't be creative," he recalled.[10]

Shortly before the Lavi's cancellation, Gross decided to leave not only IAI but the whole aeronautics field. "In aerospace, you can't be an entrepreneur," he explained. "The government owns the industry, and the projects are huge. But I learned a lot of technical things there that helped me immensely later on."

This former flight engineer went on to found seventeen start-ups and develop over three hundred patents. So, in a sense, Yossi Gross should thank France. Charles de Gaulle hardly intended to help jump-start the Israeli technology scene. Yet by convincing Israelis that they could not rely on foreign weapons systems, de Gaulle's decision made a pivotal contribution to Israel's economy. The major increase in military R&D that followed France's boycott of Israel gave a generation of Israeli engineers remarkable experience. But it would not have catalyzed Israel's start-up hothouse if it had not been combined with something else: a profound interdisciplinary approach and a willingness to try anything, no matter how destabilizing to societal norms.

## CHAPTER 12

# From Nose Cones to Geysers

*If most air forces are designed like a Formula One race car,
the Israeli Air Force is a beat-up jeep with a lot of tools
in it.... Here, you're going off-road from day one.
The race car is just not going to work in our environment.*

—TAL KEINAN

DOUG WOOD IS A NEW AND UNLIKELY RECRUIT to Israel. With his calm and reflective demeanor, he stands out among his more brash Israeli colleagues. He was hired from Hollywood to do something that's never before been tried in Jerusalem: Wood is the director of the first feature-length animated movie to be produced by Animation Lab, the start-up founded by Israeli venture capitalist Erel Margalit.

Wood worked as vice president of feature animation development and production at Turner, Warner Brothers, and Universal. When Margalit asked him to relocate to Jerusalem to create an animated feature, Wood said he would first have to see if Jerusalem had a real creative community. After spending some time in Jerusalem at Bezalel—Israel's leading academy of art and design—he was convinced. "I met with the faculty there. I met with some TV writers and [author] Meir Shalev, and some other big storytellers," he told us. "They were as good if not better than the people you would meet at the world's top art schools."

But he also identified something different about Israel. "There's a multitask mentality here. We've consulted with a lot of the Israeli technical people and they come up with innovative ways to improve our pipeline and do things more directly. And then there was this time I was working on a creative project with an art graduate from Bezalel. He looked the part—long hair, an earring, in shorts and flip-flops. Suddenly a technological problem erupted. I was ready to call the techies in to fix it. But the Bezalel student dropped his graphic work and began solving the problem like he was a trained engineer. I asked him where he learned to do this. It turns out he was also a fighter pilot in the air force. *This art student? A fighter pilot?* It's like all these worlds come colliding here—or collaborating—depending how you look at it."[1]

It's not surprising that multitasking, like many other advantages Israeli technologists seem to have, is fostered by the IDF. Fighter pilot Tal Keinan told us that there is a distinct bias against specialization in the Israeli military. "If most air forces are designed like a Formula One race car, the Israeli Air Force is a beat-up jeep with a lot of tools in it. On a closed track, the Formula One's going to win," Keinan said. But, he noted, in the IAF, "you're going off-road from day one.... The race car is just not going to work in our environment."[2]

The difference between the Formula One and the jeep strategies is not just about numbers; each produces divergent tactics and modes of thinking. This can be seen in the different "strike packages" that each air force constructs for its missions. For most Western air forces, a strike package is built from a series of waves of aircraft whose end goal is to deliver bombs on targets.

The United States typically uses four waves of specialized aircraft to accomplish a specific component of the mission: for example, a combat air patrol, designed to clear a corridor of enemy aircraft; a second wave that knocks out any enemy antiaircraft systems that are firing missiles; a third wave of electronic warfare aircraft, tankers for refueling, and radar aircraft to provide a complete battle picture; and, finally, the strikers themselves—planes with bombs. These are guarded by close air-support fighters "to make sure nothing happens," Keinan explained.

"It's overwhelming and it's very well coordinated," Keinan said of the U.S. system. "It's very challenging logistically. You've got to meet the tanker at the right place. You've got to rendezvous with the electronic warfare—if one guy's off by a few seconds, it all falls apart. The IAF could not pull off a system like this even if it had the resources; it would just be a big mess. We're not disciplined enough."

In the Israeli system, almost every aircraft is a jack-of-all-trades. "You don't go into combat without air-to-air missiles, no matter what the mission is," said Keinan. "You could be going to hit a target in southern Lebanon, with zero chance of meeting another aircraft, and if you do, the home base is two minutes' flying time away and someone else can come and help you. Still, there's no such thing as going into hostile territory without air-to-air missiles."

Similarly, nearly every aircraft in the IAF has its own onboard electronic warfare system. Unlike the U.S. Air Force, the IAF does not send up a special formation to defeat enemy radars. "You do it yourself," Keinan noted. "It's not as effective, but it's a hell of a lot more flexible." Finally, in a typical Israeli strike package, about 90 percent of the aircraft are carrying bombs and are assigned targets. In a U.S. strike package, only the strikers in the final wave are carrying bombs.

In the Israeli system, each pilot learns not only his own target but also other targets in separate formations. "If an aircraft gets hit, for example, and two aircraft split off to go after a downed pilot or to engage in air-to-air combat... the other pilots have to take over those targets," Keinan explained. "You're expected to do that—it's actually a normal outcome. About half the time you're hitting somebody else's target."

The differences in the two countries' systems are most obvious when Israelis and Americans fly together in joint exercises. Keinan was surprised to find, in one such exercise, that American pilots were given a "dance card" that diagrammed the maneuvers the pilot was supposed to use in the fight. "We see that and say, *What the hell is that?* How many times do you know what the other guy is going to do?" For Keinan, who now is an investor, the American system seems "like going into a trading day saying, 'Whatever the market does, I'm buying.'"

The multitasking mentality produces an environment in which job titles—and the compartmentalization that goes along with them—don't mean much. This is something that Doug Wood noticed in making the transition from Hollywood to Jerusalem: "This is great because conventional Hollywood studios say you need a 'projection major' and you need a 'production coordinator' or you need a 'layout head.' But in Israel the titles are kind of arbitrary, really, because they are interchangeable in some ways and people do work on more than one thing.

"For example," he told us, "we have a guy who is in the CG team, the computer-generated-image team, but he also works on clay 3-D models of the characters. And then we're doing a sequence, and he came up with a funny line for the end of this thirty-second sequence that we're producing. And I actually liked the line so much I rewrote the script and put it in there. So the CG guy crossed the disciplinary walls and ventured into modeling and into scriptwriting."

The term in the United States for this kind of crossover is a *mashup*. And the term itself has been rapidly morphing and acquiring new meanings. Originally referring to the merging of two or more songs into one, it has also come to designate digital and video combinations, as well as a Web application that meshes data from other sites—such as HousingMaps.com, which graphically displays craigslist rentals postings on Google Maps. An even more powerful mashup, in our view, is when innovation is born from the combination of radically different technologies and disciplines.

The companies where mashups are most common in Israel are in the medical-device and biotech sectors, where you find wind tunnel engineers and doctors collaborating on a credit card–sized device that may make injections obsolete. Or you find a company (home to beta cells, fiber optics, and algae from Yellowstone National Park) that has created an implantable artificial pancreas to treat diabetes. And then there's a start-up that's built around a pill that can transmit images from inside your intestines using optics technology taken from a missile's nose cone.

Gavriel Iddan used to be a rocket scientist for Rafael, a company that is one of the principal weapons developers for the IDF. He specialized in the sophisticated electro-optical devices that allow missiles to "see" their target. Rockets might not be the first place one would look for medical technology, but Iddan had a novel idea: he would adapt the newest miniaturization technology used in missiles to develop a camera within a pill that could transmit pictures from inside the human body.

Many people told him it would be impossible to cram a camera, a transmitter, and light and energy sources into a pill that anyone could swallow. Iddan persisted, at one point going to the supermarket to buy chickens so he could test whether the prototype pill could transmit through animal tissues. He started a business around these pill cameras, or PillCams, and named his company Given Imaging.

In 2001, Given Imaging became the first company in the world to go public on Wall Street after the 9/11 attacks. By 2004, six years after its founding, Given Imaging had sold 100,000 PillCams. In early 2007, the company hit the 500,000 PillCams mark, and by the end of 2007 it had sold almost 700,000.

Today, the latest generation of PillCams painlessly transmit eighteen photographs per second, for hours, from deep within the intestines of a patient. The video produced can be viewed by a doctor in real time, in the same room or across the globe. The market remains large and has attracted major competitors; the camera giant Olympus now makes its own camera in a pill. That other companies would get into the act is not surprising, since ailments of the gastrointestinal tract are responsible for more than thirty million visits to doctors' offices in the United States alone.

The story of Given Imaging is not just one of technology transfer from the military to the civilian sectors, or of an entrepreneur emerging from a major defense technology company. It is an example of a technology mashup, of someone combining not only the disparate fields of missiles and medicine but integrating a staggering array of technologies—from optics, to electronics, to batteries, to wireless data transmission, to software, in order to help doctors analyze what they are seeing. These types of mashups are the holy grail of technological innovation. In fact, a recent study by Tel Aviv University revealed that patents originating from Israel are distinguished globally for citing the highest number and most diverse set of precedent patents.[3]

One such mashup, a company that has bridged the divide between the military and medicine, is Compugen, whose three founders— president Eli Mintz, chief technology officer Simchon Faigler, and software chief Amir Natan—met in the IDF's elite Talpiot program.

Another Talpiot alumnus at Compugen, Lior Ma'ayan, said that twenty-five of the sixty mathematicians in the company joined through their network of army contacts.

In the IDF, Mintz created algorithms for sifting through reams of intelligence data to find the nuggets that have been so critical to Israel's successes in hunting terrorist networks. When his wife, a geneticist, described the problems they had in sifting through enormous collections of genetic data, Mintz thought he might have a better way to do it.

Mintz and his partners were about to revolutionize the process of genetic sequencing. Merck bought Compugen's first sequencer in 1994, a year after the start-up was founded and long before the human genome had been successfully mapped. But this was just the beginning. In 2005, Compugen transformed its business model and moved into the drug discovery and development arena, and did so using techniques different from those that dominate the pharmaceutical industry.

Combining mathematics, biology, computer science, and organic chemistry, Compugen has been pioneering what it calls "predictive" drug development. Rather than testing thousands of compounds, hoping to hit upon something that "works," Compugen's strategy is to begin at the genetic level and develop drugs based on how genes express themselves through the production of proteins.

A major aspect of Compugen's approach is its unusual combination of "dry" (theoretical) and "wet" (biological) labs. "Imagine working with Big Pharma overseas or in another part of the country," Alon Amit, Compugen's VP for technology, explained. "The back and forth that you can expect is a lot slower than if you have the biologists and mathematicians literally on the same floor discussing what to test, how to test, and inform the models."[4]

Though Israel's largest company, Teva, is in pharmaceuticals, as are Compugen and a number of new Israeli companies, the more crowded field for Israeli start-ups is that of medical devices, many of them related to drug delivery. This field seems to nicely fit the Israeli penchant for multidisciplinary thinking, as well as Israelis' characteristic lack of patience—since drugs take so long to develop.

One such mashup-based company is Aespironics, which has developed an inhaler the size and shape of a credit card that includes a breath-powered wind turbine. The problem with many inhalers is that they are tricky and expensive to manufacture. A way must be found to release the drug effectively through a wire mesh. In addition, this process must be timed perfectly with the breath of the patient to maximize and regulate the drug's absorption in the lungs.

Aespironics seems to have solved all these problems at once. Inside the "credit card" is a fanlike propeller that is powered by the flow of air when the patient inhales from the edge of the card. As the propeller turns, it brushes against a mesh with the drug on it, thereby knocking the drug off the mesh and into the air flow in a measured manner. Since the propeller works only when the user inhales, it automatically propels the drug into the patient's lungs.

Putting this together required an unorthodox combination of engineering skills. In addition to experts on inhalers, Aespironics' team includes Dan Adler, whose specialty is designing gas turbines and jet engines. He was a professor at the Technion and at the U.S. Naval Graduate School and a consultant to such companies as General Dynamics, Pratt & Whitney, and McDonnell Douglas.

Mixing missiles and pills, jets and inhalers may seem strange enough, but the true mashup champion may be Yossi Gross. Born in Israel and trained in aeronautical engineering at the Technion, Gross worked at Israel Aircraft Industries for seven years before leaving to pursue more entrepreneurial endeavors.

Ruti Alon of Pitango Venture Capital, which has invested in six of Gross's seventeen start-ups, argues that his multidisciplinary approach is the key to his success. "He has training in aeronautical engineering and electronics. He also knows a lot about physics, flow, and hemodynamics, and these things can be very helpful when thinking about devices that need to be implanted in the human body." Plus, Alon reminded, "he knows a lot of doctors."[5]

Some of Gross's companies combine such wildly diverse technologies that they border on science fiction. Beta-$O_2$, for example, is a start-up working on an implantable "bioreactor" to replace the defective pancreas in diabetes patients. Diabetics suffer from a disorder that causes their beta cells to cease producing insulin. Transplanted beta cells could do the trick, but even if the body didn't reject them, they cannot survive without a supply of oxygen.

Gross's solution was to create a self-contained micro-environment that includes oxygen-producing algae from the geysers of Yellowstone Park. Since the algae need light to survive, a fiber-optic light source is included in the pacemaker-sized device. The beta cells consume oxygen and produce carbon dioxide; the algae does just the opposite, creating a self-contained miniature ecosystem. The whole bioreactor is designed to be implanted under the skin in a fifteen-minute outpatient procedure and replaced once a year.

Combining geothermal algae, fiber optics, and beta cells to treat diabetes is typical of Gross's cross-technology approach. Another of his start-ups, TransPharma Medical, combines two different innovations: using radio frequency (RF) pulses to create temporary microchannels through the skin, and the first powder patch ever developed. "It's a small device," Gross explains, "like a cell phone, that you apply to the skin for one second. It creates RF cell ablation, hundreds of microchannels in the skin. Then we apply on top a powder patch, not a regular patch. Most patches out there are gel- or adhesive-based. We print the drug on the patch, and it's dry.

When we apply the patch to the skin, the interstitial fluid comes out slowly from the microchannels and pulls the lyophilized [freeze-dried] powder from the patch under the skin."

Gross claims that this device solves one of the most intractable problems of drug delivery: how to get large molecules, such as proteins, through the outer layer of the skin without an injection. The first products will deliver human growth hormone and a drug for osteoporosis; patches to deliver insulin and other drugs, hormones, and molecules—most of them currently delivered by injections—are in the works.

The Israeli penchant for technological mashups is more than a curiosity; it is a cultural mark that lies at the heart of what makes Israel so innovative. It is a product of the multidisciplinary backgrounds that Israelis often obtain by combining their military and civilian experiences. But it is also a way of thinking that produces particularly creative solutions and potentially opens up new industries and "disruptive" advances in technology. It is a form of free thinking that is hard to imagine in less free or more culturally rigid societies, including some that superficially seem to be on the cutting edge of commercial development.

# CHAPTER 13

# The Sheikh's Dilemma

*The future of the region is going to depend on our teaching our young people how to go out and create companies.*

—FADI GHANDOUR

EREL MARGALIT'S BACKGROUND would not normally predict a future in venture capital. He was born on a kibbutz, fought in Lebanon in 1982 as an IDF soldier, studied math and philosophy at the Hebrew University of Jerusalem, and then pursued a doctorate in philosophy at Columbia University. He wrote his dissertation on the attributes of historical leaders—he thinks of them as "entrepreneurial leaders"—who profoundly affected the development of their nations or even civilizations (he profiled Winston Churchill and David Ben-Gurion, among others, as exemplars).

Along the way, he went to work for Teddy Kollek, the mayor of Jerusalem from 1965 to 1993. Shortly before Kollek was defeated in the 1993 municipal election, Margalit pitched an idea to help encourage start-ups in Jerusalem, which, then as now, was struggling to keep young people from leaving for nearby Tel Aviv, Israel's vibrant business capital. With Kollek gone, Margalit decided to implement his plan himself, but in the private sector. He called his new venture capital fund Jerusalem Venture Partners (JVP). It was seed-funded with capital from the Yozma program.

Since he founded JVP, in 1994, Margalit has raised hundreds of millions of dollars from France Telecom SA, Germany's Infineon Technologies AG, as well as Reuters, Boeing, Columbia University, MIT, and the Singapore government, to name a few sources. He has backed dozens of companies, many of which have held public offerings (IPOs) or been sold to international players, producing windfall returns. JVP was behind PowerDsine, Fundtech, and Jacada, all currently listed on the NASDAQ. One of its big hits was Chromatis Networks, an optical networking company, which was sold to Lucent for $4.5 billion.

In 2007, *Forbes* ranked Margalit sixty-ninth on its Midas List of "the world's best venture capitalists." He is among three Israelis on this top one hundred list, which is populated mostly by Americans.

But Margalit's contribution to Israel goes beyond business. He is investing huge sums of his personal fortune—and entrepreneurial know-how—to revitalize Jerusalem's arts scene. He launched the Maabada, the Jerusalem Performing Arts Lab, which is leading in the exploration of the link between technology and art, and is co-locating artists and technologists side by side in a way not done anywhere else in the world.

Next door to the nonprofit theater he founded, which was built in an abandoned warehouse, Margalit has converted a printing house into the headquarters for a burgeoning animation company, Animation Lab, which aims to compete with Pixar and others in the production of full-length animated films.

Jerusalem might seem like the last place to build a world-class movie studio. As a center for the three monotheist religions, the ancient city of Jerusalem is about as different from Hollywood as one could imagine. Filmmaking is not an Israeli specialty, though

Israeli movies have recently been prominently featured in international film festivals. Further complicating matters is the fact that the Israeli arts scene is centered in secular Tel Aviv, rather than Jerusalem, known more for holy sites, tourists, and government offices. But Margalit's vision for creating companies, jobs, industries, and creative outlets was specifically a vision *for Jerusalem.*

This cultural commitment can be central to the success of economic *clusters*, of which Israel's high-tech industry is a case in point. A cluster, as described by the author of the concept, Harvard Business School professor Michael Porter, is a unique model for economic development because it's based on "geographic concentrations" of interconnected institutions—businesses, government agencies, universities—in a specific field.[1] Clusters produce exponential growth for their communities because people living and working within the cluster are in some way connected to each other.

An example, according to Porter, is northern California's "wine cluster," which is populated by hundreds of wineries and thousands of independent grape growers. There are also suppliers of grape stock, manufacturers of irrigation and harvesting equipment, producers of barrels, and designers of bottle labels, not to mention an entire local media industry, with winery advertising firms and wine trade publications. The University of California at Davis, also near this area, has a world-renowned viticulture and oenology program. The Wine Institute is just south, in San Francisco, and the California legislature, in nearby Sacramento, has special committees dealing with the wine industry. Similar community structures exist around the world: in Italy's fashion cluster, Boston's biotech cluster, Hollywood's movie cluster, New York City's Wall Street cluster, and northern California's technology cluster.

Porter argues that an intense concentration of people working in and talking about the same industry provides companies with better access to employees, suppliers, and specialized information. A cluster does not exist only in the workplace; it is part of the fabric of daily life, involving interaction among peers at the local coffee shop, when picking up kids from school, and at church. Community connections become industry connections, and vice versa.

As Porter says, "the social glue" that binds a cluster together also facilitates access to critical information. A cluster, he notes, must be built around "personal relationships, face-to-face contact, a sense of common interest, and 'insider' status." This sounds just like what Yossi Vardi described: in Israel "everybody knows everybody, and there is a very high degree of transparency."

Margalit would point out that Israel has just the right mix of conditions to produce a cluster of this kind—and that's rare. After all, attempts to create clusters don't always succeed. Take, for example, Dubai. Searching for a Dubai equivalent of Erel Margalit, one thinks of Mohammed Al Gergawi. Al Gergawi is the chairman and chief executive of Dubai Holding, one of the larger businesses owned by Sheikh Mohammed bin Rashid Al Maktoum, the ruler of Dubai (and also the prime minister and defense minister of the United Arab Emirates). For all intents and purposes, Sheikh Mohammed is the chairman of "Dubai Inc." There is no distinction between Dubai's public finances and the sheikh's private wealth.

Al Gergawi's leap to prominence came in 1997 when he went to meet Sheikh Mohammed in the *majlis*, a forum for average citizens to come to see the sheikh—think of it as the Arab world's version of a town hall meeting, only far less interactive. During the visit, Sheikh Mohammed pointed out Al Gergawi and declared, "I know you and you'll go far."[2]

It turns out that Al Gergawi, then a midlevel government bureaucrat, had been identified months earlier by one of Sheikh Mohammed's "mystery shoppers," whose job it is to scour the kingdom for potential business leaders. Soon after the *majlis* meeting, Al Gergawi was put on an accelerated path to management of one of the sheikh's three major companies. Others within Dubai's government told us that Al Gergawi was selected because he was regarded as a competent technocrat—he could execute extremely well but would not challenge the ruler's vision.

Dubai's economic system is based largely on patronage, which has kept the local citizens pliant (only 15 percent of Dubai's 1.4 million residents are actually Emirati citizens). Like Singapore, it is an extremely orderly society, and there are no outlets for protest—even peaceful ones—against the government. Many of the founders of Dubai's first human rights organization are also employed by the government and are dependent on Sheikh Mohammed's largesse.

Freedom of speech is constitutionally "guaranteed," but it does not cover criticism of the government or anything deemed offensive to Islam. When it comes to government transparency, especially as it relates to the economy, the trend is moving in the wrong direction. A new media law makes tarnishing the UAE's reputation or economy a crime punishable by fines of up to 1 million dirhams (approximately $270,000). The government maintains a list of banned Web sites; the ban is enforced by state censorship of the Internet (users do not dial directly into the Web but go through a proxy server monitored by the state telecom monopoly). In compliance with the Arab League boycott, neither visitors nor residents can call Israel from landlines or cell phones—the 972 country code is blocked.

Sheikh Mohammed recently decreed that his twenty-five-year-old son, Sheikh Hamdan, would be crown prince; a younger son and a brother were named as his two deputies. There is no path for an Emirati equivalent of Erel Margalit to play a senior leadership role in government or run for office. Mohammed Al Gergawi himself is one of only 210,000 Emiratis in the entire country, and only people from this limited pool are eligible to serve in senior government positions or in leadership roles in the sheikh's businesses.

Other than its official leadership circles, Dubai is open to outsiders for business and has a centuries-old history as a trade hub for everything from pearls to textiles. Sheikh Mohammed's great-grandfather declared his city-state a tax-free port in the early part of the twentieth century. He wanted to attract Iranian and Indian merchants.

In the 1970s, Sheikh Mohammed's father, Rashid bin Saeed Al Maktoum, ordered the dredging of the Dubai Creek and built one of the planet's largest man-made harbors at Jebel Ali, twenty-two miles southwest of Dubai. By 1979, the Jebel Ali Port had become the Middle East's largest port and, according to some experts, ranked alongside the Great Wall of China and the Hoover Dam as the only three man-made constructions that can be seen from space. Jebel Ali is now the world's third-most-important reexport center (after Hong Kong and Singapore).

For Rashid, this liberal trade outlook was based on the reality that Dubai's economic wellspring would eventually dry up. With only .5 percent of the oil and gas reserves of neighboring Abu Dhabi, and an even tinier fraction of Saudi Arabia's, Dubai's reserves could run out as soon as 2010. As Sheikh Rashid once famously said, "My grandfather rode a camel, my father rode a camel, I drive a Mercedes, my son drives a Land Rover, his son will drive a Land Rover, but his son will ride a camel."

In addition to creating a world-class port, Sheikh Rashid also established the Middle East's first free-trade zone, which allowed foreigners to repatriate 100 percent of their capital and profits and allowed 100 percent foreign ownership of properties and businesses. This sidestepped the requirement in the UAE and much of the Arab world that all companies be majority-owned by a local national.

The royal family's next generation—led by Sheikh Mohammed—took the free-zone model even further, with the creation of business parks dedicated to specific industrial sectors. The first of these was Dubai Internet City (DIC), designed with the help of Arthur Andersen and McKinsey & Company.

DIC provided an ideal base for any technology company doing business in the Middle East, the Indian subcontinent, Africa, or the former Soviet republics—collectively a potential market of 1.8 billion people with a total GDP of $1.6 trillion. In no time 180 companies signed up as tenants, including Microsoft, Oracle, HP, IBM, Compaq, Dell, Siemens, Canon, Logica, and Sony Ericsson.

In one sense, DIC was a remarkable success: by 2006, one-quarter of the world's top five hundred companies had a presence in Dubai. Dubai then tried to replicate that success story, founding Dubai Healthcare City, Dubai Biotechnology and Research Park, Dubai Industrial City, Dubai Knowledge Village, Dubai Studio City, and Dubai Media City (where Reuters, CNN, Sony, Bertelsmann, CNBC, MBC, Arabian Radio Network, and other media companies all have a major presence).

DIC's director of marketing, Wadi Ahmed, a British citizen of Arab origin, explains, "We have made Porter's [cluster] theory a reality. If you bring all the companies from the same segment together...opportunities materialize. It's real-life networking. It is bringing the integrator together with the software developers. Our cluster includes six hundred companies working within two kilometers of each other.... Silicon Valley has some similarities but it is an area, not a single managed entity."[3]

It is true that Dubai had at first posted impressive growth rates and that it turned itself into an important commercial hub in a short time. But there was never any comparability between the number of start-ups in Israel and in Dubai, or the amount of venture capital Dubai has been able to attract compared to Israel, not to mention the number of new inventions and patents. So what makes Israel and Dubai different in this way?

Drill down a bit into what is going on in Dubai's Internet City, for example, and the answer begins to emerge. In DIC you will not find any R&D or new innovation-based companies. Dubai opened its doors to innovative global companies, and many have come. But they have come to spread innovations made elsewhere to a particular regional market. Dubai, therefore, has not created any thriving innovative clusters; rather, it has built large, successful service hubs. So when Mohammed Al Gergawi was handpicked by Sheikh Mohammed to help catalyze Dubai's economic miracle, the job was to grow and manage this exciting, but not necessarily innovation-generating, venture.

In Israel the story is different. Margalit is one of tens of thousands of serial entrepreneurs. No one picked him; he picked himself. All of his success came from creating innovative companies and hooking into a global venture and tech ecosystem that is constantly searching for new products and markets. And while the physical infrastructure that facilitated this process in Israel may have been inferior to Dubai's, the cultural infrastructure has proved to be vastly richer soil on which to cultivate innovation.

Attracting new members to a cluster by offering a less expensive way to do business might be sufficient to create a cluster, but not to sustain it. If price is a cluster's only competitive edge, some other country will always come along to do it more cheaply. The other qualitative elements—such as tight-knit communities whose members are committed to living and working and raising families in the cluster—are what contribute to sustainable growth. Crucially, a cluster's sense of shared commitment and destiny, which transcends day-to-day business rivalries, is not easy to manufacture.

The obstacles for Dubai, in this sense, are profound. Foreign nationals—European and Persian Gulf business adventurers or South Asian and Arab temporary laborers—are there to make money, period. Once they've done so, they have typically returned home or moved on to their next adventure. They have a transactional relationship with Dubai; they are not part of a tight-knit community, and they are not collectively laying roots or building anything new. They evaluate their standing and accomplishments vis-à-vis the communities in their home countries, not those in Dubai. Their emotional commitment and sense of rootedness lie elsewhere. This, we believe, is a fundamental obstacle to a fully functioning cluster, and it may also be an impediment to cultivating a high-growth entrepreneurial economy.

"If there is an Internet bubble in Israel, then Yossi Vardi is the bubble."[4] So says Google cofounder Sergey Brin, referring to Vardi's role in helping to rebuild Israel's Internet sector from the ashes of the global technology market crash of 2000. Vardi's name has become synonymous with the world of Israeli Internet start-ups. He is best known for ICQ, the Internet chat program founded by his son Arik Vardi and three pals when they were in their early twenties. Isaac Applbaum of The Westly Group says that ICQ—once the world's most popular chat program—was one of a handful of companies that "transformed technology forever," along with Netscape, Google, Apple, Microsoft, and Intel.

ICQ (a play on "I seek you") was introduced in November 1996, with seed funding from Vardi. It was the first program to allow Windows users to communicate with one another live. America Online (AOL) invented its own chat program, called Instant Messenger (AIM), at about the same time, but at first AOL's program was available only to its subscribers.

The Israeli program spread much faster than AOL's. By June 1997, close to half a year after ICQ's launch—when only 22 percent of American homes had Internet access—ICQ had over a million users. In six months the number of users had jumped to 5 million, and ten months later to 20 million. By the end of 1999, ICQ had a total of 50 million registered users, making it the largest international online service. ICQ became the most downloaded program in the history of CNET.com, with 230 million downloads.

Back in mid-1998, when ICQ hit about 12 million users, AOL bought the start-up for what at the time was the largest amount paid for an Israeli tech company: $407 million. (They wisely insisted on taking all cash instead of stock.)

Though Israel was already well into its high-tech swing by then, the ICQ sale was a national phenomenon. It inspired many more Israelis to become entrepreneurs. The founders, after all, were a group of young hippies. Exhibiting the common Israeli response to all forms of success, many figured, *If these guys did it, I can do it better.* Further, the sale was a source of national pride, like winning a gold medal in the world's technology Olympics. One local headline declared that Israel had become an Internet "superpower."[5]

Vardi invests in Internet start-ups because he believes in them. But his dogged focus on the Internet when almost everyone else was in either classic "Israeli" sectors, such as communications and security, or hot new areas, like cleantech and biotech, is not attributable just to profit calculation. For one, Israel is his cluster, and he is conscious of his status as an "insider" in this community—a community that he wants to succeed. And with that commitment, he is also conscious of his role in sustaining this sector through a dry spell. Investing with a personal as well as a national purpose has been called "profitable patriotism," and has been getting renewed attention of late.

More than a century ago, prominent banker J. P. Morgan almost single-handedly stabilized the U.S. economy during the Panic of 1907. At a time when there was no Federal Reserve, "Morgan was not only committing some of his own money but also organizing the entire financial community to join in the rescue," said Ron Chernow, a business historian and biographer.[6]

When the crisis of 2008 hit, Warren Buffett seemed to play a similar role, pumping $8 billion into Goldman Sachs and General Electric over just two weeks. As the panic deepened, Buffett knew that his decision to make massive investments might signal to the market that he, America's most respected investor, was not waiting for shares to plunge further and believed that the economy was not going to collapse.

Vardi's interventions are not on nearly as large a scale, of course, but even so, he has had an impact on the mix of Israeli start-ups by playing a leadership role in keeping the Internet segment of the pie afloat. His mere presence and steadfastness in a sector that everyone was writing off helped turn it around.

At the 2008 TechCrunch, an influential conference that singled out the fifty-one most promising start-ups in the world, *seven* of them were Israeli, and many of those had raised capital from Yossi Vardi. TechCrunch founder Michael Arrington is a strong supporter of Vardi's: "You [Israel] should build a statue of Yossi Vardi in Tel Aviv," he says.[7]

In the best-selling book *Built to Last*, business guru James Collins identifies several enduring business successes that all have one thing in common: a core purpose articulated in one or two sentences. "Core purpose," Collins writes, "is the organization's fundamental reason for being. [It] reflects the importance people attach to the company's work…beyond just making money." He lists fifteen examples of core purpose statements. All of them are by companies—including Wal-Mart, McKinsey, Disney, and Sony—with one exception: Israel. Collins describes Israel's core purpose as "to provide a secure place on Earth for the Jewish people." Building Israel's economy and participating in its cluster—which are interchangeable—and pitching it to the most far-flung places in the world are what in part motivates Israel's "profitable patriots."[8] As historian Barbara Tuchman observed before Israel's tech boom, "With all its problems, Israel has one commanding advantage: a sense of purpose. Israelis may not have affluence...or the quiet life. But they have what affluence tends to smother: a motive."[9]

The absence of motive is a problem in a number of the states of the Gulf Cooperation Council (GCC), which is composed of the UAE, Saudi Arabia, Bahrain, Kuwait, Qatar, and Oman. In the case of Dubai, one of the emirates in the UAE, most of the entrepreneurs that come from elsewhere are motivated by profit—which is important—but they are not also motivated by building the fabric of community in Dubai. And as we have seen in examining Michael Porter's cluster theory, a profit motive alone will get a national economy only so far. When economic times are difficult, as has been the case in Dubai since late 2008, or security becomes dicey, those not committed to building a home, a community, and a state are often the first to flee.

In the other GCC economies, the problem is somewhat different. In our travels throughout the Arabian Peninsula, we have seen firsthand how Saudi nationals—young and old—are proud of the economic and infrastructural modernization of their economy. Many Saudis have a tribal lineage that traces back centuries, and building an advanced economy that is recognized globally is a matter of tribal and national pride.

But all of these economies also face challenges that can stifle any potential for progress.

A number of business and government leaders throughout the Arab world have turned their attention to stimulating a high-growth entrepreneurial economy, and some have been quietly studying Israel. "How else are we going to create eighty million jobs in the next decade?" Riad al-Allawi asked us. Al-Allawi is a successful Jordanian entrepreneur who has done business all over the region. Eighty million is the number we kept hearing from experts during our travels to Arab capitals.

The Arab economies of North Africa (Egypt, Algeria, Morocco, and Tunisia), the Middle East (Lebanon, Syria, Palestine, Iraq, and Jordan), and the Persian Gulf (Saudi Arabia, the UAE, Qatar, Bahrain, Kuwait, and Oman) comprise approximately 225 million people, just over 3 percent of the world's population. And the total GDP of the Arab economies in 2007 was $1.3 trillion—almost two-fifths the size of China's economy. But wealth distribution varies widely: there are oil-rich economies with tiny populations (such as Qatar, with 1 million people and a per capita GDP of $73,100) and oil-poor economies with large, dense populations (such as Egypt, with 77 million people but a per capita GDP of just $1,700). Generalizations about development strategies for the region are risky since the sizes, structures, and natural resources of the Arab economies vary widely.

But even with all the differences, the unifying economic challenge for the Arab Muslim world is its own demographic time bomb: approximately 70 percent of the population is under twenty-five years old. Employing all of these people will require the creation of eighty million new jobs by 2020, as al-Allawi told us.[10] Meeting this goal means generating employment at twice the U.S. job growth rate during the boom decade of the 1990s. "The public sector isn't going to create these jobs; big companies aren't going to create these jobs," says Fadi Ghandour, a successful Jordanian entrepreneur. "The stability and future of the region is going to depend on our teaching our young people how to go out and create companies."[11]

But entrepreneurship has played only a negligible part in Arab world economies. Even before its economy imploded less than 4 percent of the UAE's adult population was working in early-stage or small enterprises. So what are the barriers to an Arab "start-up nation"? The answer includes oil, limits on political liberties, the status of women, and the quality of education.

The vast majority of the region's economic activity is driven by the production and refinement of hydrocarbons. The non-oil GDP exported by the entire Arab world—with a population of approximately 250 million people—is less than that of Finland, with a population of 5 million. Outside of oil, there are some successful multinationals, such as UAE-based Emirates Airlines, Egypt-based Orascom Telecom, and Jordan-based Aramex, a logistics support provider. (Orascom and Aramex were founded and built by savvy entrepreneurs.) Family-owned service businesses are also prominent and—in the case of countries like Egypt—textiles and agriculture, too. But the oil industry is by far the biggest contributor to the region's GDP. The region produces almost one-third of the world's oil and 15 percent of the world's gas.

There is an ever-increasing growth in demand for oil, with China and India the most prominent examples of countries that need more oil. Beginning in 1998, India and China's combined demand increased by a third in less than a decade. So however much the price of oil fluctuates, the demand is undergoing a global transformation.

But the Arab world's oil economy has stymied high-growth entrepreneurship. Distributing oil wealth largesse to the masses has insulated governments in the Persian Gulf from pressure to reform politically and economically. Oil wealth has cemented the power of autocratic governments, which do not have to collect taxes from their citizens and therefore do not need to be terribly responsive to their complaints. As historians of the Muslim world have put it, in Arab countries "the converse of a familiar dictum is true: No representation without taxation."[12]

The badly needed reforms that the elites regard as a threat—the right to free expression, tolerance of experimentation and failure, and access to basic government economic data—are necessary for a culture in which entrepreneurs and inventors can thrive. For precisely all the reasons that entrepreneurship helps economies grow and societies progress—it rewards merit, initiative, and results rather than status—the Persion Gulf governments have stifled it. This is what political scientist Samuel Huntington once called the "king's dilemma": all modernizing monarchs ultimately try to balance economic modernization with limits on liberalization, since liberalization challenges the monarch's power. In the Arab world, British journalist Chris Davidson, author of *Dubai: The Vulnerability of Success*, calls this the "sheikh's dilemma."

With the exception of Lebanon and Iraq, there has never been a genuinely free election in any of the other twenty-two Arab League countries. After one attempt at an election in the UAE in 2006 attracted low voter turnout, a prominent member of the government remarked, "This is particularly disappointing given that all of the candidates and participants were from very good families, and were all personally approved by the UAE's rulers."[13]

A number of Persian Gulf Arab governments have sought to work around the "sheikh's dilemma" by using oil wealth to modernize the hard infrastructure of their economies, while leaving the political structures virtually untouched. Income from the previous oil booms—in the 1970s—was not absorbed by the regional economies but, rather, spent on imports from the West, investments overseas, and military arms. The local economies saw little direct benefit. But since 2002, over $650 billion from this new—demand-driven—oil windfall have been reinvested in the gulf economies alone.

Alongside the cluster strategy adopted by Dubai and a number of other gulf Arab countries, much of the region's oil revenues have gone into real estate development. The GCC real estate sector has been the fastest growing in the world. Between 2000 and 2010, an estimated 19.55 million square yards of new leasable space—new office buildings, shopping malls, hotels, industrial facilities, and housing developments—will have been added in the region, mostly in Saudi Arabia and the UAE, growing at 20 percent annually during this period. (China's annual growth in leasable space was 15 percent.)

But as in much of the rest of the world, the Persian Gulf real estate bubble has burst. As of early 2009, residential and commercial values in Dubai, for example, have declined by 30 percent and are expected to plummet further. Home owners have actually been abandoning their homes and just leaving the country—to avoid the prospect of imprisonment for failure to pay a debt. Large-scale construction projects have been frozen.

Neither oil nor real estate nor clusters have built a high-growth entrepreneurial or innovation economy.

With the demographic time bomb ticking, the gulf's oil-rich governments have also tried to build academic research clusters. Every technology cluster has a collection of great educational institutions. Silicon Valley famously got its start in 1939 when William Hewlett and David Packard, two Stanford University engineering graduates, pooled their funds of $538 and founded Hewlett-Packard. Their mentor was a former Stanford professor, and they set up shop in a garage in nearby Palo Alto.

But the Arab world's cultural and social institutions, as was reported by a U.N.-sanctioned committee of Arab intellectuals, are chronically underdeveloped. The United Nations' Arab Human Development Report, which presented the organization's research from 2002 through 2005, found that the number of books translated annually into Arabic in all Arab countries combined was one-fifth the number translated into Greek in Greece. The number of patents registered between 1980 and 2000 from Saudi Arabia was 171; from Egypt, 77; from Kuwait, 52; from the United Arab Emirates, 32; from Syria, 20; and from Jordan, 15—compared with 7,652 from Israel. The Arab world has the highest illiteracy rates globally and one of the lowest numbers of active research scientists with frequently cited articles. In 2003, China published a list of the five hundred best universities in the world; it did not include a single mention of the more than two hundred universities in the Arab world.[14]

Recognizing the importance of universities for R&D, which is necessary for patents and innovation, Saudi Arabia is opening the King Abdullah University of Science and Technology, to create a research home for twenty thousand faculty and staff members and students. It will be the first university in Saudi Arabia to have male and female students in the same classes. Qatar and the UAE have established partnerships with iconic Western academic institutions. Qatar's Education City houses satellite campuses for Weill Cornell Medical College, Carnegie Mellon University's computer science and business administration programs, a Georgetown University international relations program, and a Northwestern University journalism program. Abu Dhabi—one of the seven emirates in the UAE—has established a satellite campus for New York University. The idea is that if Arab countries can attract the most innovative researchers from around the world, it will help stimulate an innovation culture locally.

But these new institutions have not made much progress. They cannot recruit a reliable stable of foreign academic talent to lay roots and make a long-term commitment to the Arab world. "It has been more about bringing education brands to the gulf than immigrating and assimilating brains," Chris Davidson told us. "These universities are focused on national reputation building, not real innovation."[15]

Israel's case was different. Top-notch universities were founded well before there even was a state. Professor Chaim Weizmann, a world-renowned chemist who helped launch the field of biotechnology with his invention of a novel method of producing acetone, commented on this oddity at the inauguration of the Hebrew

University of Jerusalem on July 24, 1918: "It seems at first sight paradoxical that in a land with so sparse a population, in a land where everything still remains to be done, in a land crying out for such simple things as ploughs, roads, and harbours, we should begin by creating a centre of spiritual and intellectual development."[16]

The Hebrew University's first board of governors included Weizmann, Israel's first president, as well as Albert Einstein, Sigmund Freud, and Martin Buber. The Technion was founded in 1912 and opened its doors in 1924. The Weizmann Institute of Science followed in 1934 and, in 1956, Tel Aviv University—the largest university in Israel today. Thus by the late 1950s, Israel's population was only around the two million mark and the country already had the seeds of four world-class universities. Other major universities, such as Bar-Ilan University, University of Haifa, and Ben-Gurion University of the Negev, were founded in 1955, 1963, and 1969, respectively.

Today, Israel has eight universities and twenty-seven colleges. Four of them are in the top 150 worldwide universities and seven are in the top 100 Asia Pacific universities. None of them are satellite campuses from abroad. Israeli research institutions were also the first in the world to commercialize academic discoveries.

In 1959 the Weizmann Institute established Yeda ("knowledge" in Hebrew) to market its research. Yeda has since spawned thousands of successful medical technology products and companies. Between 2001 and 2004, the institute amassed one billion shekels (more than $200 million) in royalty revenues. By 2006, Yeda was ranked first in income royalties among world academic institutes.[17]

Several years after the creation of Yeda, the Hebrew University founded its own technology transfer company, called Yissum (a word for "implementation" in Hebrew). Yissum earns over $1 billion annually in sales of Hebrew University–based research and has registered 5,500 patents and 1,600 inventions. Two-thirds of its 2007 inventions were in biotechnology, a tenth were in agricultural technology, and another tenth were in computer science and engineering products. The research has been sold to Johnson & Johnson, IBM, Intel, Nestlé, Lucent Technologies, and many other multinational companies. Overall, Yissum was recently ranked twelfth—after ten American universities and one British university—in global biotech patent rankings (Tel Aviv University is ranked twenty-first).

Israel, a nation of immigrants, has continually been dependent on successive waves of immigration to grow its economy. It is in large part thanks to these immigrants that Israel currently has more engineers and scientists per capita than any other country and produces more scientific papers per capita than any other nation—109 per 10,000 people.[18] Jewish newcomers and their non-Jewish family members are readily granted residency, citizenship, and benefits. Israel is universally regarded as highly entrepreneurial and—like the IDF—dismissive of the strictures of hierarchy.

In the Persian Gulf, however, governments will allow residency visas for only up to three years, nothing longer—even for fellow Muslims and Arabs. There is no path to citizenship in these countries. So globally sought-after researchers have been unwilling to relocate their families in meaningful numbers and invest their careers in an institution whose host country stifles free speech, academic freedom, and government transparency and puts a time limit on residency. While five- or ten-year residency visas have been considered in several gulf Arab countries, no government has ever ultimately allowed for them.

These residency restrictions are also symptomatic of a larger obstacle to attracting academics: the few research professionals who have shown up quickly became aware of the government's desire to keep them on the outskirts. The laws emanate from the pressure on governments to be responsive to Arab nationalism broadly, and sovereign nationalism specifically. For example, an Emirati woman who marries an expat must give up her citizenship, and their children will not be issued a UAE passport or any of the government's welfare benefits.

One of the major challenges to a high-growth entrepreneurial culture elsewhere in the Arab world—beyond just the gulf—is that the teaching models in primary and secondary schools and even the universities are focused on rote memorization. According to Hassan Bealaway, an adviser to the Egyptian Ministry of Education, learning is more about systems, standards, and deference rather than experimentation. It is much more the *Columbia* model than the *Apollo*.

This emphasis on standardization has shaped an education policy that defines success by measuring inputs rather than outcomes. For example, according to a study produced by the Persian Gulf offices of McKinsey & Company, Arab governments have been consumed with the number of teachers and investments in infrastructure—buildings and now computers—in hopes of improving their students' performance. But the results of the recent Trends in International Mathematics and Science Study ranked Saudi students forty-third out of forty-five (Saudi Arabia was even behind Botswana, which was forty-second).[19]

While the average student-teacher ratio in the GCC is 12 to 1—one of the world's lowest, comparing favorably with an average of 17 to 1 in OECD countries—it has had no real positive effect. Unfortunately, international evidence suggests that low student-teacher ratios correlate poorly with strong student performance and are far less important than the quality of the teachers. But the education ministries in most Arab countries do not measure teacher performance. Inputs are easier to measure, through a methodology of standardization.

Focusing on the number of teachers has particularly harmful implications for boys in the Arab world. Many government schools are segregated by gender: boys are taught by men, girls by women. Since teaching positions have traditionally been less appealing to men, there is a shortage of teachers for boys. As a result of the smaller talent pool, boys' schools often employ lower-quality teachers. In fact, the GCC gender gap in student performance is among the most extreme in the world.

Finally, a perhaps even larger factor in the limit on high-growth entrepreneurial economies is the role of women. Harvard University's David Landes, author of the seminal book *The Wealth and Poverty of Nations*, argues that the best barometer of an economy's growth potential lies in the legal rights and status of its women. "To deny women is to deprive a country of labor and talent... [and] *to undermine the drive to achievement of boys and men*," he writes. Landes believes that nothing is more dilutive to drive and ambition than a sense of entitlement. Every society has elites, and a number of them were born into their upper-echelon status. But there is no more widely dispersed sense of entitlement than ingraining in the minds of half the population that they are superior, which, he argues, reduces their "need to learn and do." This kind of distortion makes an economy inherently uncompetitive, and it is the result of the subordinated economic status of women in the Arab world.[20]

The economy of Israel and many of those in the Arab world are living laboratories for the economic theory of clusters and, more broadly, what it takes for nations to generate—or stifle—innovation. The contrast between the two models demonstrates that a simplistic view of clusters—one that maintains that a collection of institutions can be mechanically assembled and out will pop a Silicon Valley—is flawed. Moreover, it seems that a stake in the country, Tuchman's "motive," provides an essential glue that helps encourage entrepreneurs to build and take risks.

# CHAPTER 14

# Threats to the Economic Miracle

*We're using fewer and fewer of the cylinders to move
this machine forward.*

—DAN BEN-DAVID

THE ISRAELI ECONOMY is still in its infancy. The start-up scene
that seems so established today was born at roughly the same
time as the Internet economy itself, just over a decade ago. The
dawn of Israel's tech boom coincided not only with a global surge
in information technology but with the American tech-stock
bubble, the jump-starting of Israel's venture capital industry
through the Yozma program, the massive wave of immigration
from the former Soviet Union, and the 1993 Oslo peace accords,
bringing what seemed to be the prospect of peace and stability.
What if Israel's economic miracle were simply built on a rare con-
fluence of events and would disappear under less favorable circumstances? Even if Israel's new economy is not just the product of
happenstance, what are the real threats to Israel's long-term economic success?

One need not speculate about what would happen if the positive factors that launched Israel's tech boom in the late 1990s were to disappear. Most of them have.

In 2000, the tech-stock bubble burst. In 2001, the Oslo peace process crumbled, as a wave of suicide bombings in Israel's cities temporarily wiped out the tourism industry and contributed to an economic recession. And the massive flow of immigrants from the former Soviet Union, which swelled the Jewish population of the country by one-fifth, exhausted itself by the end of the 1990s.

These negative developments happened about as rapidly and simultaneously as their positive counterparts had just a few years earlier. And yet the new state of affairs didn't bring an end to the boom that was only about five years old. From 1996 to 2000, Israeli technology exports more than doubled, from $5.5 billion to $13 billion. When the tech bubble burst, exports dropped slightly, to a low of less than $11 billion in 2002 and 2003, but then surged again to almost $18.1 billion in 2008. In other words, Israel's technology engine was barely slowed by the multiple hits it took between 2000 and 2004 and managed not just to recover but to exceed the 2000 boom level of exports by almost 40 percent in 2008.

A similar picture can be seen in venture capital funding. When the VC bubble burst in 2000, investments in Israel dropped dramatically. But Israel's market share of the global VC flow increased from 15 to 30 percent over the next three years, even as the Israeli economy came under increasing stress.

Israel may not, however, fare as well in the current global economic slowdown, which, unlike that of 2000, is not limited to international tech stocks and venture capital funding but is being dramatically felt in the global banking system as well.

That said, the breakdown in international finance has infected almost every nation's banking system, with two notable exceptions: neither Canada nor Israel has faced a single bank failure. Since Israel's hyperinflation and banking crisis of the early 1980s—which culminated in 1985 with the trilateral intervention of the Israeli and U.S. governments and the IMF—tight restrictions have been in place. Israel's financial institutions adhere to conservative lending policies, typically leveraged 5 to 1. U.S. banks, on the other hand— precrisis—were leveraged at 26 to 1, and some European banks at a staggering 61 to 1. There were no subprime mortgages in Israel, and a secondary mortgage market never came into existence. If anything, a shortage of financing—even before the crisis—for small businesses in Israel drove even more people into the technology sector, where taxes and regulations were more friendly and venture capital was available.

As Israeli financial analyst Eytan Avriel put it, "Israeli banks were horse-drawn carts and U.S. banks were racing cars. But those racing cars crashed badly whereas the carts traveled more slowly and stayed on course."[1]

This is the good news for Israel. Yet while Israel's economy was not exposed to bad lending practices or complex credit products, it may be overexposed to venture finance, which could soon be in scarce supply. Venture capital firms are funded largely by institutional investors such as pension funds, endowments, and sovereign wealth funds. These investors set aside a specific allocation for what are called alternative investments (venture capital, private equity, hedge funds), typically in the range of 3 to 5 percent of their overall portfolios. But as the dollar value of their public equity (stock market) allocations has shrunk—due in large measure to crashing markets globally—it has shrunk the absolute dollar amount available for alternative investments. The overall pie has been downsized, reducing available funds for venture capital investments.

A diminished supply of venture capital dollars could mean less "innovation finance" for Israel's economy. Thousands of workers in Israel's tech scene have already lost their jobs, and many tech companies have shifted to four-day workweeks to avoid further layoffs.[2]

In the absence of new financing, many Israeli start-ups have been forced to close.

In addition to an overdependence on global venture capital, Israeli companies are also overdependent on export markets. Over half of Israel's GDP comes from exports to Europe, North America, and Asia. When those economies slow down or collapse, Israeli start-ups have fewer customers. Because of the Arab boycott, Israel does not have access to most regional markets. And the domestic market is far too small to serve as a substitute.

Israeli companies will also find it harder to negotiate exits—like Given Imaging's IPO on the NASDAQ or Fraud Sciences' sale to PayPal—which are often the means by which Israeli entrepreneurs and investors ultimately make their money. A global slowdown will coincide with fewer IPOs and acquisitions.

And a continued deterioration of the regional security situation could also threaten Israel's economic success. In 2006 and at the turn of 2008 to 2009, Israel fought wars against two groups trained and funded by Iran. While these wars had little effect on the Israeli economy, and Israeli companies have become adept at upholding their commitments to customers and investors regardless of security threats large and small, the next iteration of the Iranian threat could be different from anything Israel has ever experienced.

Iran, as is widely reported by international regulatory bodies and news organizations, is in pursuit of a nuclear capability. If the Iranian government establishes a nuclear-weaponization program, it could spark a nuclear arms race throughout the Arab world. This could freeze foreign investment in the region.

While much of the international focus is on the potential threat of an Iranian nuclear missile strike on Israel, the political and security leadership of Israel warns against the effect of an Iranian nuclear capability on the region even if it is never directly used. As Prime Minister Benjamin Netanyahu told us, "The first-stage Iranian goal is to terrify Israel's most talented citizens into leaving."[3]

Clearly, if the Iranian threat is not somehow addressed, the Israeli economy could be affected. So far, however, the presence or potential of such threats has not deterred foreign companies and venture funds from increasing their investments in Israel.

Indeed, when it comes to threats to the economy, discussion within Israel centers more on domestic factors. Maybe because Israel has inoculated itself against security threats to its economy in the past, or maybe because the prospect of a nuclear threat is too grave to ponder, Tel Aviv University economist Dan Ben-David is fixated on another threat—the "brain drain" from the faculties of Israeli universities.

To be sure, Israel is a leader in the international academic community. A global 2008 survey by *Scientist* magazine named two Israeli institutions—the Weizmann Institute and the Hebrew University of Jerusalem—as the top two "best places to work in academia" outside the United States.[4]

Economist Dan Ben-David pointed us to a study by two French academics that ranks nations outside the United States according to publications in top economic journals between 1971 and 2000. The United Kingdom—including the London School of Economics, Oxford, and Cambridge—came in at number two. Germany had fewer than half as many publications per faculty member as the British had. And Israel was number one. "Not five or ten percent more, but seven times more—in a league of our own," Ben-David crowed to us. "And as good as Israel's economists are, our computer scientists are apparently even better, relative to their field. We have two Nobel Prizes recently in economics, and one or two in chemistry."[5]

But despite all this success, Ben-David is worried. He told us that Israel's academic lead has lessened in recent years, and will fall further as older faculty members retire and many of the rising stars leave to teach abroad. In his own field, economics, Ben-David pointed to a study that found that of the top thousand economists in the world, as measured by citations of their work between 1990 and 2000, twenty-five were Israelis, thirteen of whom were actually based in Israel. Since that study was published, only four of these have remained in Israel full-time. And none of the twelve Israelis working abroad in 2000 have returned to Israel. In total, an estimated three thousand tenured Israeli professors have relocated to universities abroad.

Ben-David is one of those four top economists who remain in Israel. And he is sounding the alarm on Israel's continued economic growth. From 2005 through 2008, Israel grew substantially faster than most developed countries. But there was a recession the previous few years so, Ben-David argues, "all we've done is return to the long-term path. We're not in uncharted territory; we are where we should have been had we not had the recession."

The problem, according to Ben-David, is that while the tech sector has been surging ahead and becoming more productive, the rest of the economy has not been keeping up. "It's like an engine," he says. "You have all the cylinders in the engine. You have all the population in the country. But we're using fewer and fewer of the cylinders to move this machine forward." In essence, the tech sector is financing the rest of the country, which is "not getting the tools or the conditions to work in a modern economy."

This underutilization brings us to what we believe is the biggest threat to Israel's continued economic growth: low participation in the economy. A little over half of Israel's workforce contributes to the economy in a productive way, compared to a 65 percent rate in the United States. The low Israeli workforce participation rate is chiefly attributable to two minority communities: *haredim*, or ultra-Orthodox Jews, and Israeli Arabs.[6]

Among mainstream Israeli Jewish civilians aged twenty-five to sixty-four, to take one metric, 84 percent of men and 75 percent of women are employed. Among Arab women and *haredi* men, these percentages are almost flipped: 79 percent and 73 percent, respectively, are *not* employed.[7]

The ultra-Orthodox, or *haredim*, generally do not serve in the military. Indeed, to qualify for the exemption from military service, *haredim* have to show that they are engaged in full-time study in Jewish seminaries (yeshivot). This arrangement was created by David Ben-Gurion to obtain *haredi* political support at the time of Israel's founding. But while the "yeshiva exemption" first applied to just four hundred students, it has since ballooned to tens of thousands who go to yeshiva instead of the army.

The result of this has been triply harmful to the economy. *Haredim* are socially isolated from the workforce because of their lack of army experience; plus, since they are not *allowed* to work if they want a military exemption—they have to be studying—as young adults they receive neither private-sector nor military (entrepreneurial) experience; and thus *haredi* society becomes increasingly dependent on government welfare payments for survival.

There are two primary reasons why Israeli Arabs have low participation rates in the economy. First, because they are not drafted into the army, they, like the *haredim*, are less likely to develop the entrepreneurial and improvisational skills that the IDF inculcates. Second, they also do not develop the business networks that young Israeli Jews build while serving in the military, a disparity that exacerbates an already long-standing cultural divide between the country's Jewish and Arab communities.

Each year, thousands of Arab students graduate from Israel's technology and engineering schools. Yet, according to Helmi Kittani and Hanoch Marmari, who codirect the Center for Jewish-Arab Economic Development, "only a few manage to find jobs which reflect their training and skills....Israel's Arab graduates need to be equipped with a crucial resource which the government cannot supply: a network of friends in the right places."[8] And in the absence of those personal connections, Israeli Jews' mistrust of Israeli Arabs is more likely to hold sway.

Another problem is the bias within the Israeli Arab community against women in the workplace. A 2008 study by Women Against Violence, an Israeli Arab organization, found that public opinion among local Arabs may be slowly changing, but traditional attitudes are still entrenched. In a survey, even participants who "opposed older attitudes" still agreed with the statement "Arab society is predominantly patriarchal, where men are perceived as the decision-makers and women as inferior and ideally subservient....A man who treats his partner other than [according to] the acceptable norm endangers his social standing."

Despite this paradox, Women Against Violence director Aida Touma-Suleiman said that she sees men as partners for change, including a new acceptance of women who work outside the home. "There are Arab men who are unhappy with this balance of power, and wish to improve the relations between the genders. They see it as in their interest as much as anyone else's," she said.[9]

Yet because of the high birth rates in both the *haredi* and the Arab sectors, efforts to increase workforce participation in these sectors are racing against the demographic clock. According to *Israel 2028*, the report issued by an official blue-ribbon commission, the *haredi* and Arab sectors are projected to increase from 29 percent of Israel's total population in 2007 to 39 percent by 2028. Without dramatic changes in workforce patterns, this shift will reduce labor-force participation rates even further. "The existing trends are working in stark opposition to the desired development," the report warns.[10]

As he was campaigning to return to the premiership, Bibi Netanyahu made getting Israel to number among the top ten largest (per capita) economies in the world a centerpiece of his agenda. An independent think tank, the Reut Institute, has been pursuing a similar campaign called Israel 15. Gidi Grinstein, the founding president of Reut, was an adviser to former prime minister and current defense minister Ehud Barak, who had been a political rival of Netanyahu's. Yet Grinstein agrees with Netanyahu that Israel's goal should be not just to keep up with advanced nations but to rise to rank among the top nations as measured by GDP per capita.

As Grinstein sees it, "This challenge is not a luxury, it's a necessity." At a minimum, Israel must grow 4 percent per capita for a decade, he believes; the current gap in living standards between Israel and other developed countries is dangerous. He says, "Our business sector is among the world's best, and our population is rich in skills and education. At the same time, the quality of life and the quality of public services in Israel are low, and for many, emigration is an opportunity to improve their lot."[11]

This may be overstated, since record numbers of Israeli expatriates have recently been returning from the United States and other countries, in part due to a newly enacted ten-year tax holiday on foreign income for such returnees. And, of course, other factors besides income enter into "quality of life" decisions.

But the point that Israel can, should, and must grow its economy faster is crucial. Of all the threats and challenges facing Israel, an inability to keep the economy growing is perhaps the greatest, since it involves overcoming political obstacles and giving attention to neglected problems. Israel has a rare, maybe unique, cultural and institutional foundation that generates both innovation and entrepreneurship; what it lacks are policy fixes to further amplify and spread these assets within Israeli society. Fortunately for Israel, it is probably easier to change policies than it is to change a culture, as countries like Singapore demonstrate. As the *New York Times'* Thomas Friedman put it, "I would much rather have Israel's problems, which are mostly financial, mostly about governance, and mostly about infrastructure, rather than Singapore's problem because Singapore's problem is culture-bound."[12]

# Conclusion

## Farmers of High Tech

*The most careful thing is to dare.*

—SHIMON PERES

As we waited in one of the anterooms of the President's House, we were not sure how much time we would get with President Shimon Peres. At eighty-five, Peres is the last member of the founding generation still in high office. Peres began his career as a twenty-five-year-old sidekick to David Ben-Gurion and went on to serve in almost every ministerial post, including two stints as prime minister. He also picked up a Nobel Peace Prize along the way.

Abroad, he is one of the most admired Israelis. At home, his reputation is more controversial. Peres is known primarily as the father of the 1993 Oslo accords, which were famously instituted with a handshake between Yitzhak Rabin and Yasir Arafat in the presence of Bill Clinton on the White House lawn, but which came to symbolize, to many Israelis, false hopes, terrorism, and war.

It is hard to exaggerate Peres's impact on Israel's diplomacy, but this is not what we were primarily interested in talking to him about. Less well known, but no less significant, was his role as a serial entrepreneur of a very unique sort—a founder of industries. He never spent a day of his life in business. In fact, he told us that neither he nor Ben-Gurion knew anything about economics. But Peres's approach to government has been one of an entrepreneur launching start-ups.

Peres grew up on a kibbutz before the founding of the state. It wasn't just the social and economic structure of this Israeli invention that was innovative; its very means of sustenance represented a huge departure. "Agriculture is more revolutionary than industry," Peres was quick to point out as we finally settled into his book-lined office, surrounded by mementos from Ben-Gurion and world leaders.

"In twenty-five years, Israel increased its agricultural yields seventeen times. This is amazing," he told us. People don't realize this, Peres said, but agriculture is "ninety-five percent science, five percent work."

Peres seemed to see technology everywhere, and long before Israelis themselves thought in such terms. This may have been one of the reasons Ben-Gurion backed Peres so strongly; the "Old Man" was also fascinated by technology, he told us. "Ben-Gurion thought the future was science. He would always say that in the army it's not enough to be up to date; you have to be up to tomorrow," Peres recalled.

So Ben-Gurion and Peres became a technological tag team. Peres and American swashbuckler Al Schwimmer started dreaming up an aeronautics industry while flying over the Arctic in 1951. But when they got back to Israel, they were met with stiff opposition. "We can't even make bicycles," ministers told Peres, in days in which a nascent bicycle industry was indeed failing, refugees were continuing to flood into the country, and basic foodstuffs were still being rationed. But with Ben-Gurion's backing, Peres was able to prevail.

Later on, Peres's idea of starting a nuclear industry was similarly written off. It was seen as too ambitious, even by Israeli scientists in the field. The finance minister, who believed that the Israeli economy should focus on textile exports, told Peres, "It's very good you came to me. I shall make sure you won't get a penny." So with typical disregard for the rules, Ben-Gurion and Peres somehow funded the project off-budget and Peres went around the established scientists, turning instead to students at the Technion, some of whom he sent to France for training.

The result was the nuclear reactor near Dimona, which has operated since the early 1960s without mishap and has reportedly made Israel a nuclear power. As of 2005, Israel was the world's tenth-largest producer of nuclear patents.[1]

But Peres didn't stop there. As deputy minister of defense, he pumped money into defense R&D, to the dismay of the military leadership, which, perhaps understandably, was more concerned about chronic shortages of weapons, training, and manpower.

Today, Israel leads the world in the percentage of its GDP that goes to research and development, creating both a technological edge critical to national security and a civilian tech sector that is the main engine of the economy. The key, however, is the way the entrepreneurial nation building Peres embodies has morphed into a national condition of entrepreneurship.

This transformation was not easy, planned, or foreseen. It came later than Israelis would have liked—there was a "lost decade" of low growth and hyperinflation between the founders' era of high growth and the current era of high tech. But it came, and a thread runs through the founders' time of draining swamps and growing oranges to today's era of start-ups and chip designers.

Today's entrepreneurs feel the tug of this thread. While the founders' milieu was socialist and frowned on profit, now "there's a legitimate way to make a profit because you're inventing something," says Erel Margalit, one of Israel's top entrepreneurs. "You're not just trading in goods, or you're not just a finance person. You are doing something for humanity. You are inventing a new drug or a new chip. You feel like a *falah* ["farmer" in Arabic], a farmer of high tech. You dress down. You're with your buddies from the army unit. You talk about a way of life—not necessarily about how much money you're going to make, though it's obviously also about that." For Margalit, innovation and technology are the twenty-first-century version of going back to the land. "The new pioneering, Zionist narrative is about creating things," he says.

Indeed, what makes the current Israeli blend so powerful is that it is a mashup of the founders' patriotism, drive, and constant consciousness of scarcity and adversity and the curiosity and restlessness that have deep roots in Israeli and Jewish history. "The greatest contribution of the Jewish people in history is dissatisfaction," Peres explained. "That's poor for politics but good for science.

"All the time you want to change and change," Peres said, speaking of both the Jewish and the Israeli condition. Echoing what we heard from almost every IDF officer we interviewed, Peres said, "Every technology that arrives in Israel from America, it comes to the army and in five minutes, they change it." But the same thing goes on outside the IDF—an insatiable need to tinker, invent, and challenge.

This theme can be traced to the very idea of Israel's founding. The modern state's founders—or national *entrepreneurs*—were building what might be called the first "start-up nation" in history.

Many other nations, of course, have emerged from scratch, at the stroke of a departing colonial power's pen. Neighboring Jordan, for example, was created in 1921 by Winston Churchill, who decided to hand the Hashemite clan a kingdom.

Other countries, like the United States, were the product of a truly entrepreneurial or revolutionary process, rather than a national amalgamation that had accrued slowly over centuries, such as England, France, and Germany. None, however, were the result of such a conscious effort to build from scratch a modern reincarnation of an ancient nation-state.

Some modern countries, of course, can trace their heritage back to ancient empires: Italy to the Romans, Greece to the Greeks, and China and India to peoples who lived in those areas for thousands of years. But in all these other cases, either the original commonalty continued in an unbroken chain from the ancient generations to the modern one, without ever completely losing control of its territory, or the ancient people simply disappeared, never to be heard from again. Only Israel's founders had the temerity to try to start up a modern first-world country in the region from which their ancestors had been exiled two thousand years earlier.

So what is the answer to the central question of this book: What makes Israel so innovative and entrepreneurial? The most obvious explanation lies in a classic cluster of the type Harvard professor Michael Porter has championed, Silicon Valley embodies, and Dubai has tried to create. It consists of the tight proximity of great universities, large companies, start-ups, and the ecosystem that connects them—including everything from suppliers, an engineering talent pool, and venture capital. Part of this more visible part of the cluster is the role of the military in pumping R&D funds into cutting-edge systems and elite technological units, and the spillover from this substantial investment, both in technologies and human resources, into the civilian economy.

But this outside layer does not fully explain Israel's success. Singapore has a strong educational system. Korea has conscription and has been facing a massive security threat for its entire existence. Finland, Sweden, Denmark, and Ireland are relatively small countries with advanced technology and excellent infrastructure; they have produced lots of patents and reaped robust economic growth. Some of these countries have grown faster for longer than Israel has and enjoy higher standards of living, but none of them have produced anywhere near the number of start-ups or have attracted similarly high levels of venture capital investments.

Antti Vilpponen is a Finnish entrepreneur who helped found a "start-up movement" called ArcticStartup. Finland is home to one of the great technology companies of the world, Nokia, the cell phone maker. Israelis often look to Finland and ask themselves, "Where's our Nokia?" They want to know why Israel hasn't produced a technology company as large and successful as Nokia. But when we asked Vilpponen about the start-up scene in Finland, he lamented, "Finns produce lots of technology patents but we have failed to capitalize on them in the form of start-ups. The initial investment in Finland into a start-up is around three hundred thousand euros, while it's almost ten times higher in Israel. Israel also produces ten times more start-ups than Finland and the turnover of these start-ups is shorter and faster. I'm sure we'll see a lot of growth, but so far we're way behind Israel and the U.S. in developing a start-up culture."[2]

While the high turnover of start-ups concerns Israelis, Vilpponen sees them as an asset. What is clear is that Israel has something that's sought by other countries—even countries that are considered on the forefront of global competitiveness. In addition to the institutional elements that make up clusters—which Finland, Singapore, and Korea already possess—what's missing in these other countries is a cultural core built on a rich stew of aggressiveness and team orientation, on isolation and connectedness, and on being small and aiming big.

Quantifying that hidden, cultural part of an economy is no easy feat, but a study by professors comparing the cultures of fifty-three countries captured part of it. The study tried to categorize countries according to three parameters that particularly affect the workplace: Are they more hierarchical or more egalitarian, more assertive or more nurturing, more individualist or more collectivist?[3]

The study found in Israel a relatively unusual combination of cultural attributes. One might expect that a country like Israel, where people are considered individualistic, would accordingly be less nurturing. Personal ambition might be expected to conflict with teamwork. And one would also anticipate that such a type A–driven society would be more hierarchical. In fact, Israel scored high on egalitarianism, nurturing, and individualism. If Israelis are competitive and aggressive, how can they be "nurturing"? If they are so individualistic, how does that reconcile with the lack of hierarchies and "flatness"?

In Israel, the seemingly contradictory attributes of being both driven and "flat," both ambitious and collectivist make sense when you throw in the experience that so many Israelis go through in the military. There they learn that you must complete your mission, but that the only way to do that is as a team. The battle cry is "After me": there is no leadership without personal example and without inspiring your team to charge together and with you. There is no leaving anyone behind. You have minimal guidance from the top and are expected to improvise, even if this means breaking some rules. If you're a junior officer, you call your higher-ups by their first names, and if you see them doing something wrong, you say so.

If you stood out in high school for your leadership skills, scientific test scores, or both, you will be snapped up by one of the IDF's elite units, which will turbocharge your skills with intensive training and the most challenging possible on-the-job experience. In combat, you will be given command of dozens of people and millions of dollars' worth of equipment and be expected to make split-second life-and-death decisions. In the elite technology units, you will be put in charge of development projects for cutting-edge systems, giving you experience that someone twice your age in the private sector might not have.

And when you complete your military service, everything you need to launch a start-up will be a phone call away, if you have the right idea. Everyone knows someone in his or her family, university, or army orbit who is an entrepreneur or understands how to help. Everyone is reachable by cell phone or e-mail. Cold-calling is acceptable but almost never fully cold; almost everyone can find some connection to whomever he or she needs to contact to get started. As Yossi Vardi told us, "Everybody knows everybody."

Most importantly, launching a start-up or going into high tech has become the most respected and "normal" thing for an ambitious young Israeli to do. Like the stereotypical Jewish mother, an Israeli mother might be satisfied with a child who becomes a doctor or a lawyer, but she will be at least as proud of her son or daughter "the entrepreneur." What in most countries is somewhat exceptional in Israel has become an almost standard career track, despite the fact that everyone knows that, even in Israel, the chances of success for start-ups are low. It's okay to try and to fail. Success is best, but failure is not a stigma; it's an important experience for your résumé.

The secret, then, of Israel's success is the combination of classic elements of technology clusters with some unique Israeli elements that enhance the skills and experience of individuals, make them work together more effectively as teams, and provide tight and readily available connections within an established and growing community. For outside observers, this raises a question: If the Israeli "secret sauce" is so unique to Israel, what can other countries learn from it?

Luckily, while innovation is scarce, it is also a renewable resource. Unlike finite natural resources, ideas can spread and benefit whichever countries are best positioned to take advantage of them, regardless of where they were invented. George Bernard Shaw wrote, "If you have an apple and I have an apple and we exchange apples, then you and I will still each have one apple. But if you have an idea and I have an idea and we exchange these ideas, then each of us will have two ideas."[4]

While innovation is in principle an unlimited resource, and one that spreads on its own, almost every company wants to obtain the maximum benefit from this process. The world's major companies learned long ago that the simplest way to benefit from Israeli innovations is to buy an Israeli start-up, set up an Israeli R&D center, or both. With our increasingly global world and the movement toward open sourcing, there is little need for multinational companies to try to duplicate the business environments of countries that have a comparative advantage in manufacturing, innovation, or regional market access.

That said, most major companies understand that in a global market where change is the only constant, innovation is one of the foundations of long-term competitiveness. Further, while it is possible for countries and companies to take advantage of innovation that originates elsewhere, there are also corporate and national advantages to being the source of innovation.

For this purpose, it may be possible to simulate an "Israeli" environment. Intel Israel's Dov Frohman, for example, found it necessary to do this even in Israel itself. His original guiding slogan for Intel Israel was that it would be "the last Intel plant to close in a crisis." When his employees found this description to be too negative, he changed his slogan to "survival through success"—meaning that the goal was success but the motivation was survival, which could never be taken for granted. For Frohman, the key to the success of a large company was "maintaining the atmosphere of a precarious start-up."[5]

Further, while other democracies have no reason to institute a military draft like Israel's, a mandatory or voluntary national service program that is sufficiently challenging could give young college-age people—before they begin college—something like the leadership, teamwork, and mission-oriented skills and experience Israelis receive through military service. Such a program would also increase social solidarity and help inculcate the value of serving something larger than oneself, whether a family, a community, a company, or a nation. And when U.S. military men and women, for example, are transitioning to civilian life, they should not be advised to deemphasize their military experience when applying for a job.

For any nation and, indeed, for the world, the stakes of increasing innovation are tremendous. Paul Romer, considered one of the leading economists of "new growth theory," points out that the average annual growth rate of the United States between 1870 and 1992 was 1.8 percent—about half a percent higher than in the United Kingdom. He believes that this competitive edge has been maintained by America's "historical precedent for creating institutions which lead to better innovation."[6] Romer suggests that subsidizing graduate and undergraduate studies in science and engineering could boost economic growth. In addition, a system of "portable fellowships," which students could bring to any institution, would encourage lab directors and professors to compete over meeting the research and career needs of students, not just their own.

Romer points out that the biggest leaps in growth and productivity were produced by "meta-ideas" that increased the generation and spread of ideas. Patents and copyrights were a critical meta-idea invented by the British in the seventeenth century, while Americans introduced the modern research university in the nineteenth century and the peer-reviewed competitive research grant system in the twentieth century.

"We do not know what the next major idea about how to support ideas will be. Nor do we know where it will emerge," writes

Romer. "There are, however, two safe predictions. First, the country that takes the lead in the twenty-first century will be the one that implements an innovation that more effectively supports the production of new ideas in the private sector. Second, new meta-ideas of this kind will be found."[7]

About an hour and a half into our meeting with President Peres, we ran out of time. His next scheduled appointment had arrived, and we prepared to say our good-byes. But as we stood to do so, he paused for a moment and said, "Why don't you come back in half an hour and we can continue?" So we did, and he previewed what his message would be for Israel's entrepreneurs and policymakers in the coming years: "Leave the old industries. There are going to be five new industries. Tremendous—new forms of energy, water, biotechnology, teaching devices—there's a shortage of teachers—and homeland security to defend against terrorism." Nanotechnology research, for which Peres has also been instrumental in establishing funding, he predicted, would cut across all of these new industries and others as well.

We don't know whether Peres has picked the right industries, but that's not the point. At eighty-five, he still has the *chutzpah* to think up and advocate new industries. As they do in Israeli society (and have throughout Israel's history), the pioneering and innovative impulses merge into one. At the heart of this combined impulse is an instinctive understanding that the challenge facing every developed country in the twenty-first century is to become an idea factory, which includes both generating ideas at home and taking advantage of ideas generated elsewhere. Israel is one of the world's foremost idea factories, and provides clues for the meta-ideas of the future. Making innovation happen is a collaborative process on many levels, from the team, to the company, to the country, to the world. While many countries have mastered the process at the level of large companies, few have done so at the riskiest and most dynamic level of the process, the innovation-based start-up. Accordingly, while Israel has much to learn from the world, the world has much to learn from Israel. In both directions, the most careful thing, as Peres told us, is to dare.

# AFTERWORD

In the two years since this book was published, the Start-Up Nation economy is still going strong. In Chapter 1 we compared the amount of venture capital received by various nations' start-ups per capita. Working from the most recent data (for the year 2010), Israel is still the world's leader in venture capital dollars raised per capita—coming in at 2.5 times the next most venture capital intensive country, the United States.

This continued success has generated considerable interest in the Israeli economic model, and we have been asked to speak about the lessons from *Start-Up Nation* throughout Asia, Europe, South America, the United States, and Canada. Because many questions come up over and over again, we are addressing some of them in this paperback edition.

We have always freely acknowledged: Israel has plenty of challenges. What is more, as with any vibrant economy, there is always the danger that Israel could grow complacent and see its competitive edge diminish. Yet while it's the problems that often receive the most attention, we believe that Israel has only just begun to tap its potential, and is poised to become an even bigger player on the global innovation scene than it is today. In the questions and answers below, we consider this potential and what's next for the Start-Up Nation.

Dan Senor and Saul Singer
May, 2011

*1. What conversation has been sparked since the release of* Start-Up Nation?
As of this writing, the book has or will be translated into Chinese (in China and Taiwan), Korean, Russian, Portuguese (in Brazil), German, French, Italian, Bulgarian, Czech, Hebrew, Turkish, Spanish, and Arabic; it is a bestseller in Singapore and India. This international interest in the Israeli economic model indicates that the premium placed on innovation and entrepreneurship is not only high, but growing.

In the book we explain how a well conceived government program in Israel called Yozma helped build a venture capital sector that fueled thousands of potential start-ups. Yozma worked because it catalyzed an existing reality. It didn't create that reality, but it gave it a push. We suspect that this book is succeeding in a similar—albeit much smaller—way. We didn't create anything—we just told the story. Israel should have been known as the Start-Up Nation already, but this salient aspect of Israel had been overlooked and underappreciated.

For both developed and developing countries, one of the best ways to replace lost jobs and generate growth remains through innovation, and much of that innovation will come from start-ups. Indeed, President Barack Obama and Prime Minister David Cameron have in quick succession launched high-profile "Start-Up America" and "Start-Up Britain" initiatives. Setting aside the question of whether these particular programs will be effective, it is difficult to find a developed or emerging economy that does not want more start-ups and greater entrepreneurship.

## 2. What's next for the Start-Up Nation?

Israel is beginning to build on its strong technological base with other forms of innovation. One promising area is business model innovation. For example, the electric car system of Better Place is not based on a miracle battery but on a revolution in the structuring of car ownership that removes the current price premium on electric cars. Israel's largest food company, Strauss—a small company by global standards—is selling coffee in Brazil using an innovative business model, not new technology.

The same is true for KCPS, an investment management firm in Tel Aviv that works for a number of the world's most sophisticated investors in both developed and developing countries. The firm's founders believe that the Israeli focus on innovation could be as transformative in financial services as it has been in technology.

Globalization is also a key realm of potential growth. A Chinese company recently bought Machteshim Agan—an Israeli company that sells crop-protection products—not so much for its technology, but because the company was already operating in over one hundred countries. This partnership helped the Chinese company to globalize instantly.

Because Israelis have almost no local market and are largely shut off from the regional market, they have become experts at cultivating this kind of global reach—*all exports all the time*. For companies seeking to expand internationally, this mindset makes Israel a natural partner.

We also expect that Israel will become a "beta country" (as Better Place founder Shai Agassi puts it) for addressing seemingly insurmountable challenges in the realms of education, food, energy, water, and health care. Technology and innovation, after all, are not ends, but tools and means to a better world. Tackling global problems through innovation and entrepreneurship—and the creative energy that comes from their combination in a concentrated cluster—could become Israel's greatest export of all.

### 3. What's holding back Israel's start-up economy today?

While Israel has world-class universities—Tel Aviv University was just ranked ahead of Oxford, Cambridge, and Yale in citations per faculty member—Israeli high school students have nevertheless fallen behind in international test scores, and universities are struggling with "brain drain" as large numbers of faculty members have moved to the United States. Israel still has relatively low workforce participation rates, and large income gaps between the high-tech sector and the rest of the economy.

There is a lot of work to do. But if anything is greater than the challenges, it is the potential for the Israeli economy. Over 80 percent of foreign direct investment in Israel (or FDI, mainly development centers of big international companies) is from the United States; less than 20 percent from all of Europe, Asia, and the rest of the world. This means there is tremendous potential for companies from other regions to copy their American counterparts and benefit from Israeli innovation.

### 4. Was Start-Up Nation a snapshot reflecting a high point for the Israeli economy? Has Israel maintained its mojo?

Israel is a young country, just over sixty years old, and its innovation economy only began to achieve critical mass in the mid-1990s. Given that, a key question we've asked ourselves has been, is it sustainable? After our book was published, a column in the *Economist* acknowledged that Israel is a "high-tech superpower," but then wondered, "Can the good news last?"

The strongest evidence for the sustainability of Israel's innovation economy can be found in the country's performance during two major economic crises: the bursting of the internet bubble in 2000 and the subsequent tech/telecom collapse of 2001, and the global downturn that began in 2008. In 2000, when the Israeli start-up scene was still vulnerable, many favorable factors evaporated at the same time: the Oslo peace process fell apart, massive immigration from the former Soviet Union slowed to a trickle, global venture capital dried up and tech sectors collapsed, and a wave of terrorism helped plunge the Israeli economy into recession. By 2005, however, Israeli start-ups had bounced back so strongly that the country garnered an even *larger* share of global venture capital than it had in 2000—as noted in the preceding chapters. Far from crushed, Israel emerged stronger than ever.

A similar thing happened in 2008. As the *Economist* put it, Israel was one of the "last countries to enter recession and among the earliest to exit." Indeed, Israel had only one quarter of negative growth, and has since been leading all other OECD countries in GDP growth.

A December 2010 International Monetary Fund report led with the question, "Why was Israel so little affected by the Great Recession?" The IMF report showed how unemployment had dropped sharply from a peak far above the OECD average in 2003, to well below that average in 2010. And even more striking, Israeli exports continue to grow despite one of the strongest currencies in the world, and no commodities (yet).

While the IMF credited strong bank supervision and fiscal discipline for Israel's quick recovery, we believe these factors are only one part of the story. Israel's economy is, after all, start-up-centric, and the high-tech sector is the source of about half of Israel's exports. Technology start-ups, though small, are the catalyst at the center of a thriving ecosystem.

Israel has developed an unusual specialty: an ability not only to cope with but to leverage all sorts of adversity—a lack of local and regional markets, a scarcity of physical resources, and a barrage of boycotts and attacks. The essence of the Start-Up Nation story is a country's ability to turn adversity into a renewable source of creative energy—much of which goes into high-tech, but that is also evident in social entrepreneurship, medicine, the sciences, and the arts.

*5. Will Israel be able to build more large companies and not "just" start-ups?*

This is a question that preoccupies Israelis in the high-tech sector and government. For years, many would ask wistfully, "Where's our Nokia?"—they saw Finland as a small country that had produced a then-dominant tech branding and manufacturing powerhouse, rather than "just" small start-ups. The concern is that Israel has not continued to produce new large companies since Checkpoint, Comverse, Amdocs, and others, let alone another truly global large company like Teva, the generic pharmaceutical giant. (Incidentally, it could be said that Nokia is Finland's Teva. Teva's market cap is 1.5 times the size of Nokia's.)

What they do not fully realize is that people from countries as varied as Brazil, Finland, China, South Korea, and Singapore have been coming to Israel to look for answers to a question of their own: "Where are *our* start-ups?"

It turns out that Israel has inadvertently developed a knack for producing one of the most challenging and essential elements of the global technology ecosystem. Most start-ups make do without much in the way of revenue, employees, or customers; what they *do* have is concentrated innovation. This formative stage is harder than it looks, partly because it is so romanticized (many start-ups are depicted as a few people tinkering in a garage), and also because the *essence* of this innovation is so often misunderstood.

A search for "innovation" on Google Images produces a deluge of light bulbs. This reflects the popular perception that innovation is mainly about brilliant ideas. Our study of the Israeli model, however, indicates that *ideas are only the beginning of innovation*, and not the most essential part.

If ideas were the essence of innovation, we would expect the countries that led the world in patents per capita—including Korea, Finland, and Israel—to all have roughly the same number of start-ups.

Why does Israel, for its size, have many more start-ups than countries that, judging by patents, are producing roughly as many great ideas? It seems that Israel has two other essential ingredients: mission orientation and a cultural acceptance of the need to take risks. Those are the themes that we encourage policymakers and business leaders to focus on.

It takes a tremendous amount of time, energy, and hard work to turn a great idea into a viable company. Most start-ups fail, whether they are launched in Israel or Silicon Valley. So the question of innovation becomes one of where this determination and acceptance of risk comes from.

Most of the book is dedicated to answering this question. Part of the answer is that Israel is itself a start-up. The Zionist idea was at least as improbable as many of the business plans that today's entrepreneurs are seeking to launch. Many of those entrepreneurs say they see themselves as doing the twenty-first-century equivalent of what their grandparents did—not draining the swamps and greening the desert, but building companies.

*6. Other countries, notably China and India, are rapidly climbing the value chain. What does this mean for Israel?*

China has become the largest manufacturer of solar panels and is producing increasingly sophisticated technology. The Chinese government, not to mention the hundreds of thousands of new engineers graduating in China each year, are determined to shift from "Made in China" to "Made by China." In the next few years, we may see China leapfrog American leadership in whole industries, such as the development and manufacture of electric cars and the batteries to power them. India is also becoming a science and technology powerhouse. China and India also have the advantage of access to their own rapidly growing markets that are being jealously eyed by the developed world.

None of this is bad for Israel; in fact it represents a major opportunity. Just as Israeli start-ups and development centers have played a critical role for tech giants such as Google, Microsoft, IBM, Intel, and Cisco, Israeli companies could be ideal partners for Chinese and Indian companies—including start-ups—looking to innovate and globalize. A major challenge facing Western companies, including those in United States and Israel, is to help billions of people in countries like China and India move into the middle class and as they do, access the market potential of the largest shift in history of people into the fully modern world.

# ACKNOWLEDGMENTS

This book began as a long discussion between the two of us in April 2001, when Dan brought to Israel a group of twenty-eight Harvard Business School classmates. The purpose was to explore Israel's economy, politics, and history. It was at a time of vast business opportunity in Israel but also, with the collapse of the peace process, of escalating insecurity.

Almost none of the students had any previous ties to Israel—in fact only three were Jewish. They came from a range of countries: the United Kingdom, the United States, Canada, Spain, Italy, Portugal, and India. At the end of the week, many were asking the same question: Where did all this innovation and entrepreneurship come from?

We realized that we did not have an answer.

Over the years since then, Saul would write *Jerusalem Post* editorials about the Israeli economy and Dan would come to Israel almost every other quarter to invest in start-ups and visit family. As Dan would meet with an impressive Israeli entrepreneur or Saul would highlight one, our curiosity grew.

We assumed there must be some book that explained what made

the start-up scene so vibrant and seemingly impervious to the security situation. There wasn't. So we decided to write one.

We are indebted to many people who have helped us along the way. The greatest compliment we can pay to Jonathan Karp, the founder and force behind Twelve, is that he is a true innovator in the book world. Publishing only twelve books each year, he is the quintessential undiversified investor. Jon taught us many things, most important among them was to do less arguing and more storytelling.

With energy and creativity, Cary Goldstein thought through who might be interested in this book and how to reach them. Colin Shepherd was meticulous in every phase of the book's production and persistent as the deadline reminder. Dorothea Halliday was abundantly patient in the copyediting phase. Laura Lee Timko, Anne Twomey, Tom Whatley, and Giraud Lorber—also all part of Twelve's team—were a huge help to us.

It was never a dull moment working with Ed Victor, our agent. In promoting our proposal, as with everything he does, Ed was chock-full of *chutzpah*. Don Epstein and Arnie Hermann were trusted advisers, too.

As a rare truly independent research institution in its field, the Council on Foreign Relations is a special place. It is an honor for Dan to have a home there. Richard Haass, CFR's president, was immediately intrigued by the idea of a book on the Israeli economy. He contributed important insights and helped us draft expertise from CFR's diverse scholars and members. We are also specifically grateful to CFR's Isobel Coleman, author of the forthcoming book *Paradise Beneath Her Feet: Women and Reform in the Middle East* (Random House), for sharing her observations with us. Gary Samore, formerly of CFR, provided guidance early on. Jim Lindsay, CFR's director of studies, made several important suggestions on improving the manuscript. The CFR staff is among the most professional of any organization we've dealt with in the private, academic, or public sectors; we would like to specifically thank Janine Hill for all her patient assistance, and Lisa Shields and her communications team.

Part of our book was written in the eclectic Van Leer Institute in Jerusalem, which made an invaluable contribution by hosting Saul as a library fellow. Our thanks to director Gabriel Motzkin and librarians Yaffa Weingarten and Paul Maurer for all their gracious assistance.

We are deeply indebted to our industrious and creative team of research assistants: Michal Lewin-Epstein was our lead researcher at the Council on Foreign Relations; Dani Gilbert spent a summer at CFR with us and then continued doing part-time research while at the London School of Economics; Joshua Kram joined our team for a stint after serving as an adviser to Hillary Clinton's presidential campaign; Talia Gordis brought her own experience in IDF intelligence, and Ian Mitch and Anton Ornstein also helped at CFR as we began the project.

A number of people we interviewed, as well as one of our researchers, came from Arab countries. We respect their request for anonymity, since association with this book could prevent them from working in the Arab world; and we are grateful for their contributions.

With speed and deftness, our friend Judy Heiblum of Sterling Lord Literistic—and a Unit 8200 alumnus—made important suggestions on the structure of the manuscript.

We thank all the friends and family who read the manuscript; your sharp and candid feedback sent us back to the drawing board. We are especially grateful to Dan Allen, Stephen Backer, Max Boot, Paul Bremer, Reed Dickens, Shane Dolgin, Jonathan Ehrlich, Annette Furst, Mark Gerson, Henry Gomez, Alan Isenberg, Terry Kassel, Roger Marrero, Roman Martinez, Jim Miller, Josh Opperer, Matt Rees, Helen Senor, Seth "Yossi" Siegel, Suzanne and Max Singer, Andrew Vogel, and Pete Wehner, who read the manuscript from cover to cover under considerable time pressure.

Dale and Bill Fairbanks (Dan's in-laws) provided a quiet writing refuge in their art studio in Pensacola, Florida, keeping him well fed, highly caffeinated, and intensely focused for a long stretch leading up to the publisher's deadline.

A group of Dan's friends and business partners were extremely patient as this book was being written. Devon Archer, Dan Burrell, David Fife, Chris Heinz, and Jenny Stein deserve special thanks. Paul Singer, while never directly interviewed for this book, has been a teacher about macroeconomics without even realizing it. His very strong views about innovation economics impacted our thinking about the context for this book in the postcrash global economy.

We interviewed over one hundred people for this book, and wish to thank all of them for their time and wisdom. In particular, Hall of Fame Israeli venture investors Eli Barkat, Yigal Erlich, Yadin Kaufmann, Erel Margalit, Jon Medved, Chemi Peres, and Yossi Vardi have been living and telling the Start-up Nation story from long before we got involved; they were our guides. Jon Medved, in particular, was pitching the Israeli economy to the world before it was on anyone's map. Other extremely busy people who spent a lot of time with us in multiple interviews were Shai Agassi, Tal Keinan, and Scott Thompson. Isaac "Yitz" Applbaum and Alan Feld went out of their way to put themselves "on call" for us. Professor Shira Wolovsky Weiss helped us early on, as did Ken Pucker.

A number of U.S. companies have a strong presence in Israel and truly "get" the Start-up Nation. Current and former leaders from three in particular opened their doors to us in Israel and in Silicon Valley and provided lots of access: thank you to Google's Eric Schmidt, David Krane, Yossi Mattias, Andrew McLaughlin, and Yoelle Maarek; Intel's Shmuel Eden and David Perlmutter; and Cisco's Michael Laor and Yoav Samet.

Leon Wieseltier provided us with wise counsel on the relationship between Jewish history and the modern Israeli ethos.

Stuart Anderson, a former colleague of Dan's from the Senate Subcommittee on Immigration, has always been a source of rich analysis on immigration reform. He shared important research on the subject for this book.

We are grateful to the president of Israel, Shimon Peres, who gave us half a day in his office. He not only gave us his unique perspective as a central player throughout the entire span of Israel's history, but is still, at age eighty-five, in high office and busy working to launch whole new industries. We would also like to thank the prime minister of Israel, Benjamin Netanyahu, for spending a lot of time with us during a hectic period for him in 2008.

As we compared the Israeli and American experiences, a number of U.S. military leaders helped us think through the contrasts. In particular, we would like to thank Generals John Abizaid (ret.), Jack Keane (ret.), Mark Kimmitt (ret.), David Petraeus, H. R. McMaster, and Jim Newbold (ret.).

Our wives, Campbell Brown (Dan) and Wendy Singer (Saul), have been an integral part of our daily conversation about this book since we began writing it, and bore the brunt of the frenzied weeks before each deadline.

Campbell gave birth to the Senors' first son, Eli, two weeks before we started writing the proposal, and to their second, Asher, just before we submitted the final manuscript, all as she held down the family fort during a chaotic time. Wendy scooped up the Singer girls—Noa, Tamar, and Yarden—for week-long trips to give Saul space before deadlines. The Singer girls added to our excitement as they lapped up stories of the latest Israeli inventions with enthusiasm.

This book relied heavily on Campbell's and Wendy's criticisms and advice, and could not have been completed without their virtuoso feats of multitasking. For that, and for so much more, we dedicate it to them.

We have also dedicated this book to Jim Senor (Dan's father) and Alex Singer (Saul's brother).

Jim worked in Iran helping to organize the Jewish community, and later for the Weizmann Institute of Science, where he drafted resources for its pioneering solar energy program. Just months before the 1985 ground-breaking for the field of mirrors—now still active as a research facility—Jim passed away.

On September 15, 1987, his twenty-fifth birthday, IDF Lieutenant Alex Singer was flown by helicopter into Lebanon to intercept terrorists bound for Israel; he was killed while trying to rescue his downed company commander. Many who never knew him have since been inspired by the joy and passion of his life as seen in *Alex: Building a Life*, the book of his letters, journals, and art.

Jim's and Alex's work is part of this story. We missed their guidance, and sharing their amazement at what the Start-up Nation has become.

# NOTES

## Introduction

1. The information in this passage is largely drawn from an interview with Shimon Peres, president of Israel, December 2008; and interviews with Shai Agassi, founder and CEO of Better Place, March 2008 and March 2009.

2. Shai Agassi's blog, "Tom Friedman's Column," July 26, 2008, http://shaiagassi.typepad.com/.

3. The information about Better Place is largely drawn from interviews with Shai Agassi.

4. Daniel Roth, "Driven: Shai Agassi's Audacious Plan to Put Electric Cars on the Road," *Wired*, vol. 16, no. 9 (August 18, 2008).

5. Haim Handwerker, "U.S. Entrepreneur Makes Aliyah Seeking 'Next Big Invention,'" *Haaretz*, August 28, 2008.

6. Israel Venture Capital Research Center, www.ivc-online.com.

7. Authors' calculations based on venture capital data from Dow Jones, VentureSource.

8. Dow Jones, VentureSource.

9. Donna Rosenthal, *The Israelis: Ordinary People in an Extraordinary Land* (New York: Free Press, 2005), p. 111.

10. Standard of living comparative data from www.gapminder.com.

11. Mark Twain, *The Innocents Abroad: or, The New Pilgrims' Progress* (Hartford: American Publishing Company, 1870), p. 488.

12. Interviews with Gidi Grinstein, founder and president, Reut Institute, May and August 2008.

13. Interview with Eric Schmidt, chairman and CEO, Google, June 2009; Maayan Cohen and Reuters, "Microsoft CEO, in Herzliya: Our Company Almost as Israeli as American," *Haaretz*, May 21, 2008.

14. "The Global 2000," Forbes.com, March 29, 2007; http://www.forbes.com/lists/2007/18/biz_07forbes2000_The-Global-2000_Ind Name.html; and "Recent International Mergers and Acquisitions," http://www.investinisrael.gov.il/NR/exeres/F0FA7315-4D4A-4FD CA2FA-AE5BF294B3C2.htm; and Augusto Lopez-Claros and Irene Mia, "Israel: Factors in the Emergence of an ICT Powerhouse," http://www.investinisrael.gov.il/NR/rdonlyres/61BD95A0-898B-4F48-A795-5886 B1C4F08C/0/israelcompleteweb.pdf, p. 8. Among the top fifty software and technology companies of the two thousand largest public companies listed on Forbes, almost half have acquired Israeli companies or have opened an R&D center in Israel.

15. Paul Smith, senior vice president of Philips Medical, quoted in Invest in Israel, "Life Sciences in Israel: Inspiration, Invention, Innovation" (Israel Ministry of Industry, Trade and Labor, Investment Promotion Center, 2006).

16. Interviews with Gary Shainberg, vice president for technology and innovation, British Telecom, May and August 2008.

17. Interview with Jessica Schell, vice president, NBC Universal, Inc., April and June 2008.

18. David McWilliams, "We're All Israelis Now," April 25, 2004, http://www.davidmcwilliams.ie/2004/04/25/were-all-israelis-now.

19. Background interview with senior eBay executive.

20. Curtis R. Carlson, CEO of Stanford Research Institute International, in "We Are All Innovators Now," *Economist Intelligence Unit*, October 17, 2007.

21. John Kao, *Innovation Nation: How America Is Losing Its Innovation Edge, Why It Matters and What We Can Do to Get It Back* (New York: Free Press, 2007), p. 3.

22. Robert M. Solow, "Growth Theory and After," Nobel Prize lecture, December 8, 1987, http://nobelprize.org/nobel_prizes/economics/laureates/1987/solow-lecture.html.

23. Interview with Carl Schramm, president of the Kauffman Foundation, March 2009.

24. *Paths to Prosperity: Promoting Entrepreneurship in the Twenty-first Century*, Monitor Company, January 2009.

25. Michael Mandel, "Can America Invent Its Way Back?" *Business-Week*, September 11, 2008.

## Chapter 1. Persistence

1. Information in the following section is taken from interviews with Scott Thompson, president, PayPal, October 2008 and January 2009; Meg Whitman, former president and CEO of eBay, September 2008; and Eli Barkat, chairman and cofounder, BRM Group, and seed investor in Fraud Sciences, January 2009.

2. Leo Rosten, *The Joys of Yiddish* (New York: McGraw-Hill, 1968), p. 5.

3. Loren Gary, "The Right Kind of Failure," *Harvard Management Update*, January 1, 2002.

4. Background interview with Israeli Air Force trainer, May 2008.

5. Paul Gompers, Anna Kovner, Josh Lerner, and David S. Scharfstein, "Skill vs. Luck in Entrepreneurship and Venture Capital: Evidence from Serial Entrepreneurs," working paper 12592, National Bureau of

Economic Research, October 2006, http://imio.haas.berkley.edu/williamsonseminar/scharfstein041207.pdf.

6. Eric Weiner, *The Geography of Bliss: One Grump's Search for the Happiest Places in the World* (New York: Twelve, 2008), p. 163.

7. Ian King, "How Israel Saved Intel," *Seattle Times*, April 9, 2007.

8. Shahar Zadok, "Intel Dedicates Fab 28 in Kiryat Gat," *Globes Online*, July 1, 2008.

9. Michael S. Malone, *Infinite Loop: How Apple, the World's Most Insanely Great Computer Company, Went Insane* (New York: Doubleday Business, 1999); quoted in "Inside Intel: The Art of Andy Grove," *Harvard Business School Bulletin*, December 2006.

10. David Perlmutter in "Intel Beyond 2003: Looking for Its Third Act," by Robert A. Burgelman and Philip Meza, Stanford Graduate School of Business, 2003.

11. Interview with Shmuel Eden, vice president and general manager, Mobile Platforms Group, Intel, November 2008.

12. Ian King, "Intel's Israelis Make Chip to Rescue Company from Profit Plunge," Bloomberg.com, March 28, 2007.

13. Eliot A. Cohen, *Supreme Command: Soldiers, Statesmen, and Leadership in Wartime* (New York: Free Press, 2002), p. 144.

14. Dov Frohman and Robert Howard, *Leadership the Hard Way: Why Leadership Can't Be Taught and How You Can Learn It Anyway* (San Francisco: Jossey-Bass, 2008), p. 7.

15. This passage is based on Ian King, "Intel's Israelis Make Chip to Rescue Company from Profit Plunge," Bloomberg.com, March 28, 2007.

16. "Energy Savings: The Right Hand Turn," video presentation by John Skinner, Intel Web site, http://video.intel.com/?fr_story=542de663 c9824ce580001de5fba31591cd5b5cf3&rf=sitemap.

17. Interview with Shmuel Eden.

## Chapter 2. Battlefield Entrepreneurs

Epigraph: Interview with Eric Schmidt.

1. Interview with Abraham Rabinovich, historian, December 2008.

2. Azriel Lorber, *Misguided Weapons: Technological Failure and Surprise on the Battlefield* (Dulles, Va.: Potomac Books, 2002), pp. 76–80.

3. Interview with Michael Oren, senior fellow, Shalem Center, May 2008.

4. Interview with Edward Luttwak, senior associate, Center for Strategic and International Studies, December 2008.

5. This section is based on an interview with Major Gilad Farhi, commander, Kfir infantry unit, IDF, November 2008.

6. Interview with Brigadier General Rami Ben-Ephraim, head of Personnel Division, Israeli Air Force, November 2008. The name of the pilot is fictitious since the IDF does not allow publication of names of most pilots.

7. Interview with Major General (res.) Aharon Zeevi-Farkash, former head of 8200, IDF, May 2008.

8. Interview with Frederick W. Kagan, military historian and resident scholar, American Enterprise Institute for Public Policy Research (AEI), December 2009.

9. Interview with Nathan Ron, attorney and IDF Lieutenant Colonel (res.), Ron-Festinger Law Offices, December 2008.

10. Interview with Amos Goren, venture partner, Apax, January 2009.

11. Amos Oz, speech at the Israeli Presidential Conference, Jerusalem, May 14, 2008.

12. Interview with Michael Oren.

13. Interview with Lieutenant General (res.) Moshe Yaalon, Likud member of Knesset and former chief of staff, IDF, May 2008.

## Chapter 3. The People of the Book

1. Information in this section is from Patrick Symmes, "The Book," *Outside*, August 2005; and an interview with Darya Maoz, anthropologist, June 2009; and an interview with Dorit Moralli, owner, El Lobo restaurant and guesthouse in La Paz, Bolivia, March 2009.

2. Aaron J. Sarna, *Boycott and Blacklist: A History of Arab Economic Warfare Against Israel* (Totowa, N.J.: Rowman & Littlefield, 1986), appendix.

3. Chaim Fershtman and Neil Gandal, "The Effect of the Arab Boycott on Israel: The Automobile Market," *Rand Journal of Economics*, vol. 29, no. 1 (Spring 1998), p. 5.

4. Christopher Joyner, quoted in Aaron J. Sarna, *Boycott and Blacklist: A History of Arab Economic Warfare Against Israel*, p. xiv.

5. Sarna, *Boycott and Blacklist*, pp. 56–57.

6. Interview with Orna Berry, venture partner, Gemini Israel Funds, January 2009.

7. Interview with Gil Kerbs, venture capitalist and contributor to *Forbes*, January 2009.

8. Interview with Edward Luttwak.

9. Interview with Alex Vieux, CEO of Red Herring, May 2009.

## Chapter 4. Harvard, Princeton, and Yale

1. Interview with David Amir (fictitious name), August 2008.

2. Interview with Gil Kerbs, venture capitalist, January 2009.

3. Interview with Gary Shainberg, vice president for technology and innovation, British Telecom, August 2008.

4. *IMD World Competitiveness Yearbook* (Lausanne, Switzerland: IMD, 2005).

5. Interview with Mark Gerson, executive chairman, Gerson Lehrman Group, January 2009.

6. Interview with Tal Keinan, cofounder KCPS, May 2008.

7. Interview with Yossi Vardi, angel investor, May 2008.

8. Background interview with U.S. Army recruiter, January 2009.

9. David Lipsky, *Absolutely American: Four Years at West Point*; and interview with Lipsky in March 2009.

10. Information from this passage is largely based on an interview with Colonel (res.) John Lowry, general manager at Harley-Davidson Motor Company, November 2008.

11. Interview with Jon Medved, CEO and board member, Vringo, May 2008.

12. This experience prompted the army leadership to pursue a proactive public relations campaign to bridge the civilian-military divide, which included reaching out to *Rolling Stone* and offering access to a West Point class. This effort culminated in David Lipsky's book *Absolutely American*. This passage is also based on author interview with General John Abizaid, May 2009.

13. Interview with Tom Brokaw, author, *The Greatest Generation*, April 2009.

14. Interview with Al Chase, corporate executive recruiter and founder, White Rhino Partners, February 2009.

15. Interview with Nathaniel Fick, author of *One Bullet Away*, March 2008.

16. Interview with Brian Tice, captain (res.), U.S. Marine Corps, February 2009.

## CHAPTER 5. Where Order Meets Chaos

1. CIA, "Field Listing—Military Service Age and Obligation," *The 2008 World Factbook*.

2. Mindef Singapore, "Ministerial Statement on National Service Defaulters by Minister for Defence Teo Chee Hean," January 16, 2006.

3. Amnon Barzilai, "A Deep, Dark, Secret Love Affair," http://www
.israelforum.com/board/archive/index.php/t-6321.html.

4. Mindef Singapore, "Speech by Prime Minister Goh Chok Tong at
the 35 Years of National Service Commemoration Dinner," September 7,
2007.

5. BBC News, "Singapore Elder Statesman," July 5, 2000, http://news
.bbc.co.uk/2/hi/programmes/from_our_own_correspondent/820234
.stm; retrieved November 2008.

6. Quoted in James Flanigan, "Israeli Companies Seek Global Profile,"
*New York Times*, May 20, 2009.

7. Interview with Laurent Haug, founder and CEO, Lift Conference,
May 2009.

8. Interview with Tal Riesenfeld, founder and vice president of marketing, EyeView, December 2008.

9. The information from this passage is largely taken from Michael A.
Roberto, Amy C. Edmondson, and Richard M. J. Bohmer, "*Columbia's
Final Mission*," Harvard Business School Case Study, 2006; Charles Mur-
ray and Catherine Bly Cox, *Apollo* (Birkittsville, Md.: South Mountain
Books, 2004); Jim Lovell and Jeffrey Kluger, *Apollo 13* (New York: Mariner
Books, 2006); and Gene Kranz, *Failure Is Not an Option: Mission Control
from Mercury to Apollo 13 and Beyond* (New York: Berkley, 2009).

10. Michael Useem, *The Leadership Moment: Nine True Stories of Triumph and Disaster and Their Lessons for Us All* (New York: Three Rivers,
1998), p. 81.

11. Roberta Wohlstetter quoted in Michael A. Roberto, Richard M. J.
Bohmer, and Amy C. Edmondson, "Facing Ambiguous Threats," *Harvard Business Review*, November 2006.

12. Interview with Yuval Dotan (fictitious name), IAF fighter pilot,
May 2008.

13. Interview with Edward Luttwak.

14. Interview with Eliot A. Cohen, director of the Strategic Studies Program, Paul H. Nitze School of Advanced International Studies, Johns Hopkins University, January 2009.

15. Lieutenant Colonel Paul Yingling quoted in Thomas E. Ricks, "A Brave Lieutenant Colonel Speaks Out: Why Most of Our Generals Are Dinosaurs," *Foreign Policy*, January 1, 2009, http://ricks.foreignpolicy.com/posts/2009/01/22/a_brave_colonel_speaks_out_why_most_of_our_generals_are_dinosaurs.

16. Lieutenant Colonel Paul Yingling (United States Army), "A Failure in Generalship," *Armed Forces Journal*, 2007, http://www.armedforcesjournal.com/2007/05/2635198.

17. Interview with Eliot Cohen.

18. Giora Eiland, "The IDF: Addressing the Failures of the Second Lebanon War," in *The Middle East Strategic Balance 2007–2008*, edited by Mark A. Heller (Tel Aviv: Institute for National Security Studies, 2008).

19. Quote identified from interview with Carl Schramm, March 2009.

20. William J. Baumol, Robert E. Litan, and Carl J. Schramm, *Good Capitalism, Bad Capitalism, and the Economics of Growth and Prosperity* (New Haven: Yale University Press, 2007); and Carl Schramm, "Economic Fluidity: A Crucial Dimension of Economic Freedom," in *2008 Index of Economic Freedom*, edited by Kim R. Holmes, Edwin J. Feulner, and Mary Anastasia O'Grady (Washington, D.C.: Heritage Foundation, 2008), p. 17.

## CHAPTER 6. An Industrial Policy That Worked

1. Central Bureau of Statistics (Israel), "Gross Domestic Product and Uses of Resources, in the Years 1950–1995," in *Statistical Abstract of Israel 2008*, no. 59, table 14.1, http://www.cbs.gov.il/reader/shnaton/templ_shnaton_e.html?num_tab=st14_01x&CYear=2008.

2. Howard M. Sacher, *A History of Israel: From the Rise of Zionism to Our Time*, 2nd ed. (New York: Knopf, 1996), p. 30.

3. "Yishuv," in *Encyclopedia Judaica*, 2nd ed., vol. 10, p. 489.

4. Quoted in Time/CBS News, *People of the Century: One Hundred Men and Women Who Shaped the Last Hundred Years* (New York: Simon & Schuster, 1999), p. 128.

5. Leon Wieseltier, "Brothers and Keepers: Black Jews and the Meaning of Zionism," *New Republic*, February 11, 1985.

6. Quoted in Meirav Arlosoroff, "Once Politicians Died Poor," *Haaretz*, June 8, 2008.

7. Daniel Gavron, *The Kibbutz: Awakening from Utopia* (Lanham, Md.: Rowman & Littlefield, 2000), p 1.

8. Bruno Bettelheim, *The Children of the Dream: Communal Child-Rearing and American Education* (New York: Simon & Schuster, 2001), pp. 15–17.

9. Alon Tal, *Pollution in a Promised Land: An Environmental History of Israel* (Berkeley: University of California Press, 2002), p. 219.

10. Alon Tal, "National Report of Israel, Years 2003–2005, to the United Nations Convention to Combat Desertification (UNCCD)," July 2006, http://www.unccd.int/cop/reports/otheraffected/national/2006/israel-eng.pdf.

11. Dina Kraft, "From Far Beneath the Israeli Desert, Water Sustains a Fertile Enterprise," *New York Times*, January 2, 2007.

12. Information for this passage comes from Web sites of the Weizmann Institute, Yatir Forest Research Group, http://www.weizmann.ac.il/ESER/People/Yakir/YATIR/Yatir.htm, and the Keren Kayemeth LeIsrael / Jewish National Fund, http://www.kkl.org.il/kkl/english/main_subject/globalwarming/israeli%20research%20has%20worldwide%20implications.x.

13. Reut Institute, "Generating a Socio-economic Leapfrog," February 14, 2008, http://reut-institute.org/data/uploads/PDFVer/20080218%20-%20%20Hausman%27s%20main%20issues-%20English.pdf.

14. Reut Institute, "Israel 15 Vision," http://www.reut-institute.org/event.aspx?EventId=6.

15. Information in this passage is from Yakir Plessner, *The Political Economy of Israel: From Ideology to Stagnation* (Albany: State University of New York Press, 1994), pp. 11–31.

16. Ibid., p. 288.

17. David Rosenberg, "Inflation—the Rise and Fall," Ministry of Foreign Affairs Web site, January 2001, http://www.mfa.gov.il.

18. CNNMoney.com, "Best Places to Do Business in the Wired World," http://money.cnn.com/galleries/2007/biz2/0708/gallery.road warriorsspecial.biz2/11.html.

19. Orna Yefet, "McDonalds," *Yediot Ahronot*, October 29, 2006.

## CHAPTER 7. Immigration: The Google Guys' Challenge

1. Interview with Shlomo Molla, member of Knesset, Kadima Party, March 2009.

2. This covert rescue effort was aided by the Central Intelligence Agency, local mercenaries, and even Sudanese security officials. It was kept a secret largely for political reasons—in order to shield Sudan from any blowback from the Arab countries that would criticize the government for ostensibly aiding Israel. When the story of the airlift broke prematurely, the Arab countries pressured Sudan to stop the airlift, which it did. This left one thousand Ethiopian Jews stranded until U.S.-led Operation Joshua evacuated them to Israel a few months later.

3. Leon Wieseltier, "Brothers and Keepers: Black Jews and the Meaning of Zionism."

4. Joel Brinkley, "Ethiopian Jews and Israelis Exult as Airlift Is Completed," *New York Times*, May 26, 1991.

5. David A. Vise and Mark Malseed, *The Google Story* (New York: Delacorte, 2005), p. 15.

6. Interview with Natan Sharansky, chairman and distinguished fellow, Adelson Institute for Strategic Studies, Shalem Center, and founder of Yisrael B'Aliya, May 2008.

7. Interview with David McWilliams, Irish economist and author of *The Pope's Children*, March 2009.

8. Interview with Erel Margalit, founder of Jerusalem Venture Partners (JVP), May 2008.

9. Interview with Reuven Agassi, December 2008.

10. While the new law was already rigid, the U.S. State Department directed consular officers overseas to become even stricter in their application of the "public charge" provision of immigration law. A public charge is someone unable to support himself or his family. At the beginning of the Great Depression, in response to a public outcry for tougher immigration laws, overseas consuls were told to expand the interpretation of the "public charge clause" to prohibit admission to immigrants who just might become public charges. The designation became a completely speculative process.

11. David Wyman, *Paper Walls: America and the Refugee Crisis, 1938–1941* (New York: Pantheon, 1985), p. x.

12. Some scholars now believe that the lack of a safe haven for Jews seeking to leave Germany and other soon-to-be-occupied Nazi territories became an important factor in Nazi plans to exterminate the Jewish population of Europe. "The overall picture clearly shows that the original [Nazi] policy was to force the Jews to leave," says David Wyman. "The shift to extermination came only after the emigration method had failed, a failure in large part due to lack of countries open to refugees." From Wyman, *Paper Walls: America and the Refugee Crisis, 1938–1941* (New York: Pantheon, 1985), p. 35.

13. In 1939, the British government created a ceiling of 10,000 Jewish immigrants per year into Palestine, with an additional allotment of 25,000 possible entries. It is true that in 1945, President Harry Truman

requested a U.S. government investigation of treatment of Jewish displaced persons, many of whom were in facilities overseen by the U.S. Army. "The resulting report chronicled shocking mistreatment of the already abused refugees and recommended that the gates of Palestine be opened wide for resettlement," writes Leonard Dinnerstein in *America and the Survivors of the Holocaust* (New York: Columbia University Press, 1986). After several unsuccessful attempts to persuade Great Britain to admit the Jews into Palestine, Truman asked Congress to pass a law to bring a number of these refugees to the States.

While Truman's bill became law in 1948, the year of Israel's founding, a group of legislators, led by Nevada senator Pat McCarran, manipulated the drafting of the bill's language so that it actually had the effect of discriminating against Eastern European Jews. Ultimately, historian Leonard Dinnerstein estimates, only about 16 percent of those issued visas as displaced persons between July 1948 and June 1952 were Jewish. "Thus McCarran's numerous tricks and ploys were effective," notes Dinnerstein. "Jews who might otherwise have chosen the United States as their place of resettlement went to Israel."

14. The document can be found at http://www.jewishvirtuallibrary .org/jsource/History/Dec_of_Indep.html.

15. Interview with David McWilliams, Irish economist and author of *The Pope's Children*, March 2009.

16. This is not to suggest that there are not ethnic tensions among this very diverse country. Deep friction erupted between European Holocaust refugees and Jews from the Arab world as far back as the state's founding. Sammy Smooha, today a world-renowned sociologist at the University of Haifa, was, like Reuven Agassi, an Iraqi Jewish immigrant who spent part of his childhood in a transit tent. "We were told not to speak Arabic, but we didn't know Hebrew. Everything was strange. My father went from being a railroad official in Baghdad to an unskilled nobody. We suffered a terrible loss of identity. Looking back, I'd call it cultural repression. Behind their lofty ideals of 'one people,' they [the Jews of European origin] were acting superior, paternalistic." Quoted in Donna Rosenthal,

*The Israelis: Ordinary People in an Extraordinary Land* (New York: Free Press, 2005), p. 116.

## CHAPTER 8. The Diaspora: Stealing Airplanes

1. Fred Vogelstein, "The Cisco Kid Rides Again," *Fortune*, July 26, 2004; http://money.cnn.com/magazines/fortune/fortune_archive/2004 /07/26/377145/index.htm; and interview with Michael Laor, founder of Cisco Systems Development Center in Israel, February 2009.

2. Marguerite Reardon, "Cisco Router Makes Guinness World Records," July 1, 2004, *CNET News*, http://news.cnet.com/Cisco-router -makes-Guinness-World-Records/2100-1033_3-5254291.html?tag=nefd .top; retrieved January 2009.

3. Vogelstein, "The Cisco Kid Rides Again."

4. Marguerite Reardon, "Cisco Sees Momentum in Sales of Key Router," *TechRepublic*, December 6, 2004, http://articles.techrepublic .com.com/5100-22_11-5479086.html; and Cisco, press release, "Growth of Video Service Delivery Drives Sales of Cisco CRS-1, the World's Most Powerful Routing Platform, to Double in Nine Months," April 1, 2008, http://newsroom.cisco.com/dlls/2008/prod_040108c.html.

5. Interview with Yoav Samet, Cisco's corporate business development manager in Israel, Central/Eastern Europe, and Russia/CIS, January 2009.

6. Interview with Yoav Samet.

7. Richard Devane, "The Dynamics of Diaspora Networks: Lessons of Experience," in *Diaspora Networks and the International Migration Skills*, edited by Yevgeny Kuznetsov (Washington, D.C.: World Bank Publications, 2006), pp. 59–67. The quote is from p. 60.

8. Jenny Johnston, "The New Argonauts: An Interview with AnnaLee Saxenian," July 2006, GBN Global Business Network, http://thenewar gonauts.com/GBNinterview.pdf?aid=37652.

9. The information in this passage is drawn from Anthony David,

*The Sky Is the Limit: Al Schwimmer, the Founder of the Israeli Aircraft Industry* (Tel Aviv: Schocken Books, 2008; in Hebrew); and the interview with Shimon Peres. Regarding the accounts of Peres and Schwimmer flying over the Arctic tundra and Schwimmer's meeting with Ben-Gurion in the United States, see also Shimon Peres, *David's Sling* (New York: Random House, 1970).

## CHAPTER 9. The Buffett Test

1. Interview with Yoelle Maarek, former director, Google's R & D Center in Haifa, Israel, January 2009.

2. Joel Leyden, "Microsoft Bill Gates Takes Google, Terrorism War to Israel," Israel News Agency, 2006, http://www.israelnewsagency.com/microsoftgoogleisraelseo581030.html; retrieved November 2008.

3. Quote from a transcript of a documentary film interview conducted by the American Israel Public Affairs Committee (AIPAC) in 2007, provided to the authors.

4. Dan Senor is an investor in Vringo.

5. Interview with Alice Schroeder, author of *The Snowball*, 2008.

6. Uzi Rubin, "Hizballah's Rocket Campaign Against Northern Israel: A Preliminary Report," *Jerusalem Issue Brief*, vol. 6, no. 10 (August 31, 2006), http://www.jcpa.org/brief/brief006-10.htm.

7. Interview with Eitan Wertheimer, chairman of the board of Iscar, January 2009.

8. Dov Frohman with Robert Howard, *Leadership the Hard Way: Why Leadership Can't Be Taught—and How You Can Learn It Anyway* (San Francisco: Jossey-Bass, 2008), pp. 1–16. All quotes from Frohman in this passage come from this book.

9. Interviews in this passage with senior Intel executive were on background, December 2008.

10. Interview with Eitan Wertheimer.

## Chapter 10. Yozma: The Match

1. Jennifer Friedlin, "Woman on a Mission," *Jerusalem Post*, April 20, 1997.

2. Interview with Orna Berry, partner in Gemini Israel Funds, and chairperson of several Gemini portfolio companies, January 2009.

3. Interview with Jon Medved, CEO and board member, Vringo, May 2008.

4. Interview with Yigal Erlich, founder, chairman, and managing partner of the Yozma Group, May 2008.

5. Gil Avnimelech and Morris Tuebal, "Venture Capital Policy in Israel: A Comparative Analysis and Lessons for Other Countries," research paper, Hebrew University School of Business Administration and School of Economics, October 2002, p. 17.

6. The information about BIRD's founding is from an interview with Ed Mlavsky, chairman and founding partner of Gemini Israel Funds, December 2008.

7. BIRD (Israel-U.S. Binational Industrial Research and Development Foundation), "BIRD Foundation to Invest $9 Million in 12 Advanced Development Projects in Life Sciences, Energy, Communications, Software and Nanotechnology," http://www.birdf.com/_Uploads/255BOG08PREng.pdf.

8. Dan Breznitz, *Innovation of the State* (New Haven: Yale University Press, 2007), p. 60.

9. Ed Mlavsky in a PowerPoint slide presentation to Wharton MBA students, 2008.

10. Interview with Jon Medved.

11. Interview with Yigal Erlich.

12. Ibid.

13. Interview with Orna Berry.

14. Yossi Sela, managing partner, Gemini Venture Funds, http://www.gemini.co.il/?p=TeamMember&CategoryID=161&MemberId=197.

15. Interview with Erel Margalit.

16. David McWilliams, "Ireland Inc. Gets Innovated," *Sunday Business Post On-Line*, December 21, 2008, http://www.sbpost.ie/post/pages/p/story.aspx-qqqt=DAVID+McWilliams-qqqs=commentandanalysis-qqqid=38312-qqqx=1.asp; retrieved January 2009.

17. Interview with Tal Keinan, cofounder of KCPS, May and December 2008.

18. Interview with Ron Dermer, former economic attaché, Embassy of Israel in United States, and senior adviser to Prime Minister Benjamin Netanyahu, September 2008.

19. Interview with Benjamin Netanyahu, prime minister of Israel, December 2008.

## CHAPTER 11. Betrayal and Opportunity

Epigraph: Quoted in Julie Ball, "Israel's Booming Hi-Tech Industry," *BBC News*, October 6, 2008, http://news.bbc.co.uk/2/hi/business/7654780.stm; retrieved January 2009.

1. John Kao, *Innovation Nation* (New York: Free Press, 2007).

2. Michael Bar-Zohar, *Shimon Peres: The Biography* (New York: Random House, 2007). p. 223. Also Reuters, "Peres Biography: Israel, France Had Secret Pact to Produce Nuclear Weapons," May 30, 2007.

3. Michael M. Laskier, "Israel and Algeria amid French Colonialism and the Arab-Israeli Conflict, 1954–1978," *Israel Studies*, June 2, 2001, pp. 1–32, http://muse.jhu.edu/journals/israel_studies/v006/6.2laskier.html; retrieved September 2008.

4. De Gaulle quoted in Alexis Berg and Dominique Vidal, "De Gaulle's Lonely Predictions," *Le Monde Diplomatique*, June 2007, http://mondediplo.com/2007/06/10degaulle; retrieved September, 2008.

5. Quoted in Berg and Vidal, "De Gaulle's Lonely Predictions."

6. "Israel's Fugitive Flotilla," *Time*, January 12, 1970, http://www.time.com/time/magazine/article/0,9171,942140,00.html.

7. Stewart Wilson, *Combat Aircraft Since 1945* (Fyshwick, Australia: Aerospace Publications, 2000), p. 77.

8. Ruud Deurenberg, "Israel Aircraft Industries and Lavi," *Jewish Virtual Library*, January 26, 2009, http://www.jewishvirtuallibrary.org/jsource/Society_&_Culture/lavi.html.

9. James P. DeLoughry, "The United States and the Lavi," *Airpower Journal* vol. 4, no. 3 (1990), pp. 34–44, http://www.fas.org/man/dod-101/sys/ac/row/3fal90.htm.

10. Interview with Yossi Gross, director and cofounder of TransPharma Medical, and founder of many medical-device start-ups, December 2008.

## CHAPTER 12. From Nose Cones to Geysers

1. Interview with Doug Wood, head of creative affairs, Animation Lab, May 2008.

2. Interview with Yuval Dotan (fictitious name), December 2008.

3. Manuel Trajtenberg and Gil Shiff, "Identification and Mobility of Israeli Patenting Inventors," Discussion Paper No. 5-2008, Pinchas Sapir Center for Development, Tel Aviv University, April 2008.

4. John Russell, "Compugen Transforms Its Business," Bio-ITWorld.com, October 17, 2005, http://www.bio-itworld.com/issues/2005/oct/bus-compugen?page:int=-1.

5. Interview with Ruti Alon, partner, Pitango Venture Capital, and chairperson, boards of BioControl, BrainsGate, and TransPharma Medical, December 2008.

## CHAPTER 13. The Sheikh's Dilemma

1. Interview with Michael Porter, professor of economics, Harvard Business School, March 2009.

2. Rhoula Khalaf, "Dubai's Ruler Has Big Ideas for His Little City-State," *Financial Times*, May 3, 2007.

3. Michael Matley and Laura Dillon, "Dubai Strategy: Past, Present, Future," Harvard Business School, February 27, 2007, p. 3.

4. Quoted in Assaf Gilad, "Silicon Wadi: Who Will Internet Entrepreneurs Turn to in Crisis?" *Cataclist*, September 19, 1998.

5. Saul Singer, "Superpower in Silicon Wadi," *Jerusalem Post*, June 19, 1998.

6. Quoted in Steve Lohr, "Like J. P. Morgan, Warren Buffett Braves a Crisis," *New York Times*, October 5, 2008.

7. Quoted in Eyal Marcus, "Israeli Start-ups Impress at TechCrunch50," *Globes Online*, September 14, 2008.

8. James C. Collins and Jerry I. Porras, *Built to Last: Successful Habits of Visionary Companies* (New York: HarperCollins, 1997), pp. xix, 224.

9. Barbara W. Tuchman, *Practicing History: Selected Essays* (New York: Ballantine Books, 1982), quoted in Collins and Porras, *Built to Last*, p. xix.

10. Interview with Riad al-Allawi, Jordanian entrepreneur, March 2009.

11. Fadi Ghandour, in Stefan Theil, "Teaching Entrepreneurship in the Arab World," *Newsweek International*, August 14, 2007; also available at http://www.gmfus.org/publications/article.cfm?id=332; retrieved March 2009.

12. Bernard Lewis, "Free at Last? The Arab World in the Twenty-first Century," *Foreign Affairs*, March/April 2009. Similar observation has been made by Samuel Huntington.

13. Quoted in Christopher M. Davidson, *Dubai: The Vulnerability of Success* (New York: Columbia University Press, 2008), p. 166.

14. UNDP (United Nations Development Programme), *The Arab Human Development Report, 2005: Towards the Rise of Women in the Arab World* (New York: United Nations Publications, 2006).

15. Interview with Christopher M. Davidson, author of *Dubai: The Vulnerability of Success*, March 2009.

16. Quoted in Fannie F. Andrews, *The Holy Land Under Mandate*, vol. 2 (Boston: Houghton and Mifflin, 1931), p. 4.

17. Hagit Messer-Yaron, *Capitalism and the Ivory Tower* (Tel Aviv: Ministry of Defence Publishing, 2008), p. 82.

18. America-Israel Friendship League, "Facts About Israel and the U.S.," http://www.aifl.org/html/web/resource_facts.html.

19. McKinsey & Company, "Perspective on the Middle East, North Africa and South Asia (MENASA) region," July 2008. All of the data in this section comes from this study.

20. David Landes, *The Wealth and Poverty of Nations* (New York: Norton, 1999), pp. 412–13.

## CHAPTER 14. Threats to the Economic Miracle

1. Quoted in Joanna Chen, "The Chosen Stocks Rally," *Newsweek*, March 14, 2009, http://www.newsweek.com/id/189283.

2. Amiram Cohen, "Kibbutz Industries Also Adopt Four-Day Workweek," *Haaretz*, March 12, 2009, http://www.haaretz.com/hasen/spages/1070086.html.

3. Interview with Benjamin Netanyahu, prime minister of Israel, December 2008.

4. Jennifer Evans, "Best Places to Work for Postdocs 2009," *The Scientist.com*, vol. 23, no. 3, p. 47, http://www.the-scientist.com/bptw.

5. Interview with Dan Ben-David, Department of Economics, Tel Aviv University, June 2008.

6. Israel's overall workforce participation level is 55 percent among adults, among the lowest in the West. The overall average is pulled down mainly by the extremely low workforce-participation levels of two minority groups: ultra-Orthodox Jews (40 percent participation) and Arab women (19 percent participation). These figures are cited in the *Israel 2028* report, which recommends working to raise workforce participa-

tion rates of ultra-Orthodox Jews and Arab women to 55 percent and 50 percent, respectively, by 2028. U.S.-Israel Science and Technology Foundation, *Israel 2028: Vision and Strategy for Economy and Society in a Global World*, edited by David Brodet (n.p.: U.S.-Israel Science and Technology Foundation, March 2008).

7. Dan Ben-David, "The Moment of Truth," *Haaretz*, February 6, 2007. Also reprinted with graphs on Dan Ben-David's Web site: http://tau.ac.il/~danib/articles/MomentOfTruthEng.htm.

8. Helmi Kittani and Hanoch Marmari, "The Glass Wall," Center for Jewish-Arab Economic Development, June 15, 2006, http://www.cjaed.org.il/Index.asp?ArticleID=269&CategoryID=147&Page=1.

9. Quoted in Yoav Stern, "Study: Israeli Arab Attitudes Toward Women Undergoing Change," *Haaretz*, March 14, 2009, http://www.haaretz.com/hasen/spages/1008797.html.

10. U.S.-Israel Science and Technology Foundation, *Israel 2028*, p. 39.

11. Reut Institute, "Last Chance to Become an Economic Superpower," March 5, 2009, http://reut-institute.org/en/Publication.aspx?PublicationId=3573.

12. Thomas Friedman speech at Reut Institute conference, Tel Aviv, June 2008.

## Conclusion: Farmers of High Tech

1. Organisation for Economic Co-operation and Development (OECD) and European Patent Office, "Compendium of Patent Statistics," 2008, http://www.oecd.org/dataoecd/5/19/37569377.pdf.

2. Interview with Antti Vilpponen, founder, ArcticStartup, January 2009.

3. Craig L. Pearce, "Follow the Leaders," *Wall Street Journal/MIT Sloan Management Review*, July 7, 2008, http://sloanreview.mit.edu/business-insight/articles/2008/3/5034/follow-the-leaders/.

4. Quoted in Gallup, "Gallup Reveals the Formula for Innovation," *Gallup Management Journal*, May 10, 2007, http://gmj.gallup.com/content/27514/Gallup-Reveals-the-Formula-for-%20Innovation.aspx.

5. Dov Frohman and Robert Howard, *Leadership the Hard Way: Why Leadership Can't be Taught—and How You Can Learn It Anyway* (San Francisco: Jossey-Bass, 2008), p. 7.

6. Quoted in Ronald Bailey, "Post-Scarcity Prophet: Economist Paul Romer on Growth, Technological Change, and an Unlimited Human Future," *Reason Online*, December 2001, http://www.reason.com/news/show/28243.html.

7. Ronald Bailey, "Post-Scarcity Prophet"; and Paul Romer, "Economic Growth," both in *The Concise Encyclopedia of Economics*, edited by David R. Henderson (Indianapolis: Liberty Fund, 2007), http://www.stanford.edu/~promer/EconomicGrowth.pdf.

# BIBLIOGRAPHY

## Published Sources

Abadi, Jacob. "Israel's Quest for Normalization with Azerbaijan and the Muslim States of Central Asia." *Journal of Third World Studies*, Fall 2002.

Agassi, Shai. "Tom Friedman's Column." The Long Tailpipe: Shai Agassi's Blog, July 26, 2008, http://shaiagassi.typepad.com/.

Alamaro, Moshe. "The Economics of Peace." *Harvard Business Review*, vol. 80, no. 11 (November 2002).

Andrews, Fannie F. *The Holy Land Under Mandate*. Vols. 1 and 2. Boston: Houghton and Mifflin, 1931.

Arlosoroff, Meirav. "Once Politicians Died Poor." *Haaretz*, June 8, 2008.

Austin, Robert D., and Carl Stormer. "Miles Davis: Kind of Blue." Harvard Business School Case 609-050, October 2008. Case Library, Harvard Business Publishing.

Avishai, Bernard. "Israel's Future: Brainpower, High Tech, and Peace," *Harvard Business Review*, November 1991.

Avnimelech, Gil, and Morris Teubal. "Venture Capital Policy in Israel: A

Comparative Analysis and Lessons for Other Countries." Research paper. Hebrew University School of Business Administration and School of Economics, October 2002.

Bailey, Ronald. "Post-Scarcity Prophet: Economist Paul Romer on Growth, Technological Change, and an Unlimited Human Future." *Reason Online*, December 2001. http://www.reason.com/news/show/28243.html.

Ball, Julie. "Israel's Booming Hi-Tech Industry." *BBC News*, October 6, 2008. http://news.bbc.co.uk/2/hi/business/7654780.stm.

Barzilai, Amnon. "A Deep, Dark, Secret Love Affair," July 17, 2004. http://www.israelforum.com/board/archive/index.php/t-6321.html.

Bar-Zohar, Michael. *Shimon Peres: The Biography*. New York: Random House, 2007.

Baumol, William J., Robert E. Litan, and Carl J. Schramm. *Good Capitalism, Bad Capitalism, and the Economics of Growth and Prosperity*. New Haven: Yale University Press, 2007.

BBC News. "Singapore Elder Statesman," July 5, 2000. http://news.bbc .co.uk/2/hi/programmes/from_our_own_correspondent/820234 .stm.

Ben-David, Dan. "The Moment of Truth." *Haaretz*, February 6, 2007.

Ben-Porath, Yoram. *The Israeli Economy: Maturing Through Crises*. Cambridge: Harvard University Press, 1986.

Berg, Alexis, and Dominique Vidal. "De Gaulle's Lonely Predictions." *Le Monde Diplomatique*, June 2007.

Bettelheim, Bruno. *The Children of the Dream: Communal Child-Rearing and American Education*. New York: Simon & Schuster, 2001.

BIRD (Israel-U.S. Binational Industrial Research and Development Foundation). "BIRD Foundation to Invest $9 Million in 12 Advanced Development Projects in Life Sciences, Energy, Communications,

Software and Nanotechnology." http://www.birdf.com/_Uploads /255BOG08PREng.pdf.

Bohmer, Richard, Laura R. Feldman, Erika M. Ferlins, Amy C. Edmondson, and Michael A. Roberto. "The *Columbia*'s Final Mission." Harvard Business School Case 304090, April 2004. Case Library, Harvard Business Publishing.

Bremmer, Ian. *The Curve: A New Way to Understand Why Nations Rise and Fall.* New York: Simon & Schuster, 2006.

Breznitz, Dan. *Innovation and the State: Political Choice and Strategies for Growth in Israel, Taiwan and Ireland.* New Haven: Yale University Press, 2007.

Brinkley, Joel. "Ethiopian Jews and Israelis Exult as Airlift Is Completed." *New York Times*, May 26, 1991.

Buffett, Warren. AIPAC interview transcript provided to authors, January 8, 2007.

Burgelman, Robert A., and Philip Meza. "Intel Beyond 2003: Looking for Its Third Act." Graduate School of Business, Stanford University, 2003.

Casadesus-Massanell, Ramon, David B. Yoffie, and Sasha Mattu. "Intel Corp.—1968–2003." Harvard Business School Case 703-427, November 2002. Case Library, Harvard Business Publishing.

Central Bureau of Statistics (Israel). "Gross Domestic Product and Uses of Resources, in the Years 1950–1995." In *Statistical Abstract of Israel 2008*, no. 59. Table 14.1. http://www.cbs.gov.il/reader/shnaton/ templ_shnaton_e.html?num_tab=st14_01x&CYear=2008.

Chen, Joanna, "The Chosen Stocks Rally." *Newsweek*, March 14, 2009.

Chesbrough, Henry W., and Anthony Massaro. "Rafael Development Corp.: Converting Military Technology to Civilian Technology in Israel." Harvard Business School Case 602011, February 2002. Case Library, Harvard Business Publishing.

CIA (U.S. Central Intelligence Agency). "Country Comparisons—Population." In *The World Fact Book*, 2008. https://www.cia.gov/library/publications/the-world-factbook/rankorder/2119rank.html.

CIA (U.S. Central Intelligence Agency). "Field Listing—Military Service Age and Obligation (Years of Age)." In *The World Fact Book*, 2008. https://www.cia.gov/library/publications/the-world-factbook/fields/2024.html.

Cisco. "Growth of Video Service Delivery Drives Sales of Cisco CRS-1, the World's Most Powerful Routing Platform, to Double in Nine Months." Press release, April 1, 2008. http://newsroom.cisco.com/dlls/2008/prod_040108c.html.

Claire, Rodger W. *Raid on the Sun: Inside Israel's Secret Campaign That Denied Saddam the Bomb*. New York: Broadway Books, 2004.

CNNMoney.com. "Best Places to Do Business in the Wired World." http://money.cnn.com/galleries/2007/biz2/0708/gallery.roadwarriorsspecial.biz2/11.html.

Cohen, Amiram. "Kibbutz Industries Also Adopt Four-day Workweek." *Haaretz*, March 12, 2009.

Cohen, Avner. *Israel and the Bomb*. New York: Columbia University Press, 1999.

Cohen, Eliot A. *Supreme Command: Soldiers, Statesmen, and Leadership in Wartime*. New York: Anchor Books, 2003.

Cohen, Uri. *The Mountain on the Hill*. Tel Aviv: Tel Aviv University Press, 2006.

Collins, Jim C., and Jerry I. Porras. *Built to Last: Successful Habits of Visionary Companies*. New York: HarperCollins, 1997.

"Coping with Current Economic Challenges." Session at the Israel Venture Association Conference, Tel Aviv, December 25, 2008.

Coutu, Diane L. "How Resilience Works." *Harvard Business Review*, May 2002.

Darling, Marilyn, Charles Parry, and Joseph Moore. "Learning in the Thick of It." *Harvard Business Review*, July 2005.

David, Anthony, *The Sky Is the Limit: Al Schwimmer, the Founder of the Israeli Aircraft Industry*. (In Hebrew.) Tel Aviv: Schocken Books, 2008.

Davidson, Christopher M. *Dubai: The Vulnerability of Success*. New York: Columbia University Press, 2008.

Deffree, Suzanne. "Mobility Boosts Intel Q3, Wall Street Sighs with Relief." *Electronics Design, Strategy, News (EDN)*, October 15, 2008. http://www.edn.com/article/CA6605604.html. Retrieved January 2009.

DeLoughry, James P. "The United States and the Lavi." *Airpower Journal*, vol. 4, no. 3 (Fall 1990): pp. 34–44. http://www.fas.org/man/dod-101/sys/ac/row/3fal90.htm.

Detert, James R., and Amy C. Edmondson. "Why Employees Are Afraid to Speak." *Harvard Business Review*, May 2007.

Deurenberg, Ruud. "Israel Aircraft Industries and Lavi." *Jewish Virtual Library*, January 26, 2009. http://www.jewishvirtuallibrary.org/jsource/Society_&_Culture/lavi.html.

Devane, Richard. "The Dynamics of Diaspora Networks: Lessons of Experience." In *Diaspora Networks and the International Migration Skills*, edited by Yevgeny Kuznetsov. Washington, D.C.: World Bank Publications, 2006.

Dinnerstein, Leonard. *America and the Survivors of the Holocaust*. New York: Columbia University Press, 1986.

Dow Jones Financial Information Services, "Venture Capital Investment Outside the U.S. Up 5% to $13.4 Billion in 2008 as More Money Goes to Energy, New Regions." February 18, 2009. http://fis.dowjones.com/pdf/4q08nonusvcpr.pdf.

Drucker, Peter F. "Discipline of Innovation." *Harvard Business Review*, August 2002.

Eiland, Giora. "The IDF: Addressing the Failures of the Second Lebanon War." In *The Middle East Strategic Balance 2007–2008*, edited by Mark A. Heller. Tel Aviv: Institute for National Security Studies, 2008.

Elon, Amos, *The Israelis: Founders and Sons*. New York: Holt, Rinehart and Winston, 1971.

Enright, Michael J., and Andrew Lee. "Singapore: Committee on Singapore's Competitiveness." Harvard Business School Case HKU033, January 1999. Case Library, Harvard Business Publishing.

Erlich, Yigal. Yozma PowerPoint Presentation, 2007.

Evans, Jennifer. "Best Places to Work for Postdocs 2009." Scientist.com, vol. 23, no. 3, p. 47. http://www.the-scientist.com/bptw.

"Facing Tomorrow." Session at the Israeli Presidential Conference, Jerusalem, May 2008.

Farson, Richard E., and Ralph Keyes. "The Failure-Tolerant Leader." *Harvard Business Review*, August 2002.

Farzad, Roben. "Israel's Clean Technology Pioneers." *BusinessWeek*, May 7, 2009.

Fear, Jeffrey, and Christian H. M. Ketels. "Cluster Mobilization in Mitteldeutschland." Harvard Business School Case 707-004, August 2006. Case Library, Harvard Business Publishing.

Fershtman, Chaim, and Neil Gandal. "The Effect of the Arab Boycott on Israel: The Automobile Market." *Rand Journal of Economics*, vol. 29, no. 1 (Spring 1998): pp. 193–214.

Fick, Nathaniel. *One Bullet Away: The Making of a Marine Officer*. New York: Houghton Mifflin, 2006.

Flanigan, James, "Israeli Companies Seek Global Profile." *New York Times*, May 20, 2009.

Francisco, Bambi. "AOL's ICQ to Debut a Big Makeover." *Market Watch*,

April 20, 2004. http://www.marketwatch.com/News/Story/Story .aspx?guid={308B699C-D4E9-4CD3-A67A-389DEC028B35}&site id=google&dist=google. Retrieved January 2008.

Friedlin, Jennifer. "Woman on a Mission." *Jerusalem Post*, April 20, 1997.

Friedman, Thomas L. *The World Is Flat: A Brief History of the Twenty-first Century*. New York: Picador, 2007.

Frohman, Dov. "Leadership Under Fire." *Harvard Business Review*, December 2006.

Frohman, Dov, with Robert Howard. *Leadership the Hard Way: Why Leadership Can't Be Taught—and How You Can Learn It Anyway*. San Francisco: Jossey-Bass, 2008.

Gallup. "Gallup Reveals the Formula for Innovation." *Gallup Management Journal*, May 10, 2007. http://gmj.gallup.com/content/27514/ Gallup-Reveals-the-Formula-for-%20Innovation.aspx. Retrieved January 2009.

Gary, Loren. "The Right Kind of Failure." *Harvard Management Update*, January 1, 2002.

Gavron, Daniel. *The Kibbutz: Awakening from Utopia*. Lanham, Md.: Rowman & Littlefield, 2000.

Ghemawat, Pankaj. "Distance Still Matters: The Hard Reality of Global Expansion." *Harvard Business Review*, September 2001.

Goetzmann, William, and Irina Tarsis. "Dubailand: Destination Dubai." Harvard Business School Case 207-005, July 2006. Case Library, Harvard Business Publishing.

Goldberg, Jeffrey. "Netanyahu to Obama: Stop Iran—or I Will." *Atlantic*, March 31, 2009.

Gompers, Paul A., and Jeffrey M. Anapolsky. "The Advent Israel Venture Capital Program." Harvard Business School Case 204-156, April 2004. Case Library, Harvard Business Publishing.

Gompers, Paul A., and Sara Bergson. "The Emergence of 'Silicon Wadi.'" Harvard Business School Note 204-156, April 2004.

Gompers, Paul A., Anne Kovner, Josh Lerner, and David S. Scharfstein. "Skill vs. Luck in Entrepreneurship and Venture Capital: Evidence from Serial Entrepreneurs." Working paper 12592. National Bureau of Economic Research, October 2006. http://imio.haag.berkley.edu/williamsonseminar/scharfstein041207.pdf.

Groysberg, Boris, Tal Riesenfeld, and Eliot Sherman. "Israeli Special Forces: Selection Strategy." Harvard Business School Case 409-041, September 2008. Case Library, Harvard Business Publishing.

Haider, Don. "Ireland: Celtic Tiger." Harvard Business School Case KEL-141, January 2005. Case Library, Harvard Business Publishing.

Handwerker, Haim. "U.S. Entrepreneur Makes Aliyah Seeking 'Next Big Invention.'" *Haaretz*, August 28, 2008.

Hari, Johann. "The Dark Side of Dubai." *Independent*, April 7, 2009. http://www.independent.co.uk/opinion/commentators/johann-hari/the-dark-side-of-dubai-1664368.html.

Horovitz, Jacques, and Anne-Valerie Ohlsson. "Dubai Internet City: Serving Business." *Asian Journal of Management Cases*, vol. 2, no. 2 (2005): pp. 163–209.

*IMD World Competitiveness Yearbook*. Lausanne, Switzerland: IMD, 2005.

Intel Inside News. "Intel's Most Unforgettable X86 CPUs and 8086: The First PC Processor." October 13, 2008. http://intelinsidenews.blog spot.com/2008/10/intels-15-most-unforgettable-x86-cpus.html. Retrieved December 2008.

Invest in Israel. "Life Sciences in Israel: Inspiration, Invention, Innovation," 2006. http://www.google.com/url?sa=t&source=web&ct=res&cd=1&url=http%3A%2F%2Fwww.israeleconomicmission.com%2Findex.php%3Foption%3Dcom_docman%26task%3Ddoc_download%26gid%3D18&ei=aEfKSceDEteLtgerorixAw&usg=AFQjCN

FBb4bXAXC68RqYFbIP4Bv0YDZUnA&sig2=rxbDEjZ-W3 huiyb50qn8Xg.

———. "Recent International Mergers and Acquisitions." http://www .investinisrael.gov.il/NR/exeres/F0FA7315-4D4A-4FDC-A2FA -AE5BF294B3C2.htm.

Israel, Steve. "Broadening the Picture—Beyond America: Conclusions." Jewish Agency for Israel. http://www.60israel.org/JewishAgency/Eng lish/Jewish+Education/Compelling+Content/Worldwide+Community /israeldiaspora/Conclusions.htm.

"Israel's Fugitive Flotilla." *Time*, January 12, 1970. http://www.time .com/time/magazine/article/0,9171,942140,00.html.

Israel Venture Capital (IVC) Research Center Web site. http://www.ivc -online.com.

Johansson, Frans. *The Medici Effect: What Elephants and Epidemics Can Teach Us about Innovation.* Boston: Harvard Business School Press, 2006.

Johnston, Jenny. "The New Argonauts: An Interview with AnnaLee Sax-enian." A GBN WorldView Interview, July 2006, http://thenewargo nauts.com/GBNinterview.pdf?aid=37652.

Joyner, Christopher. In *Boycott and Blacklist: A History of Arab Economic Warfare Against Israel,* edited by Aaron J. Sarna. Lanham, Md.: Rowman & Littlefield, 1986.

Kao, John. *Innovation Nation: How America Is Losing Its Innovation Edge, Why It Matters and What We Can Do to Get It Back.* New York: Free Press, 2007.

Khalaf, Roula. "Dubai Ruler Has Big Ideas for the Little City-State." *Financial Times,* May 3, 2007. http://www.ft.com/cms/s/2/eb00cfcc -f9a0-11db-9b6b-000b5df10621.html.

Khanna, Raun, and Krishna G. Palepu. "Emerging Giants: Building World-Class Companies in Developing Countries." *Harvard Business Review,* October 2006.

King, Ian. "Intel's Israelis Make Chip to Rescue Company from Profit Plunge." *Bloomberg.com*, March 28, 2007. http://www.bloomberg .com/apps/news?pid=20601109&sid=a2mgYutwVFnM&refer=home. Retrieved December 2008.

Kittani, Helmi, and Hanoch Marmari. "The Glass Wall." The Center for Jewish-Arab Economic Development, June 25, 2006. http://www .cjaed.org.il/Index.asp?ArticleID=269&CategoryID=147&Page=1.

Kraft, Dina. "From Far Beneath the Israeli Desert, Water Sustains a Fertile Enterprise." *New York Times*, January 2, 2007.

Kranz, Gene. *Failure Is Not an Option: Mission Control from Mercury to Apollo 13 and Beyond*. New York: Berkley, 2009.

Kuznetsov, Yevgeny N., ed. *Diaspora Networks and the International Migration of Skills: How Countries Can Draw on Their Talent Abroad*. Washington, D.C.: World Bank Institute, 2006.

Landes, David S. *The Wealth and Poverty of Nations: Why Some Are So Rich and Some So Poor*. New York: Norton, 1999.

Laskier, Michael M. "Israel and Algeria amid French Colonialism and the Arab-Israeli Conflict, 1954–1978." *Israel Studies*, June 2, 2001, pp. 1–32. http://muse.jhu.edu/journals/israel_studies/v006/6.2laskier .html. Retrieved September 2008.

Leyden, Joel. "Microsoft Bill Gates Takes Google, Terrorism War to Israel." *Israel News Agency*, October 30, 2005. http://www .israelnewsagency.com/microsoftgoogleisraelseo581030.html. Retrieved November 2008.

Lipsky, David. *Absolutely American: Four Years at West Point*. New York: Vintage Books, 2004.

Lohr, Steve. "Like J. P. Morgan, Warren E. Buffett Braves a Crisis." *New York Times*, May 5, 2008.

Lopez-Claros, Augusto, and Irene Mia. "Israel: Factors in the Emergence of an ICT Powerhouse." In *The Global Information Technology Report:*

*Leveraging ICT for Development*, edited by Soumitra Dutta and Augusto Lopez-Claros. London: Palgrave Macmillan, 2006. http://www.investinisrael.gov.il/NR/rdonlyres/61BD95A0-898B-4F48-A795-5886B1C4F08C/0/israelcompleteweb.pdf.

Lorber, Azriel. *Misguided Weapons: Technological Failure and Surprise on the Battlefield*. Dulles, Va.: Potomac Books, 2002.

Lovell, Jim, and Jeffrey Kluger. *Apollo 13*. New York: Mariner Books, 2006.

Luttwak, Edward N. *The Pentagon and the Art of War*. New York: Simon & Schuster, 1984.

Luttwak, Edward N., and Dan Horowitz. *The Israeli Army*. London: A. Lane, 1975.

Malone, Michael. *Bill & Dave: How Hewlett and Packard Built the World's Greatest Company*. N.P.: Portfolio Hardcover, 2007.

———. *Infinite Loop: How Apple, the World's Most Insanely Great Computer Company, Went Insane*. New York: Doubleday Business, 1999.

Mandel, Michael. "Can America Invent Its Way Back?" *BusinessWeek*, September 11, 2008.

Manor, Hadas. "South African Visit Yields Business Worth $30M." *Globes Online*, October 25, 2004.

Marcus, Eyal. "Israeli Start-ups Impress at TechCrunch50," *Globes Online*, September 14, 2008.

Marketing Charts. "Venture Capital Investment Slips 8% in the U.S.; Up 5% Elsewhere." February 20, 2009. http://www.marketingcharts.com/topics/asia-pacific/venture-capital-investment-slips-8-in-us-up-5--elsewhere-8033/.

Maron, Stanley. "Kibbutz Demography." In *Crisis in the Israeli Kibbutz: Meeting the Challenge of Changing Time*, edited by Uri Leviatan, Hugh Oliver, and Jack Quarter. Westport, Conn.: Greenwood Publishing Group, 1998.

Matly, Michael, and Laura Dillon. "Dubai Strategy: Past, Present and Future." Harvard Business School, February 27, 2007.

McKinsey & Company. "Perspective on the Middle East, North Africa and South Asia (MENASA) Region." July 2008.

McWilliams, David. "Ireland Inc. Gets Innovated," *Sunday Business Post On-Line*, December 21, 2008. http://www.sbpost.ie/post/pages/p/story.aspx-qqqt=DAVID+McWilliams-qqqs=commentandanalysis-qqqid=38312-qqqx=1.asp. Retrieved January 2009.

———. "We're All Israelis Now." David McWilliams's blog, April 25, 2004. http://www.davidmcwilliams.ie/2004/04/25/were-all-israelis-now.

Meehan, William F., III, Ron Lemmens, and Matthew R. Cohler. "What Venture Trends Can Tell You. *Harvard Business Review*, July 2003.

Messer-Yaron, Hagit. *Capitalism and the Ivory Tower*. Tel Aviv: Ministry of Defence Publishing, 2008.

"The Midas List." *Forbes*, January 25, 2007.

Mindef Singapore. "Ministerial Statement on National Service Defaulters by Minister for Defence Teo Chee Hean," January 16, 2006. http://www.mindef.gov.sg/imindef/news_and_events/nr/2006/jan/16jan06_nr.html.

———. "Speech by Prime Minister Goh Chok Tong at the 35 Years of National Service Commemoration Dinner." September 7, 2007. http://www.mindef.gov.sg/imindef/news_and_events/nr/2002/sep/07sep02_nr/07sep02_speech.html.print.html?Status=1.

Mlavsky, Ed. PowerPoint Presentation to Wharton MBA students, 2008.

Murray, Charles, and Catherine Bly Cox. *Apollo*. Burkittsville, Md.: South Mountain Books, 2004.

NASDAQ. "NASDAQ International Companies." http://www.nasdaq.com/asp/NonUSOutput.asp.

Nelson, Richard R., ed. *National Innovation Systems: A Comparative Analysis*. New York: Oxford University Press, 1993.

Organisation for Economic Co-operation and Development. "Compendium of Patent Statistics," 2008. http://www.oecd.org/dataoecd /5/19/37569377.pdf.

Oz, Amos. Speech at the Israeli Presidential Conference, Jerusalem, May 14, 2008.

———. *A Tale of Love and Darkness*. Orlando: Harcourt, 2005.

Pagonis, William G. "Leadership in a Combat Zone." *Harvard Business Review*, December 2001.

Parayil, Govindan. "From 'Silicon Island' to 'Biopolis of Asia': Innovation Policy and Shifting Competitive Strategy in Singapore." *California Management Review*, vol. 47, no. 2 (February 2005): pp. 50–73.

Patinkin, Don. *The Israel Economy: The First Decade*. Jerusalem: Maurice Falk Institute for Economic Research in Israel, 1960.

Pearce, Craig L. "Follow the Leaders." *Wall Street Journal/MIT Sloan Management Review*, July 7, 2008, http://sloanreview.mit.edu/busi ness-insight/articles/2008/3/5034/follow-the-leaders/.

Peres, Shimon. *David's Sling*. New York: Random House, 1970.

———. *From These Men: Seven Founders of Israel*. New York: Wyndham Publications, 1979.

———. "Speech to the United Nations General Assembly." *Haaretz*, September 24, 2008.

Plessner, Yakir. *The Political Economy of Israel: From Ideology to Stagnation*. Albany: State University of New York Press, 1994.

Porter, Michael E. "Clusters and Competition: New Agendas for Companies, Governments, and Institutions." Harvard Business School, June 1999.

———. "Clusters and the New Economics of Competition." *Harvard Business Review*, November–December 1998.

———. *The Competitive Advantage of Nations*. New York: Free Press, 1998.

Porter, Michael E., and Gregory C. Bond. "California Wine Cluster." Harvard Business School Case 799-124, June 1999. Case Library, Harvard Business Publishing.

Porter, Michael E., and Niels W. Ketelhohn. "Building a Cluster: Electronics and Information Technology in Costa Rica." Harvard Business School Case 703-422, November 2002. Case Library, Harvard Business Publishing.

Porter, Michael E., and Orjan Solvell. "Finland and Nokia: Creating the World's Most Competitive Economy." Harvard Business School Case 702-427, January 2002. Case Library, Harvard Business Publishing.

Reardon, Marguerite. "Cisco Router Makes Guinness World Records." *CNET News*, July 1, 2004. http://news.cnet.com/Cisco-router-makes -Guinness-World-Records/2100-1033 3-5254291.html?tag=nefd.top.

———. "Cisco Sees Momentum in Sales of Key Router." *TechRepublic*, December 6, 2004. http://articles.techrepublic.com.com/5100-22_11 -5479086.html.

Reuters. "Peres Biography: Israel, France Had Secret Pact to Produce Nuclear Weapons." *Haaretz*, May 30, 2007.

Reut Institute. "Generating a Socio-economic Leapfrog: Prof. Ricardo Hausmann's Visit to Israel—a Summary," February 14, 2008. http:// reut-institute.org/data/uploads/PDFVer/20080218%20-%20 %20Hausman%27s%20main%20issues-%20English.pdf.

———. "Israel 15 Vision." December 10, 2006. http://www.reut-institute .org/Publication.aspx?PublicationId=992. Retrieved October 2008.

———. "Last Chance to Become an Economic Superpower." March 5, 2009. http://reut-institute.org/en/Publication.aspx?PublicationId=3573.

Rivlin, Paul. *The Israeli Economy*. Boulder, Colo.: Westview Press, 1992.

Roberto, Michael A., Richard M. J. Bohmer, and Amy C. Edmondson. "Facing Ambiguous Threats." *Harvard Business Review*, R0611F, November 2006.

Roberto, Michael A., Amy C. Edmondson, and Richard M. J. Bohmer. "*Columbia*'s Final Mission." Harvard Business School Case Study, 2006.

Romer, Paul M. "Economic Growth." In *The Concise Encyclopedia of Economics*, edited by David R. Henderson. Indianapolis: Liberty Fund, 2007; also available at http://www.stanford.edu/~promer/Economic Growth.pdf.

Rosenthal, Donna. *The Israelis: Ordinary People in an Extraordinary Land*. New York: Free Press, 2005.

Rosten, Leo. *The Joys of Yiddish*. New York: McGraw-Hill, 1968.

Rubin, Uzi. "Hizballah's Rocket Campaign Against Northern Israel: A Preliminary Report." *Jerusalem Issue Brief*, vol. 6, no. 10 (August 31, 2006). http://www.jcpa.org/brief/brief006-10.htm.

Rubinstein, Amnon. "Return of the Kibbutzim." *Jerusalem Post*, July 10, 2007.

Sacher, Howard M. *A History of Israel: From the Rise of Zionism to Our Time*. 2nd ed. New York: Knopf, 1996.

Sarna, Aaron J. *Boycott and Blacklist: A History of Arab Economic Warfare Against Israel*. Totowa, N.J.: Rowman & Littlefield, 1986.

Schramm, Carl J. "Economic Fluidity: A Crucial Dimension of Economic Freedom." In *2008 Index of Economic Freedom*, edited by Kim R. Holmes, Edwin J., Feulner, and Mary Anastasia O'Grady. Washington, D.C.: Heritage Foundation, 2008.

———. *The Entrepreneurial Imperative: How America's Economic Miracle Will Reshape the World*. New York: HarperCollins, 2006.

Scott, Bruce R., and Srinivas Ramdas Sumder. "Austin, Texas: Building a High-Tech Economy." Harvard Business School Case 799-038, October 1998. Case Library, Harvard Business Publishing.

Singer, Saul. "Superpower in Silicon Wadi." *Jerusalem Post*, June 19, 1998.

Solow, Robert M. "Growth Theory and After." Nobel Prize lecture, December 8, 1987. http://nobelprize.org/nobel_prizes/economics/laureates/1987/solow-lecture.html.

Snook, Scott A., Leslie J. Freeman, and L. Jeffrey Norwalk. "Friendly Fire." Harvard Business School Case 404-083, January 2004. Case Library, Harvard Business Publishing.

Steil, Benn, David G. Victor, and Richard R. Nelson, eds. *Technological Innovation and Economic Performance*. Princeton: Princeton University Press, 2002.

Stern, Yoav. "Study: Israeli Arab Attitudes Toward Women Undergoing Change." *Haaretz*, March 14, 2009. http://www.haaretz.com/hasen/stages/1008797.html.

Sternhell, Zeev. *The Founding Myths of Israel*. Translated by David Maisel. Princeton: Princeton University Press, 1998.

Symmes, Patrick. "The Book." *Outside*, August 2005. http://outside.away.com/outside/features/200508/the-israeli-guidebook-1.html. Retrieved November 2008.

Tal, Alon. "National Report of Israel, Years 2003–2005, to the United Nations Convention to Combat Desertification (UNCCD)." July 2006. http://www.unccd.int/cop/reports/otheraffected/national/2006/israel-eng.pdf.

———. *Pollution in a Promised Land: An Environmental History of Israel*. Berkeley: University of California Press, 2002.

Theil, Stefan. "Teaching Entrepreneurship in the Arab World." *Newsweek International*, August 14, 2007. Also available at: http://www.gmfus.org/publications/article.cfm?id=332. Retrieved March 2009.

*Time* /CBS News. *People of the Century: One Hundred Men and Women Who Shaped the Last Hundred Years.* New York: Simon & Schuster, 1999.

Trajtenberg, Manuel, and Gil Shiff. "Identification and Mobility of Israeli Patenting Inventors." Discussion Paper No. 5-2008, Pinchas Sapir Center for Development, Tel Aviv University, April 2008. http://sapir.tau .ac.il/papers/sapir-wp/%D7%9E%D7%A0%D7%95%D7%90%D7%9C%20 %D7%98%D7%A8%D7%9B%D7%98%D7%A0%D7%91%D7%A8% D7%92%205-08%20%D7%9E%D7%A9%D7%95%D7%9C%D7%91.pdf.

Twain, Mark. *The Innocents Abroad, or The New Pilgrims' Progress.* Hartford: American Publishing Company, 1870.

UNDP (United Nations Development Programme). *The Arab Human Development Report, 2005: Towards the Rise of Women in the Arab World.* New York: United Nations Publications, 2006.

———. "Research and Development Expenditure (% of GDP)." *Human Development Reports,* 2007–08.

Useem, Michael. *The Leadership Moment: Nine True Stories of Triumph and Disaster and Their Lessons for Us All.* New York: Three Rivers, 1998.

Vietor, Richard H. K., and Rebecca Evans. "Saudi Arabia: Getting the House in Order." Harvard Business School Case 404-083, March 2002. Case Library, Harvard Business Publishing.

Vietor, Richard H. K., and Emily J. Thompson. "Singapore Inc." Harvard Business School Case 703-040, February 2003. Case Library, Harvard Business Publishing.

Vise, David A., and Mark Malseed. *The Google Story.* New York: Delacorte, 2005.

Vogelstein, Fred. "The Cisco Kid Rides Again." *Fortune,* July 26, 2004. http://money.cnn.com/magazines/fortune/fortune_archive/2004/ 07/26/377145/index.htm.

Volansky, Ami. *Academy in a Changing Environment.* Kav Adom–Kibbutz Meuchad Publisher, 2005.

"We Are All Innovators Now." Economist Intelligence Unit, October 17, 2007. http://www.eiu.com/index.asp?layout=ib3PrintArticle&article_id=292663614&printer=printer&rf=0. Retrieved January 2009.

Weick, Karl E. "Prepare Your Organization to Fight Fires." *Harvard Business Review*, May 1996.

Weiner, Eric. *The Geography of Bliss: One Grump's Search for the Happiest Places in the World*. New York: Twelve, 2008.

Weizmann Institute of Science. "Moving with the Times." *Weizmann Wonder Wander*, Fall–Winter 1997. http://wis-wander.weizmann.ac.il/site/en/weizman.asp?pi=422&doc_id=567&interID=562&sq=562.

"Weizmann's Patent Royalties." *Israel High-Tech and Investment Report*, September 2004. http://www.ishitech.co.il/0904ar5.htm.

Wieseltier, Leon. "Brothers and Keepers: Black Jews and the Meaning of Zionism." *New Republic*, February 11, 1985.

Wilson, Stewart. *Combat Aircraft Since 1945*. Fyshwick: Aerospace Publications, 2000.

World Economic Forum. "Utility Patents (Hard Data)." *Global Information Technology Report 2008–2009*.

———. "Venture Capital Availability." *World Economic Forum Executive Opinion Survey 2007, 2008*.

Wyman, David S. *Paper Walls: America and the Refugee Crisis, 1938–1941*. New York: Pantheon, 1985.

Yefet, Orna. "McDonalds." *Yediot Ahronot*, October 29, 2006.

"Yossi Sela, Managing Partner." Gemini Israel Funds Web site. http://www.gemini.co.il/?p=TeamMember&CategoryID=161&MemberId=197.

Zadok, Shahar. "Intel Dedicates Fab 28 in Kiryat Gat." *Globes Online*, July 1, 2008.

Zuckerman, Ezra, and Janet Feldstein. "Venture Capital in Israel: Emergence and Globalization." Harvard Business School Case SM88, November 2001. Case Library, Harvard Business Publishing.

## INTERVIEWS

Abizaid, General John (ret.), former commander, U.S. Central Command; May 2009.

Agassi, Reuven (Shai's father), member of the start-up council for Technion; December 2008.

Agassi, Shai, founder and CEO, Better Place; March 2008 and March 2009.

Air Force trainer, IDF; May 2008.

al-Allawi, Riad, Jordanian entrepreneur; March 2009.

Alon, Ruti, partner, Pitango Venture Capital; chairperson, boards of Bio-Control, BrainsGate, and TransPharma Medical; December 2008.

Amir, David (fictitious name), pilot, Israeli Air Force; August 2008.

Andreessen, Marc, founder, Netscape; July 2009.

Applbaum, Isaac (Yitz), venture partner, The Westly Group; May 2008.

Ariav, Yoram, director general, Israel Ministry of Finance; January 2009.

Asa-el, Amotz, founding president, *BusinessWeek Israel*, and former executive editor, *Jerusalem Post*; May 2008.

Avner, Yehuda, adviser to Israeli prime ministers Levi Eshkol, Golda Meir, Yitzhak Rabin, Menachem Begin, and Shimon Peres; ambassador to the United Kingdom, Ireland, and Australia; April 2008.

Bachar, Yossi, former director general, Ministry of Finance; May 2008.

Barkat, Eli, chairman and cofounder, BRM Group; January 2009.

Ben-David, Dan, Department of Economics, Tel Aviv University; June 2008.

Ben-Ephraim, Brigadier General Rami, head of personnel division, Israeli Air Force; November 2008.

Berry, Orna, venture partner, Gemini Israel Funds; January 2009.

Bialkin, Kenneth J., partner, Skadden, Arps; January 2009.

Brodet, David, former director general, Ministry of Finance; May 2008.

Brokaw, Tom, author, *The Greatest Generation*; April 2009.

Catalano-Sherman, Joni, corporate director of technology transfer and academic relations, Johnson and Johnson, Corporate Office of Science and Technology (COSAT); December 2008.

Chaliva, Colonel Aaron, commander of officer training base, Bahad 1, IDF; December 2008.

Chase, Al, founder, White Rhino Partners; February 2009.

Cohen, Eliot A., counselor to the State Department; former director of the Strategic Studies Program, Paul H. Nitze School of Advanced International Studies, Johns Hopkins University; January 2009.

Davidson, Christopher M., author of *Dubai: The Vulnerability of Success*; March 2009.

Davis, Tim, director, Entrepreneurship Indicators Project, OECD; March 2009.

De Haan, Uzi, William Davidson Faculty of Industrial Engineering and Management, Technion; July 2008.

Dermer, Ron, former economic attaché, Embassy of Israel in Washington, D.C., and senior adviser to Prime Minister Benjamin Netanyahu; September 2008.

Dilian, Colonel Tal (res.), former 8100 chief; member of the board of directors, Atidim; May 2008.

Doron, Daniel, president, Israel Center for Social and Economic Progress; August 2008.

Edelstein, Yuli, former minister of absorption; member of Knesset; May 2008.

Eden, Shmuel (Mooly), vice president and general manager, Mobile Platforms Group, Intel; November 2008.

Edry, Illy, founder and chief strategist, Poptok; May 2008.

Eisenberg, Michael, partner, Benchmark Capital; May 2009.

Elias, Asher, Tech Careers; March 2009.

Epstein, Asher, director, Dingman Center for Entrepreneurship, University of Maryland; May 2008.

Erlich, Yigal, founder, chairman, and managing partner, Yozma Group; May 2008.

Farhi, Major Gilad, commander in the Kfir infantry unit, IDF; November 2008.

Fick, Nathaniel, chief operating officer, Center for a New American Security; author, *One Bullet Away*; March 2008.

Friedman, Thomas, columnist, *New York Times*; April 2009.

Galil, Uzia, chairman and CEO, Uzia Initiatives & Management Ltd; July 2008.

Gerson, Mark, executive chairman, Gerson Lehrman Group; January 2009.

Gidron, Rafi, and Orni Petruschka, cofounders, Precede Technologies, Chromatis Networks, and Scorpio Communications; December 2008.

Giladi, Brigadier General Eival (res.), CEO, Portland Trust; March 2009.

Goren, Amos, venture partner, Apax Partners; January 2009.

Grinstein, Gidi, founder and president, Reut Institute; May and August 2008.

Gross, Yossi, director and cofounder, TransPharma Medical; founder of many medical-device start-ups; December 2008.

Hamed, Colonel Ramiz, head of the Minorities Unit, Human Resources Branch, IDF; November 2008.

Harris, Clinton P., founder and managing partner, Grove Street Advisors; founder and former managing director, Advent International; January 2009.

Haug, Laurent, founder and CEO, Lift Conference; May 2009.

Hausmann, Ricardo, former Venezuelan minister of state and current director of the Harvard Center for International Development; February 2009.

Ivri, David, former ambassador to the United States and former chief commander of the Israeli Air Force; December 2008.

Kagan, Frederick W., military historian; resident scholar, American Enterprise Institute for Public Policy Research (AEI); December 2008.

Kaplinsky, Major General Moshe (res.), CEO, Better Place Israel; November 2008.

Kaufmann, Yadin, founding partner, Veritas Venture Partners; December 2008.

Keinan, Tal, cofounder, KCPS; May and December 2008.

Kerbs, Gil, venture capitalist and contributor to *Forbes*; January 2009.

Ketels, Christian H. M., economist, member of the Harvard Business School faculty and of the Institute for Strategy and Competitiveness; March 2009.

Kohlberg, Isaac T., senior associate provost and chief technology development officer, Harvard University; January 2009.

Kranz, Eugene (Gene) F., former flight director and manager, NASA; May 2009.

Laor, Michael, founder of Cisco Systems Development Center in Israel; February 2009.

Lipow, Jonathan, Department of Economics, Oberlin University; May 2008.

Lipsky, David, author, *Absolutely American*; March 2009.

Lowry, Colonel John (res.), general manager, Harley-Davidson Motor Company; November 2008.

Luttwak, Edward, senior associate, Center for Strategic and International Studies (CSIS); December 2008.

Luttwak, Yael, former commander in tank gunnery course, IDF; documentary filmmaker; August 2008.

Maarek, Yoelle, former director, Google's R&D Center in Haifa, Israel; January 2009.

Maoz, Darya, anthropologist, the Hebrew University; June 2009.

Margalit, Erel, founder of Jerusalem Venture Partners (JVP); May 2008.

Matanya, Aviatar, senior officer, Talpiot program; December 2008.

Matias, Yossi, director, Google's R&D Center in Tel Aviv, Israel; January 2009.

McLaughlin, Andrew, director, public policy and government affairs for Google; January 2009.

McMaster, Brigadier General H. R., U.S. Army; May 2009.

McWilliams, David, Irish economist; July 2009.

Medved, Jon, CEO and board member, Vringo; May 2008.

Messer-Yaron, Hagit, president, Open University; January 2009.

Mitchell, Lesa, vice president, Kauffman Foundation; March 2009.

Mlavsky, Ed, chairman and founding partner, Gemini Israel Funds; December 2008.

Molla, Shlomo (Neguse), member of Knesset, Kadima Party; March 2009.

Moralli, Dorit, owner, El Lobo restaurant and guesthouse in La Paz, Bolivia; March 2009.

Nagel, Brigadier General Jacob (res.), deputy director of Mafat, IDF; December 2008.

Netanyahu, Benjamin, prime minister of Israel; December 2008.

Newbold, General Gregory (ret.), former director of operations, Joint Chiefs of Staff; May 2009.

Ofer, Idan, chairman of the board, Better Place; December 2008.

Oren, Michael, senior fellow, Shalem Center; May 2008.

Peled, Dan, Department of Economics, University of Haifa; July 2008.

Peres, Chemi, cofounder and managing general, Pitango VC; December 2008.

Peres, Shimon, president of Israel; December 2008.

Peretz, Shay, CEO, DefenSoft Planning Systems; December 2008.

Perlmutter, David, executive vice president and general manager, Mobility Group, Intel Corporation; January 2009.

Petraeus, General David, commander, U.S. Central Command; May 2009.

Porter, Michael E., professor of economics, Harvard Business School; founder and chairman, Initiative for a Competitive Inner City (ICIC); institute director, Institute for Strategy and Competitiveness; cofounder, Monitor Group; March 2009.

Pulver, Jeff, founder and chief executive, Pulver.com; August 2008.

Rabinovich, Abraham, author of *The Yom Kippur War: The Epic Encounter That Transformed the Middle East*; May 2009.

Rezk, Amr, EFG-Hermes; March 2009.

Riesenfeld, Tal, IDF Special Forces (res.); cofounder, EyeView; December 2008.

Ron, Lieutenant Colonel Nathan (res.), IDF; attorney, Ron-Festinger Law Offices; December 2008.

Rosenberg, David, Bloomberg Jerusalem bureau; former business editor, *Jerusalem Post*; former chief North American economist, Merrill Lynch; May 2008.

Samet, Yoav, corporate development manager for Israel, Central/Eastern Europe, and Russia/CIS, Cisco Systems Inc.; January 2009.

Schell, Jessica, vice president of NBC Universal, Inc.; April and June 2008.

Schmidt, Eric, chairman and CEO, Google; June 2009.

Schramm, Carl J., president and CEO, Ewing Marion Kauffman Foundation; March 2009.

Schroeder, Alice, author of *The Snowball*; January 2009.

Sela, Michael, Department of Immunology, Weizmann Institute of Science; December 2008.

Senior eBay executive, background interview; September 2008.

Shainberg, Gary, vice president for technology and innovation, British Telecom; May and August 2008.

Sharansky, Natan, chairman and distinguished fellow, Adelson Institute for Strategic Studies, Shalem Center; founder of Yisrael B'Aliya Party; May 2008.

Solomon, Ian, partner, Profile Group; vice president of business development, Aespironics; December 2008.

Swersky Sofer, Nava, former CEO, Yissum; December 2008.

Thompson, Scott, president, PayPal; October 6 and October 16, 2008; January 2009.

Tice, Captain Brian (res.), U.S. Marine Corps; February 2009.

Vardi, Yossi, Israeli Internet guru; founder of more than fifty high-tech companies; May 2008.

Vieux, Alex, CEO, Red Herring; May 2009.

Vilenski, Dan, former chairman of the board, Applied Materials Israel, Israel National Nanotechnology Initiative (INNI); July 2008.

Vilpponen, Antti, founder, ArcticStartup; January 2009.

Vise, David A., coauthor of *The Google Story*; January 2009.

Vitman, Assaf, economic attaché, Embassy of Israel in Washington, D.C.; January 2009.

Wertheimer, Eitan, chairman of the board, Iscar; January 2009.

Whitman, Meg, former president and CEO, eBay; September 2008.

Wolfe, Josh, cofounder and managing partner, Lux Capital; December 2008.

Wood, Doug, head of creative affairs, Animation Lab; May 2008.

Yaalon, Lieutenant General Moshe (res.), Likud member of Knesset; IDF chief of staff in 2002–05; May 2008.

Zeevi-Farkash, Major General Aharon (res.), former head of Intelligence Unit 8200, IDF; May 2008.

# INDEX

# ABOUT THE AUTHORS

**Dan Senor**, adjunct senior fellow for Middle East studies at the Council on Foreign Relations, has been involved in policy, politics, and business in the Middle East. As a senior foreign policy adviser to the U.S. government, he was one of the longest-serving civilian officials in Iraq, for which he was awarded the highest civilian honor by the Pentagon. He also served as a Pentagon adviser to Central Command in Qatar and as a foreign policy and communications adviser in the U.S. Senate. He has studied in Israel and at Harvard Business School and has traveled extensively throughout the Arab world. In his business career, he has invested in a number of Israeli and American start-ups, and today is with a New York–based global investment fund. Senor's analytical pieces are frequently published by the *Wall Street Journal*; he has also written for the *New York Times*, the *Washington Post*, the *Weekly Standard*, and *Time*. Mr. Senor lives in New York City with his wife and two sons.

**Saul Singer** is a columnist and former editorial page editor at the *Jerusalem Post*. Historian Michael Oren called his book *Confronting Jihad: Israel's Struggle and the World After 9/11* "mandatory reading for anyone, layman or expert, interested in the Middle East." He has written for the *Wall Street Journal*, *Commentary*, *Moment*, the *New Leader*, *bitterlemons* (an Israeli/Palestinian e-zine), and the *Washington Post*'s international blog, *PostGlobal*. Before moving to Israel in 1994, he served as an adviser in the United States Congress to the House Foreign Affairs and Senate Banking Committees. Mr. Singer lives in Jerusalem with his wife and three daughters.

You can visit the authors' website at www.startupnationbook.com.

The Council on Foreign Relations (CFR) is an independent, non-partisan membership organization, think tank, and publisher dedicated to being a resource for its members, government officials, business executives, journalists, educators and students, civic and religious leaders, and other interested citizens in order to help them better understand the world and the foreign policy choices facing the United States and other countries. Founded in 1921, CFR carries out its mission by maintaining a diverse membership, with special programs to promote interest and develop expertise in the next generation of foreign policy leaders; convening meetings at its headquarters in New York and in Washington, DC, and other cities where senior government officials, members of Congress, global leaders, and prominent thinkers come together with CFR members to discuss and debate major international issues; supporting a Studies Program that fosters independent research, enabling CFR scholars to produce articles, reports, and books and hold roundtables that analyze foreign policy issues and make concrete policy recommendations; publishing *Foreign Affairs,* the preeminent journal on international affairs and U.S. foreign policy; sponsoring Independent Task Forces that produce reports with both findings and policy prescriptions on the most important foreign policy topics; and providing up-to-date information and analysis about world events and American foreign policy on its website, www.cfr.org.

The Council on Foreign Relations takes no institutional position on policy issues and has no affiliation with the U.S. government. All statements of fact and expressions of opinion contained in its publications are the sole responsibility of the author or authors.

# ABOUT TWELVE
## MISSION STATEMENT

TWELVE

TWELVE was established in August 2005 with the objective of publishing no more than one book per month. We strive to publish the singular book, by authors who have a unique perspective and compelling authority. Works that explain our culture; that illuminate, inspire, provoke, and entertain. We seek to establish communities of conversation surrounding our books. Talented authors deserve attention not only from publishers but from readers as well. To sell the book is only the beginning of our mission. To build avid audiences of readers who are enriched by these works—that is our ultimate purpose.

For more information about forthcoming TWELVE books, you can visit us at www.twelvebooks.com.